IN-SCHOOL EVALUATION

In-School Evaluation

MARTEN SHIPMAN

Professor of Education, Warwick University

formerly

Director of Research and Statistics,
Inner London Education Authority

HEINEMANN EDUCATIONAL BOOKS
LONDON

Heinemann Educational Books
LONDON   EDINBURGH   MELBOURNE   AUCKLAND
TORONTO   HONG KONG   SINGAPORE   KUALA LUMPUR
IBADAN   NAIROBI   JOHANNESBURG
NEW DELHI   LUSAKA   KINGSTON

Shipman, Marten Dorrington
In-School Evaluation.
 1. Educational surveys—England
 I. Title
 371.2   LB2823
 ISBN   0–435–80800–1

Published by
Heinemann Educational Books Ltd
22 Bedford Square, London WC1B 3HH
Photoset and printed in Malta by
Interprint (Malta) Ltd

Contents

Acknowledgements

The author and publishers wish to thank the following for permission to reproduce copyright material:

Oliver & Boyd for the extract from *Match and Mismatch* by W. Harlen; NFER Publishing Company for the extracts from *Educational Research* and *A Critical Appraisal of Comprehensive Education*; The Controller of Her Majesty's Stationery Office for the DES extracts from the *1977 Green Paper, Ten Good Schools, Form 7d, Statistics of Education Vol. 2*, and for the HMSO extracts from *Social Trends*; the Southern Regional Examinations Board for the Certificate of Secondary Education for the extract from *Examinations Bulletin 31, Continuous Assessment in the CSE: Opinion and Practice*; The Scottish Council for Research in Education for the extract from *Profile Assessment System: Manual*; Maurice Temple Smith Ltd for the extract from *Running a School* by Barry and Tye; Ward Lock Educational Ltd for the table from *Oversubscribed* by R. Boyson; the Open University for the extracts from their Course E321, Unit 2.

Author's Note

The views presented in this book are written from a strictly personal viewpoint. It is right however to acknowledge the generosity of the Inner London Education Authority in encouraging open debate in this controversial aspect of education.

Foreword

The *Heinemann Organization in Schools Series* is a systematic attempt to help schools improve the quality of the school experience by a methodical study of aspects of the ways in which schools can be organized. The series has been planned as a whole, so that the central philosophy and every aspect of the planning and running of schools is methodically covered. However, each book has been written by a different author and from a different point of view out of his or her own observation, experience, and conviction. Since each book is written to stand on its own, there is inevitably some overlapping between the volumes, as certain topics (such as pupil choice, or the responsibilities of senior staff) need to be included in a number of books, though with varying degrees of detail and from different points of view.

In-School Evaluation is a pioneering book of great importance to all of us working in education, for no aspect of schooling can be considered adequately without some attempt to establish how effective our efforts have been. In particular, the relative autonomy of the British school is a mere empty freedom if there is no way of taking advantage of it by effective in-school decision-making; and this demands a serious attempt by the staff of the school to evaluate their work and the results of previous decisions in the school. Even the most subjective judgements are helped by methodical evaluation procedures, for, paradoxically, subjectivity can flourish best when what can be objectively evaluated has been.

Arguably, one of the major faults of most of us in schools most of the time is that we have not developed more than fragmentary in-school evaluation methods. We have lacked the guidance, and there has been no 'do-it-yourself manual' to help. That is how Professor Marten Shipman describes this simple but far-reaching book. He is the ideal person to undertake the task of offering guidance, having a rare combination of experience and skills. He writes from the unique position of having run the country's largest Education Authority's Research and Statistics Department, but also as someone who always holds in the front of his mind the human and educational needs of the pupil, the teacher, and the school organization.

For many people 'evaluation' is something other people do to schools; Marten Shipman shows us in simple but powerful ways how schools can help themselves by straight-forward ways of organizing their own evaluation of their own work. His book is thus central to our theory and our practice.

MICHAEL MARLAND

Introduction

This book is about ways of making schools more effective and about ways of ensuring that they are seen to be effective. It is not about the ends of education. It is not about the organization or impact of secondary schooling. Those who enjoy philosophy, appreciate the subtleties of sociology, or revel in debates over the curriculum should go elsewhere. Those who like to dispute over what school is for, how children learn, or who should be educated in this or that way should pass by. The concern here is with means not ends, on how to do it more effectively rather than what to do. Whether education should be traditional or progressive, open or closed, formal or informal I leave to the mountain of available work. This is a contribution to the molehill of work about making any of these forms of schooling more effective.

Education is always competing for scarce resources against social services, housing, health, and so on. This competition occurs at central and local government level. The intensity of that competition has been increased by educational researchers who have repeatedly produced evidence to show that attainment depends on social background. It is difficult to claim resources for education in the face of competing demands from services that could improve that background. Suddenly we are in a buyer's market for schooling. Each school has to retain public confidence or that public is likely to assume that it is failing. We can no longer assume that lack of information will be taken as a sign of confidence and efficiency. All who educate are under pressure to assess their effectiveness and to make that assessment public. You can label this accountability. It is really a move to an open schooling. It is no use being effective without being responsive.

This book was not however written to provide the means of selling schools to their publics. It was written in the conviction that, after a quarter of a century in which secondary schooling in Britain has become largely comprehensive, we should forget the debate over the merits of selective and non-selective schools and get on with tackling the problems of the last quarter of this century. How do we ensure that the new secondary schools, usually comprehensive, are effective organizations? Curiously, there is much published work on the aims of education, helping teachers to decide on targets. There is little on how to hit them.

The contribution of the academic world to the evaluation of everyday, routine schooling has been negligible. Test constructors and statisticians produce techniques and instruments that tend not to fit curricula, and to present them in books that have an opening chapter on the need to assess, and a remainder that concentrates on elementary statistics and descriptions of standardized tests. Curriculum theorists have proliferated but have provided even less guidance. Yet the increased rate of introduction of new developments in secondary schooling has increased the demand for new forms of evaluation. This is only partly the result of anxiety over the impact of new courses and teaching methods. It is more the result of the need for evaluation to be an integral part of these new, mainly learner-centred developments to secure continuity of learning.

This is not therefore a contribution to any academic discipline. It is a do-it-yourself manual. The menu offered covers a broad sweep of curricular and extra-curricular activities. It is offered as a partial solution to the persisting difficulty in an education system where teachers have the freedom to determine curricula and where no levels of expected attainment are laid down from the centre as targets. This arrangement allows teachers to innovate and aim high, uninhibited by central control of curricula, textbooks, and expected standards. But this freedom, while allowing many to aim high, allows others to aim low or to be aimless. Centrally established average standards can easily become ceilings. There are pros and cons in centralized and decentralized systems. The freedom to determine curricula is dear to teachers in Britain. It is accompanied by the responsibility to set targets and to organize ways of showing that they have been attained. The right to autonomy rests on the duty to evaluate.

As a start to planning this book, secondary school teachers and headteachers were consulted in London and the Midlands. They were asked about existing arrangements for evaluation in their schools. They were asked about new arrangements that they would like to make. All accepted the need to evaluate their work. They wanted information that would indicate how well they were doing compared with schools with similar intakes and in similar areas. They wanted a form of evaluation that would reflect their own broad ideas about the objectives of education. They wanted to inform the public, but not at the cost of inviting intervention in their professional role.

Out of these discussions came a series of questions. These have been gathered together in pairs below. These questions guided the writing of the book. The answers are summarized in Chapter 8.

Question 1(a) How do we set about evaluating the performance of our schools?

(*b*) What are the first steps in evaluating whether our pupils are really learning?

Question 2(*a*) Isn't it true that most of what goes on in a school can not be measured?

(*b*) Does evaluation have to increase the amount of testing of pupils?

Question 3(*a*) Is it best to start with a few easy parts of the curriculum to evaluate or to try to work out a comprehensive programme?

(*b*) Are we to evaluate the attainment of pupils, the efforts they make, their improvement or deterioration, or some other attribute?

Question 4(*a*) How can we evaluate the work of a school when there is nothing we can meaningfully compare with it?

(*b*) How can we make the assessment of pupils useful to them, to teachers, to parents, and to prospective employers?

Question 5(*a*) Does systematic evaluation involve many changes in the way assessments are usually made in the school?

(*b*) Do there have to be special arrangements for evaluation beyond those usually organized in schools?

Question 6(*a*) What information about the school should be made public?

(*b*) Is it fair to label pupils by releasing their marks?

Question 7(*a*) Given the little time that we have left after actually teaching in school, how can we get the most out of the remainder that we devote to evaluation?

(*b*) How do we get a quick review of the performance of the school without setting up an elaborate system of evaluation?

Behind all these questions there was agreement that new forms of evaluation were needed in schools. This was not primarily a response to public pressure for accountability. It was the result of experienced teachers reviewing the changes that had taken place in secondary schooling. These changes were not only related to the advent of comprehensive schools, but to the introduction in such schools of new curricula and teaching methods. The attempt to tailor education to pupils with wide variations in backgrounds, attitudes, aptitudes, and abilities meant that assessment and record-keeping were needed to ensure that learning experiences were matched to stages reached by pupils. Evaluation was seen as a necessary part of a less selective and more individualized organization of learning. The evaluation had to face two ways. First, it had to provide information for pupils and teachers in the classroom. Secondly, it had to provide teachers and others with some idea of the success of the methods adopted. The book is an approach to a new form of in-school evaluation to match new forms of education.

I am most grateful to the teachers consulted for their encourage-ment. I am particularly indebted to Michael Marland and George Phipson for comments on early drafts and for their encouragement throughout.

1. A Basis for Evaluation

Evaluation is a basic management tool in all organizations. Throughout this book the search is for information on performance that will help in decision-making. This information, produced by evaluation, does not determine the decisions. But the judgements that lead to decisions are informed by the evaluation. While this is a practical book making suggestions for teachers, it is based on insights from books on management theories. These are often written in a style that suggests that they are not relevant to education, even when the author is trying to write about schools. But they contain important messages for teachers.

There are a number of approaches to the study of management that provide useful guides to decision-making in schools. They have been summarized by Cyril Poster as a practical guide to the way schools may be organized.[1] These approaches have formidable titles and initials such as Management by Objectives (MBO), Programme, Planning and Budgeting Systems (PPBS), or Critical Path Analysis (CPA). In practice these systems simply make the implicit explicit. When a headteacher, senior teacher, a head of department, or an assistant teacher makes a decision about resources or personnel, he often follows, albeit in an unsystematic way, the path recommended in management theory. It is possible for management techniques to de-humanize by focussing attention on the system not the individual. Their use could over-simplify complicated teacher-learner interactions, or might focus attention on measurable processes to the neglect of more important aspects that might be destroyed by too much testing. But they are a model for planning education in a school. They provide a checklist for making decisions that have to be made by all, including the most humane. Consider this sequence of events:

Decide on what you want to achieve.
Work out ways of achieving these goals.
Set a time limit for this achievement.
Assess how much this will cost.
Have a look at alternative ways of achieving the same goals.
Work out a way of checking whether what you decide to do has worked.

[1] Poster, C. D. (1976), *School Decision-Making: Educational Management in Secondary Schools*. London, Heinemann Educational Books.

This is probably what every headteacher puzzles about when thinking how to allocate the school's allowances for the next school year. As soon as staff ask for resources for a new humanities course, or for a different length of lesson, or a new teacher has to be appointed, some sequence similar to that above runs through someone's head. For more major changes in a school it runs through many heads. It is the sequence of thoughts while planning a course, a lesson, or while helping a pupil. Yet this, in simplified language, was the PPBS system used by the Rand Corporation when Secretary of Defence McNamara asked that Corporation to reorganize the US Department of Defence.

In Figure 1:1 this sequence of events has been re-organized into a flow diagram, a simplified model of the evaluation process.

It is doubtful if any school staff fail to think through a similar sequence of events as they plan the allocation of next year's budget, plan the time-table, prepare new courses, or write out reports on pupils or their work. This sequence may be implicit and even casual, but it is not a new, alien management technique for teachers. It is a useful *aide-mémoire*, a reminder of the steps that should be taken before important decisions are made. From it, an immediate and important conclusion about the organization of school programmes can be drawn. A systematic approach makes it certain that objectives, teaching programmes, and evaluation itself are open to continuous feed-back and hence to change.

It is assumed that in-school evaluation will be concentrated on aspects of the school deemed central by the staff. Priority will be given to objectives that are agreed unanimously, to the key concepts, skills, and knowledge of subject areas and to central aspects of school organization. Evaluation is time-consuming and has to be concentrated where it will have most effect. But judgements about effectiveness are always being made. It is safest to ensure that they are based on dependable data.

The rest of this book has been written as a possible menu to be sampled in the heat of the school. It tries to meet the requirements of

Figure 1:1

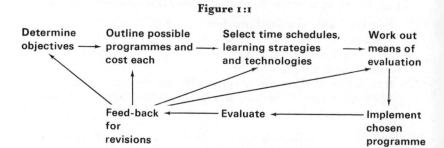

the teachers who contributed the questions in the Introduction. They were pragmatists. They saw that some evaluation is better than none, that one priority will lead to the next, that once a start is made the chances are increased that other aspects will be evaluated systematically. Their interest was in techniques that could be tried out to see if they worked. They were reluctant to accept the need to discuss the theoretical base for evaluation, but this follows and is a crucial first step.

Aims, objectives, and indicators

The purpose of evaluation is to increase the effectiveness of schooling. Effectiveness is judged by the degree to which objectives have been attained. A school could be successful without anyone spelling out any objectives. But this success would still be judged against implicit criteria. These are likely to be shared by many of the staff of the school and perhaps by other professionals. But the public for education is unlikely to share these priorities. Even more important, if nobody has spelled them out, there is no way of knowing whether there is any agreement. Confidence in an organization such as a school depends on knowing what it is supposed to be achieving.

Ask a teacher why pupils are doing something and you can receive an answer that ranges from 'to get them to think for themselves' to 'to pass examinations', or 'to keep them occupied'. It is possible to rank statements of aims into a hierarchy from the general to the specific. It is more useful to stick to the term aim for the general end, and objective for the specific. An aim then is a broad statement of purpose and intention which can provide some direction to an educational programme. An objective is a specific, verifiable result which can provide a basis for planning.

Aims

There have been many studies asking samples of people to list aims for schools. You would not expect much agreement. In a society where people hold differing social, economic, political, and religious views they will want differing emphases in schools. Aims for voluntary and county schools will differ. So will aims for suburban, inner city, and rural schools. Even in apparently similar areas, teachers, parents, employers, and other groups concerned with schools will hold contrasting views. For example, the Schools Council *Enquiry 1*, *Young School Leavers* found that fifteen-year-olds and their parents gave priority to the provision of knowledge and skills necessary for jobs.

Teachers tended to give priority to developing character and personality, ethical values, and social skills. [1]

The variety of aims expressed by those interested in schools means that teachers will not be able to satisfy everyone. The results obtained will always seem irrelevant to someone. This is why it is useful for a school staff to spell out aims for their public as well as themselves. Faced with a questionnaire, many teachers spell out aims in moral terms—'To turn out good citizens', 'a Christian community', 'a caring community', 'a respect for learning and for others', 'high standards in all things' and 'to produce honest, open, and useful adults' are all examples of aims actually expressed by teachers. Sometimes the aims are even broader, concentrating on the preparation of pupils for the modern changing world—'To give each pupil the experience that will help him through the changing world he will face as an adult' and 'to help pupils fulfil themselves in a world that we cannot anticipate', are examples of aims that look not to the experience of the past but to the unknown situation of the future.

The statement of these aims is the starting-point of evaluation. Consider the two sets outlined in the previous paragraph. The first states a moral position and implies that teachers can draw on accumulated wisdom, morals, religion, learning, caring, and skill. The curriculum derived from such aims will be geared to passing on truths as interpreted by the staff of the school. The curriculum is likely to be different in a school where the staff leans towards preparation for the twenty-first century. Here the emphasis is on change. The curriculum will be orientated less to the accumulated learning of the past, than to preparing pupils to anticipate continuous re-learning; it will teach children how to learn rather than how to absorb past learning, and should help them to appreciate the relativity of values in a particular culture.

Both sets of aims can be found in contemporary schools. But the High Master of Manchester Grammar School and the Warden of Countesthorpe College are aiming at a very different education. The public are liable to have difficulty in assessing what the staff of the comprehensive school around the corner is aiming at. Here, as a start, are eight aims of schools detailed in the 1977 DES Green Paper, *Education in Schools: a Consultative Document.* [2]

   1. To help children develop lively, inquiring minds; giving them the ability to question and to argue rationally, and to apply themselves to tasks.
   2. To instil respect for moral values, for other people and for oneself, and tolerance of other races, religions, and ways of life.

[1] Schools Council (1968), *Enquiry Number 1, Young School Leavers.* London, HMSO.
[2] Department of Education and Science (1977), *Education in Schools: a Consultative Document.* Cmnd. 6869. London, HMSO.

3. To help children understand the world in which we live, and the interdependence of nations.

4. To help children to use language effectively and imaginatively in reading, writing and speaking.

5. To help children to appreciate how the nation earns and maintains its standard of living and properly to esteem the essential role of industry and commerce in this process.

6. To provide a basis of mathematical, scientific and technical knowledge, enabling boys and girls to learn the essential skills needed in a fast-changing world of work.

7. To teach children about human achievement and aspirations in the arts and sciences, in religion, and in the search for a more just social order.

8. To encourage and foster the development of the children whose social or environmental disadvantages cripple their capacity to learn, if necessary by making additional resources available to them.

It is unlikely that any staff of a school would agree with all this list. Discussions over aims are a quick way to uncover political, moral, and social, as well as educational differences among a staff. But this list can serve as a starting-point for discussion.

Another source of aims has come from Tim McMullen, the first Warden of Countesthorpe College.[1] McMullen sees the mapping out of aims and objectives as an *aide-mémoire*, a framework for thinking through the problems of organizing a school. He is concerned with the needs of pupils in the last two decades of this century. His aims are divided into social and individual and are sub-divided as follows:

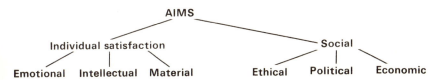

Yet another basis for a discussion of aims comes from Albert Rowe, when he was the head of David Lister School, Hull.[2] Rowe's three aims, described as long-term objectives are that a school should:

Make it possible for a pupil to gain experience of as high as possible a quality of living and so be in a position later if he chooses to go on pursuing it.

Provide the milieu in which a pupil can develop social sensitivity and awareness, and a complementary non-ideological, non-party political consciousness.

[1] McMullen, T. M. (1970), 'The Classification of Aims and Objectives as an Aid to Making Decisions', in Taylor, G. (ed.), *The Teacher as Manager*. London, National Council for Educational Technology.

[2] Rowe, A. (1971), *The School as a Guidance Community*. Hull, Pearson Press.

Lay the foundations upon which a pupil later can build to earn his daily bread.

A very full set of aims has been prepared for Sydney Stringer School and Community College, Coventry.[1] The aims specified for the pupils follow:

WHAT THE ENTERPRISE AIMS TO DO

For Its Pupils

The School is helping to build the rising generation. It is only one of many agencies influencing the way young people grow up. The School must recognize those other agencies and work closely with those that are helpful and counteract those which are unhelpful. The home is the greatest influence but church, clubs, press, TV, cinema and other adults and the environment all play their part alongside the School, sometimes helpful and sometimes not.

The School aims to equip them for life, both now and later as adults, so that whilst they are at school they are happy and secure and motivated to develop themselves to the full; and when they leave:

(*a*) They are adequately prepared to get an appropriate job or go on to Higher Education.
(*b*) They know how to cope with the problems of being a young adult.
(*c*) They are acceptable to society and can take a place in it, and play a part in changing it for the better.
(*d*) They can live with themselves.

All these headteachers are defining at a general level. Each goes on to use these aims as the first step to more precise, more specific objectives. But the aims are still an important first step. The easiest way of illustrating this is to try to conceive of an effective school where staff did not share some common aims, however general. The DES study, *Ten Good Schools*, is an affirmation of the importance of school staff being able to state aims.[2] Even more important was the willingness of these successful staffs to plan to achieve the aims. The DES expresses this as follows:

Most schools would wish to claim that they had fundamental and broad objectives that were not lost to sight in the effort to attain more immediate results in the examination room or on the games field. The schools chosen proposed such broad aims as the establishment of good relationships and tension-free discipline; the development of self-confidence and self-respect; the acquisition of knowledge and skills in terms of literacy, numeracy, aesthetic sensibility and physical well-being; the perception through the curriculum of social, moral and religious values and standards for healthy living—and all these things in a context which takes account of what has

[1] Open University, 'A Case Study in Management: Sydney Stringer School and Community College'. Unit 2 of course E321, *Management in Education*. Milton Keynes, Open University, p. 18.

[2] Department of Education and Science (1977), *Ten Good Schools: A Secondary School Enquiry*. London, HMSO.

gone before at the primary stage and, through careers education, what is to come in the world of work or continued education.

It is easy to pay lip-service to such high-sounding ideals. What is impressive about the schools in the sample is the ways in which they seek to achieve them by deliberate planning.

The common elements in the aims stressed above are a concern for the pupil as an individual in every sense, and a concern that there should be adequate preparation for the adult world. This balance is important. It is easy for teachers to adopt a humane attitude that protects pupils from the harsh, competitive world outside the school. This ensures comfortable pupil-teacher relations but leaves the sometimes difficult preparation for adulthood to someone else, and may leave it until the pupil has left school or realizes, with his parents, that he or she has little to offer in the job market or in the competition for places in further and higher education. On the other hand an excessive stress on academic qualifications and on competition in the classroom and examination hall is equally unbalanced. Schools do not seem to be very powerful influences in raising attainment where the social background is adverse. But schools may strongly influence a pupil's social development.

Thus most teachers will respond to these examples of aims because they emphasize the need to equip a pupil to earn a living and to become a useful adult, while simultaneously stressing the need to promote a consciousness of the rights of others, or self-discipline, and the need to care about the community inside and outside the school. In every staffroom there will be very different views expressed on aims for the school, but most will be on the side of the angels who specified those above.

So far, the aims have been general. But clearly they will have to be defined as specific objectives before they can be translated into action. At this point generalities should be broken down into targets defined so that the degree of success in hitting them can either be measured or assessed against some tangible standard.

Objectives

A single aim will need to be divided into several objectives before it can serve as a basis for curriculum planning. These objectives will be derived from the aim, but others will be formulated pragmatically from experience. Similarly, objectives will be changed while the aim is likely to persist. Staff turnover, changes in the catchment area, in local authority policy, in higher education, in employment, and so on will necessitate adaptations.

Once the staff of a school has agreed on some broadly defined aim or set of aims, there is a need to bridge the gap between those that are likely to be somewhat vague aspirations and the detailed curriculum planning that will finally result in a time-table, a range of subjects, a selection of learning strategies, and an identifiable form of school organization. The specification of objectives should fill some of these gaps. However, it is useless being unrealistic. Most texts on this subject assume more time, energy, motivation, and academic expertise than could be mobilized among most school staffs. They over-emphasize the measurable. They also over-estimate the amount of agreement that is likely to be found among staffs who will span forty years, different subjects, and different political and religious views. Significantly the effort to spell out even the objectives of particular curriculum projects has now been abandoned by those who first stressed their indispensability. The only practical solution is to define objectives that will serve as a guide for actual practice, while being open to evaluation, even if not immediately measurable. The definition determines the choice of suitable indicators of attainment, whether these are qualitative or quantitative. Throughout this book objectives stated by teachers in conversation about evaluation will be listed. These are specific, spontaneous statements, not finished versions stated to give measurable outputs. They reflect what teachers want to achieve in practice. They are operational, working definitions, a starting-point for an exercise that should bring later refinement. This approach, leaving the objectives to be defined by the teachers with indicators chosen to check their attainment, seemed preferable to re-defining the teachers' statements into forms that were suitable for direct measurement. The result may be imprecise, intuitive objectives, but here it is better to travel hopefully than not to start. The indicators may be blunt, but they will be reflecting a real school situation.

The sequence from defining aims to specifying more concrete objectives can be seen in this extract from a layout for a Mode 3 submission to the Southern Regional Examinations Board in 1972.[1] The subject was 'Science for Living' and the submission included a description of the origins and rationale of the course, the teachers who would be involved, the range of material to be used, the facilities and time available, a detailed syllabus, and a scheme of assessment including details of moderation and the weighting of different elements. The key to the letters used can be found in the centre of the list of objectives.

AIMS AND OBJECTIVES

The broad aims of the course are as follows:

1. To give pupils an understanding of themselves, both physically and in terms of human relationships.
2. To develop an awareness of the relationship between man and his environment and an awareness of environmental problems.

---

[1] Schools Council (1975), *Examination Bulletin 31, Continuous Assessment in the CSE* London, Evans/Methuen Educational, pp. 120–1.

3. To give pupils an understanding of the methods of scientific enquiry.
4. To emphasize common dangers and safeguards.

It will be seen that the course is envisaged as a contribution to adequacy in citizenship, but with an emphasis upon pupil involvement which ought to be the primary method of learning at the mature stage of the pupils concerned. The approach will be that of practice whenever possible.

The work will require not only the acquisition of essential knowledge but also skills and abilities, the nature of which is outlined below. The assessment pattern has been devised to measure the three aspects of the work and also, to a limited extent, attitudes which pupils adopt during the course.

Objectives
Knowledge and understanding of: *Assessable by:*
  1. Specific facts   W
  2. Simple relationships   W
  3. Systems   W
  4. Nomenclature, units, conventional representations   W
  5. Simple generalizations   W
  6. Techniques   W   P   C

Ability to identify and apply knowledge to:
  7. Simple problems   W   P   C
  8. New situations   W   P   C

Ability to:
  9. Form concepts   W
  10. Draw conclusions from information   W   P   C
  11. Recognize a problem and devise a solution   W   P   C

Practical skills:
  12. To handle apparatus   P   C
  13. To observe   P   C
  14. To follow instructions   P
  15. To measure   P   C
(W indicates Written Paper;
P indicates Practical Paper;
C indicates Course Work Assessment)

  16. To record systematically   P   C
  17. To process results   W   P   C
  18. To devise simple experiments   W   P   C

Attitudes:
  19. Will work independently   C
  20. Will co-ordinate work with others   C
  21. Persistence   P   C
  22. Enthusiasm and interest   C
  23. Industriousness   C
  24. Reliability   C

Geoffrey Holroyde has listed specific targets for Sydney Stringer School and Community College, Coventry.[1] These were based on

[1] Open University, *op. cit.*, p. 43.

Peter Drucker's key objectives translated into educational terms and refined into targets for this school. [1] Holroyde introduces these specific targets as follows:

SPECIFIC TARGETS

In 1972 I listed a number of specific targets which we should set out to achieve within the eight areas of objectives identified by Peter Drucker. Now, two years later, it is interesting to read them and note how many of them still apply.

I would like staff to read them, and keep these targets in mind as a check-list of what we should be doing. A useful monthly exercise would be to read through the list and ask oneself what one has done either as an individual or as a team to improve our performance in any of these target areas.

This sort of thinking might form the basis of useful discussions with US tutor groups and with parents—and in a watered-down way with Lower School tutor groups too. I would appreciate it if staff came up with additions to the list, or with good ideas about how we might do better in any of the target areas.

GEOFFREY HOLROYDE

The eight areas, with examples of specific targets were:

Reputation, containing 19 targets, the first and last being 'Establish reception area. Parents and visitors courteously received and welcomed. Effective sign posting' and 'Co-operation with Social Services and police'.

Innovation, containing 14 targets, the first and last being 'Team teaching is working well, providing flexibility and achievement, and responsibility delegated to the teams' and 'Consultative procedures believed in by staff'.

Effectiveness, containing 2 targets. 'Examination results above average' and 'Enterprise recognized as an effective agency in the area and has impact on the Environment and the quality of family life locally'.

Productivity, containing 10 targets, the first and last being 'Staff not used for clerical and routine work' and 'Colleges of Education, Universities and Employers help in the Education process'.

Resources, containing 7 targets, the first and last being 'Generate income from tuck shop, coffee bar, parents' associations, simulated business and service to local organizations, use of resources' and 'Generate attitude of economy in use of resources'.

Staff development, containing 9 targets, the first and last being 'Frequent in-house workshop sessions for staff. (i) General Education practice, and organization development. (ii) Sydney Stringer curriculum' and 'Establish effective communication processes'.

[1] Drucker, P. F. (1954), *The Practice of Management*. London, Heinemann.

Community relations, containing 7 targets, the first and last being, 'Every pupil and user knows at least one staff member very well' and 'Minimum punishment requirement'.

Public responsibility, containing 3 targets, the first and last being 'Little vandalism. Building is clean' and 'Effective security measures'.

These targets are the product of one headteacher convinced of the benefits to be derived from using the insights of management theory. Yet the full list of 81 targets would probably be agreed with minor changes of emphasis by the staff of most secondary schools. They are a mixture of measurable indicators and those that must rely on the judgement of the staff. A similar list would serve as the start of evaluation in any school.

The move from broad, often vague aims to more specific objectives brings the explication of ends down to the concrete level where teachers are directly concerned. Holroyde's targets are a second, more specific level of objective. There is no need to agonize too long over philosphical matters of aims. The need is for a set of working objectives that can focus evaluation. The objectives establish a tactical position that enable the staff to get on with evaluation. But the objectives have not got the means of assessing results defined into them. These means of assessment have to be both qualitative and quantitative. Thus a third stage is needed to establish criteria for success. There has to be some indication of what will be accepted by staff as signs of success or failure in achieving objectives. However, before outlining this step a reconciliation must be attempted between the view adopted here and that to be found in more academic textbooks.

Clearly we are a long way from the behavioural objectives that were once seen as the lynch-pin of efficient education when Robert Mager published a programmed text showing how to prepare them. [1] Far from specifying the terminal behaviour and the criterion for recognizing success, those who have managed to follow some of the short, unhappy history of curriculum evaluation will realize that I have been naïve and dogmatic over the use of objectives when the dispute over their use has kept many academics employed for the last quarter of a century. There are several excellent summaries of the debate over objectives. [2] They follow this debate from Tyler's advocacy of the use of objectives, defined as having sufficient clarity for the teacher '. . . if he can describe or illustrate the kind of behaviour the student is expected to acquire, so that one could recognize such

[1] Mager, R. F. (1962), *Preparing Instructional Objectives*. Palo Alto, Fearon Press.

[2] Jenkins, D. and Shipman, M. D. (1976), *Curriculum: an Introduction*, London, Open Books.

behaviour if he saw it'. [1] This means that objectives should be spelled out in terms of expected learning outcomes. Curriculum evaluators were encouraged in such actions by the industry of Bloom and others in producing classifications of objectives in the cognitive, affective, and experimental areas or domains. [2]

Having put forward a very limited notion that objectives should be spelled out in lucid, measurable form or otherwise stamped out, curriculum evaluators have now swung to the other extreme. Evaluation tends to be now seen by latter-day measuring fiends as akin to anthropology, with the evaluator mingling in the classroom until insight occurs, when he writes a personal account of what has really occurred between teachers and pupils. Illuminative evaluation is now the vogue. The lantern has replaced the slide rule. Yet it is hard to see why the evaluator can claim to have a definitive interpretation of what is going on in the school or the classroom compared to that of the teacher who has more experience of the situation. The evaluator adds a different perspective not a superior one.

For the teacher, illumination is not enough. It has to be accepted that many important objectives will never be open to measurement, that some will only be recognized as important as teaching goes on, and that many cannot be identified or defined in advance. But judgements have to be made and those judgements have to be based on some recognizable reference if they are to be convincing. Figures are useful, not because they do not incorporate judgement, but because they can often be referred to a source that gives an idea of the confidence that can be placed in them. Public examination results are widely used as indicators of success or failure in a secondary school, not because they are presented in statistical detail, but because they are derived from a recognizable exercise organized by examination boards that have established and moderated procedures, which are outside the control of any one school staff. Much of this book will be concerned with ways in which similar references can be obtained for quantitative and qualitative indicators available to teachers.

Indicators

Social scientists usually distinguish between objective and subjective indicators. The former are usually statistics of the behaviour of groups of persons—crime rates, the price of goods in the shops, or the

[1] Tyler, R. W. (1971), *Basic Principles of Curriculum and Instruction*. Chicago, University of Chicago Press.
[2] Bloom, B. S., *et al.* (1956), *Taxonomy of Educational Objectives: Cognitive Domain*, London, Longman. *See also* Kratwohl, D. R. (1964), *Taxonomy of Educational Objectives: The Affective Domain*. London, Longman; and Steinaker, N. and Bell, M. R. (1975), 'A Proposed Taxonomy of Educational Objectives: The Experiential Domain', *Educational Technology*, vol. 1, pp. 14–16.

number of births per thousand of the population. Subjective indicators are expressions of satisfaction obtained by asking people about aspects of their lives. These opinions can be aggregated into statistics, but they are obtained directly from people, not derived from measures of their behaviour. Thus indicators can be in the form of statistics, but can also be judgements. Computer analyses of business data may give an indication of the direction of the stock market, but many prefer the advice of a stockbroker. The Great Debate over education was argued over a few available statistics and a lot of professional opinions. Indicators can be soft or hard, numbers or words, objective or subjective.

While recommending caution and a pragmatic approach, I have returned to the traditional position that evaluation has to start with a broad set of aims and a progressive specification of these until one has a set of working objectives whose attainment can be judged by qualitative or quantitative indicators. To illustrate this process here is a single aim (in italics) and three accompanying objectives extracted from an extensive set of such aims and objectives chosen by Barry and Tye.[1]

> *In so far as it lies within the resources of the school, to illustrate the inter-relationship of all human knowledge, to foster an appreciation of man's creative skills, and to stimulate a conception of learning as a life-long process.*
>
> (a) By appropriate design of the curriculum, and of subject syllabuses, and by courses of general studies for senior pupils, to furnish some understanding and knowledge of the physical universe, together with some appreciation of man's achievements in the arts and in science, and of the importance of preserving the heritage of our environment.
>
> (b) To encourage co-operation between subjects, and to develop cross-fertilisation and integrated courses between subject disciplines.
>
> This might involve team-teaching, sponsored reading from a staff library, inter-departmental meetings and study groups, and staff attendance at courses and conferences.
>
> (c) So to design the curriculum and time-table that, throughout his school career, every child shall spend a significant part of every week on a creative activity or pursuit appropriate to his interests and skills.

For comparison, here is one of Mager's examples—'Given a list of 35 chemical elements, the learner must be able to recall and write the valences of at least 30'.[2] This instructional objective contains both the behaviour that is expected and the criterion of minimum acceptable performance. But a look at Barry and Tye's list shows that broader objectives are not open to such direct measurement. Objective (b) might only require an annual check that the time-table did contain the necessary integrated work, team-teaching, and meetings.

[1] Barry, H. and Tye, F. (1972), *Running a School*. London, Temple Smith.
[2] Mager, *op. cit.*, pp. 28–31.

But no such count of time-tabled subjects labelled 'creative' would indicate the amount of creative activity, objective (c), in the school. Similarly, objective (a) is not open to any obvious numerical indication. Nevertheless, it is still possible to spell out objectives so that the behaviour expected is defined and to indicate levels of performance that are considered to be significant.

The sequence of events in planning evaluation is therefore to plan the indicators at the time that the objectives are being decided. The indicators must have three properties:

1 They must be relevant to the objective under review.
2 They must be spelled out at the same time as the objectives.
3 They must have specified levels of what will be considered as degrees of success or failure.

The range of available indicators stretches from standardized tests to externally set examinations, Mode 3 examinations, reports by inspectors or external moderators or assessors, rating scales, checklists, inventories, teacher-made questionnaires, internal examinations under standard conditions, classroom tests, controlled, and particularly scaled assessments by teachers, and impressionistic ratings. These range from objective to subjective and from externally to the internally referenced.

The in-school evaluation programme will eventually consist of a selection of indicators, collected as routine every year. Collectively they should give an idea of how well the school is running in every aspect of its work. This means that indicators have to cover the academic work in the school, but also the social, the behavioural, the sporting, the cultural, the extra-mural, the relationships with parents, employers, and the public for the school, communications, staff development, and all the elements that comprise the organization necessary for achieving the objectives that lie behind the selection of indicators. The activities sampled will be determined by the staff as they articulate objectives. They will change as objectives change. Indeed, the decision to take evaluation seriously is liable to speed up this change by adding information that will indicate strengths and weaknesses.

The indicators may be selected from data that is already collected for internal use or at the request of DES, local education authority, or governors. It may be specially collected for evaluation. It may consist of objective measures or the subjective views of teachers. These views may occasionally be supplemented by those of inspectors, advisors, pupils, parents, or employers. The main use of the information derived by specifying indicators and organizing the regular collection of data will be by teachers to plan the future work of the school. But the information can also be used as the basis for a balance sheet of the activities of the school, for reports to governors and the local education authority. It can serve as the source for information to the public. This is normal practice in schools. In-school evaluation is not new. The object of this exercise is to share ideas.

It is always difficult to explain to foreigners that teachers in this country carry the responsibility for organizing curricula that is usually firmly in the hands of government elsewhere. But it is also difficult to appreciate the extent of the responsibility carried if you have been educated, and are teaching, in a country where such teacher autonomy is taken for granted. The teachers consulted before the writing of this book took this responsibility seriously and were concerned to evaluate their efforts as part of the burden of that responsibility. They were also prepared to accept the need to work towards a set of indicators that would reflect the broad objectives that they held for their schools. They saw the difficulty, but appreciated that if they claimed responsibility and objected to narrowly based evaluations focused on examination results or test scores only, then they had to present an evaluation programme that was sufficiently broad and representative of their aims for their schools.

In many countries, expected levels of performance in schools are laid down from outside. Test programmes are organized to check the schools. Such an arrangement determined the wages of teachers under the Revised Code of 1862 in England. Many states in the USA lay down aims for their schools, break these up into objectives, and test to check attainment. They go through the process recommended here for evaluation in the school, by the staff. For example, in the Minnesota Statewide Education Assessment Program information is fed to the state government, the Board of Education, local school administrators, and interested citizens.[1] Resources are then allocated to remedy revealed weaknesses. The Assessment Advisory Council who are responsible for the programme consists of twenty-five representatives drawn from teachers, administrators, higher education, and citizens. Special tests were designed to cover reading, mathematics, literature, social studies, science, art, music, writing, career and occupational development, citizenship, health, and physical education. The objectives in these areas were specified by experts in higher education, by teachers, and by citizens. Many American states have organized similar test-based ways of allocating resources.[2]

Such a centralized programme would be incompatible with the freedom of teachers to determine the curriculum in their schools. Furthermore, despite the long list of tests that can be used, some curricular areas can not or should not be measured. Moral behaviour, the wonder of science as distinct from its content or methods, appreciation of beauty, the motivation to read and the love of reading as

[1] Womer, F. B. (1973), *Developing a Large Scale Assessment Program*. Denver, Co-operative Accountability Project.

[2] Department of Education and Science (1978), *Assessment—The American Experience*, London, HMSO.

distinct from being able to read, are examples of objectives valued by many teachers but which would be distorted by measurement. Nevertheless if they are important to teachers it should be possible to agree on criteria, on indicators that would give an idea of whether the staff were being successful in their efforts.

Here we are at the heart of the evaluation problem. If it is to cover all the activities which are considered important, evaluation has to go beyond numerical measures, tests, and examination results. It has to depend on judgements. Much of this book is devoted to ways of improving these judgements. Objectives can be specified to give levels of performance that can then be used in judging how well those objectives are being attained. Throughout the book there is stress on the value of peer evaluation, the use of fellow teachers from within a school or from other schools, and of other professionals and interested parties, in assessing attainment. Such assessments depend on the specification of objectives and agreement on indicators defined to enable the evaluators to say whether an objective has been reached, or to specify that there has been an identifiable level of attainment.

This section has been deliberately titled Indicators. Many of the indicators discussed later will be test scores and statistical evidence that look solid enough to be the characteristic under discussion, rather than merely indicating it. But any grades, scores or assessments relating to the performance of individual pupils or to the standards attained by a school should be treated as data needing interpretation in the light of other available evidence. An intelligence test score may indicate something about the child other than ability to do intelligence tests well or badly, but should not be taken as measuring intelligence as that term is commonly used. The level of attendance may indicate the motivation of pupils but interpretation in the light of other events may show that other explanations are more tenable. Examination results may give a measure of the academic successes of a school, but are reliable indicators only if presented and interpreted alongside other evidence about the intake into the school and curricular objectives. Teacher turnover may indicate the morale of the staff, but will also be a reflection of job opportunities elsewhere in the teaching profession. Each indicator needs a context for interpretation. Each set of indicators still only points to the probable state of play. Once indicators have been collected for a few years, once a set of connected indicators has been worked out, and once these indicators are presented within a broader assessment they can be a valuable means of suggesting future policy. But they still only indicate. Most of the indicators in this book are in the form of numbers. This follows from the interests of those consulted. Teachers asked for ways of producing statistics that had some objective basis. They were sceptical of opinions and impressions under the label of evaluation. But it would be wrong to imply that even a major part of any school evaluation programme would be quantitative. Few aspects of school life lend themselves readily to measurement. The sequence of planning must never be to look for available measures and build them into the evaluation programme. The indicators are selected after an aspect has been agreed upon as deserving priority. They should be used only after their relation to the performance expected has been agreed. They should also contain levels of performance specified in advance. If evaluation is to include judgements, there are still procedures for raising the level of objectivity.

The list of possible indicators will need to match the items of school life that teachers consider important. This will mean a long list. Here are the goals of the Oregon Board of Education. [1]

Reading	Scientific processes	Responsible behaviour
Writing	Moral and ethical choice	Rights and respon-
Computation	Management of personal	sibilities as citizen
Spelling	resources	of community, state,
Listening	Family life	nation, world
Problem-solving	Dignity and value of work	Understand, respect, interact with
Self-direction	Personal aptitudes, interests	cultures, generations, races
Occupations	Physical and mental health	
Arts	Career choice	
Humanities	Career skills	

Most English teachers would produce a list at least this long.

Throughout the rest of this book the need to evaluate after some consideration of objectives is repeatedly stressed. Evaluation has to be parsimonious to ensure that the maximum information is collected and used with the minimum effort. It has to reflect on the priorities of staff. Yet there is a need for the collection of routine data. First, decisions are best made after looking at the facts of the situation. The allocation of resources, the reorganization of the curriculum, the in-service training of teachers, the formation of new teaching groups, indeed, all the decisions that have to be made as conditions within or around the school change, require information that should be stored ready for use, preferably in the form of time series so that changes across the years can be detected. But this detection points to another reason for collecting and storing data regardless of any decision over objectives. The data itself, displayed as graphs or tables, can indicate unforeseen, unanticipated developments, problems that are just arriving or successes that have not been noticed. The scrutiny of regularly collected information can point to the need to reconsider objectives. This point is taken up again in Chapter 8 when the organization of evaluation is considered. It is not that there is infor- mation for monitoring developments and separate information for

[1] *ibid.*, p. 13.

assessing the attainment of objectives. A glance back at Figure 1:1 will show that it is rather a matter of where you start in the cycle of evaluation, and whether that evaluation is implicit or explicit. Even in the most casually run school data is collected and decisions are made after its interpretation. Those decisions take into account objectives, even if these are only implicit. Information leads to the consideration of objectives. The consideration of objectives leads to the articulation of information needs.

To be realistic, many teachers will want to move immediately to the collection of indicators without labouring over a discussion of objectives. This is merely to enter the cycle of planning at a different point and will soon lead back to a discussion of aims, objectives, learning strategies, and new indicators. Short-circuiting is inevitable in the busy world of the school. Sooner or later, implicitly or explicitly, the sequence of events in this chapter is followed.

Finally an obvious point has to be made. Evaluation is a means to an end, not an end in itself. There is a fascination about figures. But evaluation should serve only as an aid to decision-making. The information collected serves this end and as an early-warning system, through the regular scrutiny of data. But that data and the evaluation arrangements can fossilize and be for show only. At times it is wise to evaluate the evaluation.

2. The School Assessment Programme: internally referenced

This book attempts to provide means whereby the staff of schools can evaluate their efforts and provide dependable information for their public to make informed judgements. This involves the production of reliable and if possible quantitative data. But, while it is easy to write a book outlining the technical, quantitative aspects of assessment, it is probably useless. There is no point in yet another unread book laying down methods not only beyond the interests of many teachers, but overtaxing their free time and patience. The most promising starting-point seemed to be the questions that teachers ask themselves about their work in the school rather than the answers provided by statisticians in academia. The questions that follow were asked by the teachers consulted about in-school evaluation.

How am I doing as a teacher, compared with other teachers? How do we, as a staff, compare with other staff in other schools? Is it possible to mark objectively and yet not label pupils? How can you inform parents of the real ability of their child without making yourself seem inefficient, and possibly harming the child? How do standards in my department compare with those in others? How do standards this year compare with those in previous years? How does this school perform compared with similar schools?

Behind these questions lie a number of dilemmas. Objectivity is a necessary feature of teaching. But early, possibly premature labelling may reinforce other handicaps and ensure that the label eventually fits. Giving objective information to the public of the school will make it easy for hostile judgements to be substantiated. Like may not be being compared with like, either when comparing schools or looking at trends in the same school. Evaluation focuses the spotlight on the school and its teachers.

The questions asked by teachers also reveal different purposes for evaluation, and different audiences. The questions refer to the assessment of pupils as well as to the assessment of the staff, and hence of the school as an organization. The information is required for pupils, for teachers, but also for the public for the school. Most of the data for use in evaluation is derived from the attainment of pupils, but some indicators will reflect only on the school as a whole. But there are also different reference points for these questions. Some refer to the situation inside the school only. Some refer to other schools and make external comparisons. Different purposes, audiences, and reference points may require different forms of assessment data on which evaluation can be based.

The questions in the Introduction were concerned with the difficulties in moving from academic advice on evaluation to what is practicable in a school. Out of the mass of assessments that go on in a school, only a few will form part of the evaluation programme. It is on these few per cent of the total that the efforts of the staff to evaluate should be concentrated. But even those few per cent need to be related to different reference points. These references can be inside or outside the school. They can be against some absolute standard of performance or against the performance of other schools or other pupils. They can be against the current performance of schools or pupils, or against the past performance of the pupils in the school, or the school itself.

All teachers are experts in grading, marking, and assessing. So much practice is obtained that an experienced teacher can give a mark out of ten or an A to E grade for any activity or product. From a detached position this may seem facile, yet it is an integral part of teaching. But the marks or grades given have little value as bases for anything but immediate action in the classroom. Where the assessments are to be used to rank, stream, set, select, or report, there is a need for some common standard of marking between teachers. But even marks given by different teachers in a school, based on the same assumptions and fixed in average and range, may be unsuitable as a record of the performance of a child outside the context of a particular school or for evaluating a school against the achievements of other schools or against national norms. The choice of techniques in assessing depends firstly on the purposes for which assessment is being made.

A look at the actual practice of assessment in schools reveals three levels. Each serves a different purpose. None is inferior to the other. The choice between them is made according to the time and trouble involved, and the degree of objectivity required for the job in hand. Generally, the higher the degree of objectivity required, the greater is the need for careful design. It is possible to design and use objective instruments for all assessment purposes, but there would be little time left for teaching. The solution is to be clear about the purposes of assessing, the appropriate techniques for each purpose, and to avoid confusing off-the-cuff measures with more objective scores. Three levels of assessment can, and should, be separated:

1 *The running assessment programme* used by teachers as part of their classroom technique.
2 *The controlled assessment programme* used when teachers agree to use comparable standards of assessment, or to use marks, grades, or comments that can be referred to some agreed standard of performance for interpretation.
3 *The externally referenced assessment programme* when attainments are

related to standards laid down outside the school in standardized test norms, public examinations, or by external assessors.

The running assessment programme

Teachers use assessments to motivate, control, and guide, as well as to give themselves and their pupils some idea of strengths and weaknesses, progress and regress. This is the way difficult parts of a course are identified. It is the way successful and unsuccessful teaching methods are identified. It is the way the teacher gauges when to move on to the next part of the syllabus. It is a key part of the dialogue of teaching. Such assessments can range from the instantaneous recognition of an understanding look in the eye of a pupil, or an interpretation of the number of hands up for an answer, through the 'Well done', 'Good', and 'Wake-up' that are the language of the classroom, to the marks out of ten that serve as assessment, guide, and early-warning system. These marks are based on impressions only. Given their purposes they do not need elaboration. However systematic a planned evaluation is in a school, the majority of assessments will remain impressionistic and cost-effective for the purposes they serve. But these purposes are related to the immediate teaching situation and are not suitable for public consumption or as a basis for important decisions by teacher or pupil involving comparisons between different options. There is no guarantee that the assessments between teachers are comparable.

There are assessments confined to internal teaching situations that do need elaboration. For example, while all teachers diagnose strengths and weaknesses in pupils as they mark, and add comments to help improve performance, there are often times when more thorough diagnosis is necessary. There are many standardized diagnostic tests available, and an examination of scores on the individual items of any test can yield information that will guide the teacher in helping a pupil. Teacher-made tests are also worth the investment where basic skills are involved. For example, The Bullock Committee in *A Language for Life* recommends the use of an informal reading inventory.[1] Here the teacher chooses a suitable passage of some 200 to 300 words and prepares questions to test comprehension skills, word recognition, and passage reading.[2] The pupil is classified as capable of reading at three levels of mastery. The 'Independent' classification means that no support from the teacher is needed. The

[1] *A Language for Life*, Report of the Committee of Enquiry, Chairman Sir A. Bullock (1975). London, HMSO.
[2] Vincent, D. and Cresswell, M. (1976), *Reading Tests in the Classroom*. Windsor, NFER Publishing Co., pp. 58–9.

'Instructional' classification means that occasional teacher help is needed. The 'Frustrational' classification means that the pupil can not read on his own. In addition to this basis of diagnosis, this informal inventory can be used to see if a pupil is likely to be able to cope with a particular book. Numerical criteria for judging how to classify a pupil have been produced, based on the percentage of correct answers given. This technique of assessing pupils against some previously defined level of performance to gauge how well they have mastered a skill will be developed further in this chapter and is recommended in many parts of this book. This technique does not yield information on how a pupil is doing compared with others, but gauges attainment against some pre-determined standard.

Marks recorded from impression marking should only be used to give impressions of attainment or effort. Each mark relates to an instantaneous judgement by the teacher without reference to any standard beyond an impression that one piece of work is good or bad compared with other pieces of work presented by other pupils as part of the same exercise or stored up in the mind of the teacher. This is adequate as an ongoing check on the standard of work of pupils. The marks of each teacher may be comparable with that teacher's previous marking. But it is the equivalent of measuring length by pacing. There is no guarantee that the length of one teacher's pace is the same as that of another. When pupils are being compared to see where their strengths lie between different subjects, or reports are being prepared for parents, or the level of attainment between different school classes is being compared, a yardstick is needed for common use by the teachers involved. For there to be comparability in the level of marking between teachers of the same subject, or between teachers in different subjects, there has to be some standard in common use in the school, restraining the impressions of individual teachers. As soon as marks are to be collected together from more than one teacher, comparability has to be ensured.

The distinction made earlier between the various bases of evaluation has however to be remembered. Instantaneous assessments often include consideration of a variety of qualities manifested by the pupils or the school. They are often an expression of the general feeling that a teacher, or a parent, or an employer may have at that time of the pupil, class, or school. Attainment and effort, current or past performance, assessment against set standards or against peers, against in-school, or local, or national standards, may all be confused. Running assessments should not be made public because they are usually not comparable between teachers in a department or in a school, or between different schools. But they should also remain private because they contain many unsorted qualities. This is not a criticism of such impressionistic assessment as a teaching device. But where important decisions are to be made for or by pupils, or by or for teaching staff, the bases of the assessment must be sorted out.

The controlled assessment programme

Here are four subject grades extracted from an annual report on an eleven-year-old pupil, sent to his parents in July.

Craft   B-   Grades are based on the year's work in
Home Economics   B   which A = Well above average; B = Above
Music   A   average; C = Average; D = Below average.
Science   B-

In order to interpret these grades, the parents, or other teachers using this information in the following year would need to ask for more information:

1 What is being assessed?
2 (a) What standards have been applied?
  (b) What group has the average with whom the pupil is being compared?
  (c) What other characteristics has this group, particularly what spread of grades was there?

Asking these questions is a first step towards interpreting the grades. To anticipate the questions and to present assessments that are immediately useful for fellow-teachers or for parents, the teacher must accept the need for control of marking, grading, and commenting over the small part of his assessing that is to be used for giving information to others about the pupils. The first question to ask about any evidence is 'how has its collection been controlled'? We expect a detective to be able to spell out evidence so that its credibility can be assessed. We expect a doctor's diagnosis to be based on standard diagnostic practices that can be checked through a second opinion if necessary. Teaching assessments that are used to pass on important information about a child should be referable to procedures and standards that enable its credence to be established and the information given to be interpreted.

What is being assessed

The most obvious weakness of a single grade, not referenced to anything but an unexplained average, is that there is no way of telling whether it refers to attainment, persistence, effort, ability, promise, or some other characteristic. Yet it is common for the basis of assessments to be left unexplained. As an example, here is the way a school gives a separate grade for attainment and effort.

The attainment scale used is: A = Excellent.   B = Above average.   C = Average.   D = Below average.   E = Poor.   The effort scale used is: 1 = Exceptionally hard working.   2 = Works harder than average.   3 = Puts in an average amount of work.   4 = Does less work than average.   5 = Lazy.

This is an advance on a single scale, but still gives a minimum of information. First, it does not contain any way that the 'average' can be interpreted. But even more immediate, it does not define 'effort'. The implication of the definitions 1 to 5 is that the effort of any one pupil is being compared with that of others, although whether this is a form or a year-group is not made clear. But effort can refer to how this pupil was working last term or last year. It can mean effort against personal standards, or against some standard defined by the teachers. Usually an effort grade is meant to give a comparison against some standard established through the experience of the teacher concerned. But this standard is often a confusion of assessment against a group of pupils, against some anticipated level of effort, and against the previous work of the pupil concerned.

To separate out these aspects of 'effort' or any other characteristics, the basis for interpretation should be spelled out before the assessment is made and before the grades are released. In the example above the group against which the effort is being assessed should be listed and it should be made clear that this is the basis of the grade. If the basis is to the previous performance of the individual pupil it might be better to use a +2, +1, 0, −1, −2 scale with 0 spelled out as no change and the other four grades defined in terms of improved or deteriorating effort. If the basis is to be some set of standards set by the teachers, the criteria have to be spelled out again. Thus a 3 grade could be defined as 'pupil has made a similar effort as the average pupil in his or her class'. Whatever the basis of the grade, it should be discussed and preferably agreed between staff in advance of use.

Marking to a common standard

The grades for Craft, Home Economics, Music, and Science reported above might be the result of very different standards being applied from subject to subject. Furthermore, different teachers within these subjects might use very different standards. The consequence of this use of personal rather than agreed standards can be unfair to pupils and provide misleading information for making decisions about them. This is not a problem for running assessment, but control over standards, however slight, is necessary if assessment is used for making decisions outside the classroom. This standardization can range from mathematical scaling to a loose agreement to spell out the standards to which assessments will be referred. For the present only tests designed to spread pupil marks around an average will be considered. Tests designed to check the attainment of specified levels of performance will be considered later.

It is easy to demonstrate the need to bring marks that are to be used as the basis of decisions about pupils to some known scale. Here are the scores of ten pupils, A to J, on two tests in subjects x and y.

	A	B	C	D	E	F	G	H	I	J
Test x	50	20	25	85	55	35	90	30	70	40
Text y	60	55	55	40	45	90	50	20	45	40

The temptation on receipt of marks like these is to make assumptions that could be misleading. Pupil J seems to be equally good or bad at subject x and y. But has the teacher of x marked harder or softer than the teacher of y? A staff can determine this by agreeing that they mark to an average of 50. This is so in this case. But an average of 50 can be obtained by five marks of 49 and five of 51, as well as by five of 90 and five of 10. Yet being top with 51 surely means something different from being top with 90? To be meaningful a mark has not only got to be related to the average, but to the spread, the range of all the marks. But the range on our subject tests in x and y is the same at 70, from 20 to 90. But a further look will show that if we exclude these extreme scores there is a marked difference in the distribution of the remaining marks on the two tests. In x they are spread out from 25 to 85. In y they are concentrated between 40 and 60. The scores on the two tests are still not comparable.

The simplest way of ensuring some comparability of marks between teachers in the same subject departments, or between teachers in different subjects, is for the staff to agree in advance to the use of a common method of allocating marks for a whole year-group or for groups of similar ability. This usually means fixing an average and a distribution of scores around this average. Some teachers will accept that marking is such a chancy business that it is not a sacrifice of professional skill to agree to fixing the average and spread of marks in advance. Others will oppose any constraint. There is, however, no guarantee that all teachers will be able or willing to keep to an agreed marking scheme. This can be overcome by scaling marks after they have been initially awarded. In both cases there has to be agreement of staff over a method of making marks and grades comparable.

Table 2.1 shows a marking scheme for comparisons between pupil attainments on an examination agreed in advance by teachers for the top band of three forms totalling 75 pupils out of a year-group of six forms. The agreement was to aim to place equal numbers of pupils above and below a score of 50. In technical terms a score of 50 was to be the median, that is, the score of the pupil or pupils with half those taking the test scoring more and the other half less. The spread of marks is also fixed in this agreement. The marking scheme was to serve as a rough guide, but it was agreed that any major shift away from the distribution should be justified. The comparability was considered to be essential as the marks on the third-year examinations were used as a basis of subject options. The pupils and their teachers and parents had to choose between subjects and this choice had to be made on dependable evidence. With no control over the average and the spread, the wrong decisions could be made. There are objections to constraining marks in this way, particularly where the numbers involved, in this case 75 pupils, is small. But it gave some assurance that it was the attainments of the pupils that were reflected in the marks, not the particular marking standards used by the teachers.

Table 2:1   Marking scheme for third year top band of 75 pupils in an urban comprehensive school

Range of marks	Over 75	58–74	42–57	26–41	Under 25
Grade	A	B	C	D	E
Numbers of pupils	4	19	30	19	3

Many teachers will object to having to accept an arbitrary scale for their marking. There will be few objections where examination marks for a whole year-group are scaled, but many will argue with justice that one class does differ from another, that there are good and bad years. They will maintain that their impressions should not be adjusted to an arbitrary marking scheme. If these objections prove insurmountable, scaling marks after they have been awarded can be considered. In either case it is correct to be cautious about scaling. Not only does it make mathematical assumptions about the distribution of marks among groups taking a test which might not be borne out in practice, but it can conceal weaknesses in the test. No mathematical treatment can overcome flaws in the design of a test, but the figures can make the results of a poor test look too convincing.

If no prior agreement can be reached about the average and spread of marks, or the proportion to fall into grades, it may be possible to reach agreement on scaling after initial marks have been given. In this way each teacher can preserve his or her own marks, but those marks are brought to a common basis before being used for comparisons with other sets of marks. The simplest method, percentile scoring, is illustrated here. There are many other methods, some using formula for conversion, some graphs. They all share the common purpose of eliminating differences in standards of marking.

The easiest way of avoiding the appearance of consistency and comparability in what are actually impression marks is merely to rank the pupils in order of attainment. But the best pupil may get nothing wrong on a mathematics test while the second pupil only gets 60 per cent right, the third 59 per cent, and so on. The ranks ignore the size of differences. This is, once again, a problem that arises with small groups. Percentile scores spread ranks out on a scale of 100, enable comparisons to be made on this basis, and convert ranks in small groups into what they would be in a group of 100. The first step is to rank the pupils. Here are ten pupils, A to J, in rank order on a test:

Pupil	A	B	C	D	E	F	G	H	I	J
Rank	3	4	1	7	2	6	5	10	9	8

The formula for converting these ranks into percentile scores is percentile rank $= 100 \times [(N + 1) - R]/N$ where $N =$ number in group and $R =$ rank of single pupil. So for pupil A, percentile rank $= 100 \times [(10 + 1) - 3]/10 = 100 \times 8/10 = 80$. The percentile ranks for the ten pupils will be:

Pupil	A	B	C	D	E	F	G	H	I	J
Percentile rank	80	70	100	40	90	50	60	10	20	30

(Where ranks are equal as with two pupils on seventh place, place the next pupil in the ninth rank. Then average the two tied pupils $[(7 + 8)/2 = 7.5]$ and proceed as before.)

The advantage of percentile scoring can be seen if we ask whether pupil G above has done better on the test than in coming 14th out of a group of 31 on another test. His percentile score on the latter would be $100 \times [(31 + 1) - 14]/31 = 100 \times 18/31 = 58$. The safest conclusion is that there is no difference between the performance of G on the two tests.

With large numbers of pupils it is easiest to convert raw to percentile ranks by the use of a graph through the good offices of the mathematics department. Percentiles are useful when comparisons between results in different subjects have to be made. They should not be used for making comparisons between groups which are not comparable on the attainment being assessed. They should never be added together or averaged.

There are many different ways of scaling marks. But, given the constraints of time in a school, it is unrealistic to assume that more than a few of the important internal examinations and gradings should be assessed on an arbitrary scale to ensure comparability. It is best to be parsimonious because scaling is time-consuming and teachers resent having to adopt arbitrary scales. In practice, however, the use of standardized tests and public examinations means that some scores are obtained that are comparable. The 'standardized' aspect of standardized tests means that the raw score of any pupil is referred to a table of norms and converted to a score which takes account of age and sometimes sex. This score usually has two known characteristics. Its mean (arithmetical average) and spread of marks around that mean are known. Because all scores on the test have these same known characteristics they can be compared one with another and with scores on other tests which give scores having the same characteristics. As most standardized tests are designed to have common characteristics they are a useful way of comparing performance in different areas of attainment. But comparisons of scores on such tests should only be made once it has been confirmed that the characteristics are the same. The usual mean is 100 and the usual spread is a standard deviation of 15. This standard deviation is a measure of the spread of the marks around the mean. In a conventionally standardized test with a mean of 100 and a standard deviation of 15, the design ensures that in a large sample some two thirds of scores will fall between 85 and 115 and all but 5 per cent fall between 60 and 130. Designing tests with these characteristics means that the results on each can be compared.

We can now answer the remaining questions on the grades given for the four subjects on page 23. As soon as it is known whether marks or grades have been given for relative performance in a form, a set, a whole year-group and so on, the grades begin to have meaning. They become comparable when we know that they have been based on an agreed scale in advance of grading, or have been scaled after ranking. This approach is based on comparing each pupil with the performance of a group of pupils, whether a single class, a year-group, or, in the case of a standardized test, a sample of pupils having known characteristics and who are representative of a wider grouping. The individual pupil is graded on performance relative to the norm or standard of a group. Technically this is norm-referenced assessment.

Criterion referencing

Assessment may often be more meaningful if it is made against some set standard rather than by comparison with other pupils. Teachers often use simple norm-referenced assessments such as 'work of average quality', or 'above' or 'below average'. But they also refer to standards of attainment or behaviour for assessment. Conduct for example is frequently assessed against some standard held internally by the teacher. In other cases levels of performance can be laid down in advance and their attainment determines the grade given. Assessment is made against a set of previously established criteria or objectives, not against the performance of other pupils. Technically this is criterion-referenced assessment.

A simple set of examples are found in Scouting. Badges are given when a skill such as knotting, handcraft, or safety is mastered. The skill is defined in advance and the badge is given, not by performance relative to other Scouts, but to mastery of the skill. Another example are grades in music awarded by the Associated Examining Board of the Royal Schools of Music. Grades are awarded on performance judged against standards laid down by the Royal Schools. The grades are criterion-referenced. The candidates do not compete against each other, but strive to achieve one of the previously defined levels of competence.

The establishment of criteria is part of the same exercise as establishing objectives. The first step is to identify the knowledge, the skills, performances, behaviour, or products which are agreed by the staff concerned. Listing objectives is the first step to judging success in learning. The second step is to agree on a standard of performance that will be accepted by staff as indicating mastery. This is usually set at some arbitrary number or percentage of correct or satisfactory responses. This is not of course an easy task. There are criterion-referenced tests that have been constructed with the same care as the more conventional standardized tests that are familiar to all teachers for use in selection and which are generally norm-referenced. [1] Just as it is easy to give grades relating to 'average', so it is easy to specify a number of criteria and to assess whether pupils have achieved these or not. It is possible to move from these impressionistic assessments to others that are agreed among staff, tested against other assessments, and scrutinized for consistency. But the principle behind each kind of assessment is important. If it is accepted that in-school evaluation has to start with a consideration of objectives, despite all the difficulties and dangers involved, then criterion-referenced assessment will play a large part in the evaluation programme. This accounts for the emphasis given to this approach in the chapters that follow.

There is however another advantage in assessing against criteria. Because they spring from the objectives of the teachers and because the assessment is in terms of mastery, the criteria serve as useful teaching devices. This is why criterion-referenced testing was developed in relation to instructional technology. Here it was essential that the student received information on success or failure in a step in the learning process, as a guide to whether to go on or go back. It was also a way of assessing the success of the various learning strategies used. Norm-referenced tests are useful for selecting and differentiating, but do not yield information that enables learning sequences to be followed and the success of teaching methods to be assessed. Criterion-referenced assessment also yields readily interpretable information. To know that so many pupils have attained a defined level of performance is often a more useful piece of information than grades arranged around an average but unrelated to any actual attainment, performance, or skill. For example, areas of basic skills as defined by a school staff may be divided up into agreed levels of attainment. These could be indicated by statements defining the particular level, or by a specified score on a test. The choice would come through agreement among the staff involved. Thus it might be agreed that the top of five grades in social studies should be 'capable of assessing evidence to draw conclusions and of using that evidence to hypothesize about social relations'. Pupils showing this capacity are graded A. This grade then has meaning in relation to the course.

---

[1] Sumner, R. and Robertson, T. S. (1977), *Criterion Referenced Measurement and Criterion Referenced Tests*. Windsor, NFER Publishing Co.

Often a level of attainment is specified as mastery. This can once again be defined by a statement, or by a proportion of questions answered correctly on a test, or the ability to reproduce a skill. It is an old idea. The masterpiece that qualified the apprentice was criterion-referenced and was scored to indicate mastery of the craft.

The stress laid on establishing criteria in the chapters that follow arises from the need to monitor levels of performance in in-school evaluation. But norm-referenced and criterion-referenced assessments are not alternatives. Both have their places. This applies across the whole spectrum of tests from impressionistic to standardized. It is useful for teachers to inform pupils of where they stand in relation to others in a class, year group, or some national sample. It is also useful to inform them of attainments they have mastered. Once again this can be achieved through crude reference to some specified level of attainment based on some subjective standards held by the teacher, or can be a level determined on a carefully designed test developed outside the school. The important question to ask about any assessment is 'what is its reference?'. The grade, score, or percentage has meaning only when referred to some set of standards or norms, or to some set of criteria. Interpretation can only follow reference. Most of the assessment techniques that will be used by teachers will not have high reliability or validity. But it should always be made clear that assessments have frames of reference whether based on norms or criteria. These should always be made explicit.

One of the problems of norm-referenced assessment applied to teacher-made tests taken across a single class or year-group is that scaling to facilitate comparability between different scores means fixing the distribution of marks around the mean in an arbitrary way. In large groups this is less of a problem. Most marks on attainments will bunch in the middle around the mean and taper on either side, giving a bell-shaped, normal curve. But no assumptions can be made about the distribution of marks in small groups and teachers rightly object to the distortion that can result from scaling where some such assumption is necessary. Classes do differ across a year-group or year by year. Criterion-referenced assessment does not have to overcome this difficulty. The interest is not on distribution around the mean but in determining who has passed, or failed some pre-determined criteria of attainment. The test is anchored at the ends not the middle, and performance is judged without reference to any average for the group. However, although scaling problems do not arise with criterion-referenced testing they are still difficult and time-consuming to construct. They depend on agreement among professionals liable to disagree, particularly over whether test items really represent the skills being assessed. The standards of construction applied to conventional norm-referenced standardized tests are also applicable to those that are criterion-referenced. These standards are dealt with in Chapter 3.

Profiles and pupil records

The scaling of marks to produce comparability enables profiles of pupil attainments to be built up between and within subjects. Here for example is a hypothetical profile of a pupil in mathematics (Figure 2:1). Instead of presenting a single score, each aspect of the subject is kept separate. The assessment is norm-referenced yet gives detail on strengths and weaknesses.

Figure 2:1   Mathematics profile

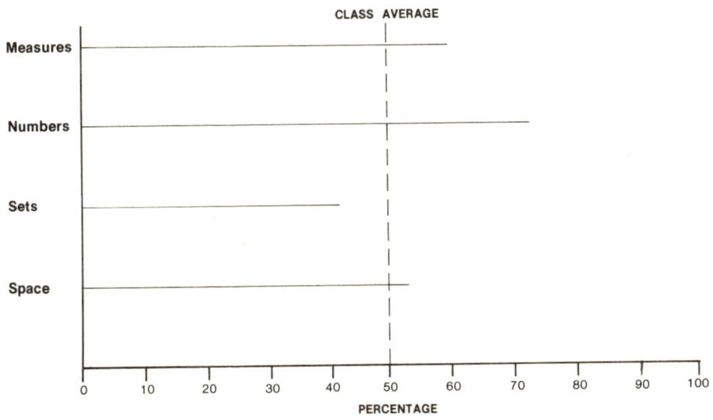

[1] SCRE, *Profile Assessment System: Manual, op. cit.*

This profile (Figure 2:1) is more useful as a learning device than as a score summarizing overall performance in mathematics. Most subjects are suitable for this first step in specifying important areas which should be mastered. However, the most common method of recording performance on pupil records is to place an A to E, 1 to 10, or a percentage into one box per subject. Frequently this assessment has no reference and has meaning only to the teacher who has used a personal, intuitive standard. Some school staffs refer grades to a previously agreed scale. The sequence is then first to rank and then to allocate pupils to grades according to some agreed distribution. It is rare to find criterion-referenced assessment in secondary schools. Primary school teachers are more used to recording progress on reading or mathematics checklists. These consist of sequences of standards of progress that serve as means of assessment, but more importantly, as teaching devices.

There are various ways in which norm- and criterion-referenced assessments can be combined. For example, the most thorough attempt to produce a secondary school assessment system uses norm-referenced assessment, but has guides for teachers on the levels of performance signified by each of the grades given.[1] This pupil profile system was produced by a working party of Scottish head-teachers, representatives from industry, education authorities, colleges of education, further education, Her Majesty's Inspectors, and the Scottish Council for Research in Education. The records are available commercially in two versions, one for manual and one for computer use.[2]

The aim of this ambitious exercise was to produce assessments along a number of dimensions. These are recorded on sheets designed to facilitate easy retrieval of the grades. After two or three assessments each year have been recorded along each dimension for the years of secondary schooling, a school-leaving report can be prepared from the data. The dimensions cover basic skills of listening, speaking, reading, writing, visual understanding and expression, use of number, physical co-ordination, and manual dexterity. There are also assessments of work-related skills. Enterprise and perseverance are included on the profile with suggestions that such aspects as co-operation, responsibility, confidence, self-reliance, and adaptability be written in by teachers. Finally, teachers fill in subject areas to be assessed on another form.

The impression of this system from a look at the forms involved suggests a mechanical filling in of grades, ending up with a matrix of 1 to 5 marks that might have little meaning beyond the standards applied by the teachers concerned. The guidance given for assessment is that teachers should judge across an age group. The top 10 per cent will be graded 1, the next 20 per cent 2, the middle 40 per cent 3, the next 20 per cent 4, and the bottom 10 per cent 5. This norm-referencing is however left to the teacher and is not supposed to be arbitrary. Any such profile system can degenerate into giving grades without much thought, so that the important assessments at the end of a pupil's school career are made off-the-cuff without reference to the record that has been so carefully accumulated. It is often the existence of unused or mechanically completed records that wastes time. But this profile system has the benefit of criteria to guide teachers as they grade. They are asked to visualize five pupils who fall into each of the grades. Each of the grades is then defined by a criterion, a standard of performance. The main interest of this Scottish system lies in these criteria.

Here is an example of this referencing of grades to statements defining the qualities judged to have been attained by pupils of five grades in the learning of English.[1] These criteria were prepared by a panel of English teachers. It is one of nine aspects of English teaching, each being covered in a similar way.

[1] Scottish Council for Research in Education (1977), *Pupils in Profile*. London, Hodder and Stoughton. *See also* SCRE (1977), *Profile Assessment System: Manual*. Edinburgh, SCRE.
[2] Safeguard Business Systems, Loomer Road, Chesterton, Newcastle, Staffs

CREATIVITY

To our minds, this refers to originality and imagination. We see it as applying to all aspects of work in the English classroom including writing, drama, drawing, dance, model-making and so on.

1. He is full of ideas and consistently responds in new, exciting and unusual ways. He shows signs of (at least the beginnings of) an inimitable personal style.
2. He does not lack ideas and can be relied upon for a vivid response.
3. He may create clear and even vivid responses to a variety of stimuli, but his efforts may often be uninspired.
4. He makes limited imaginative responses and *occasionally* produces original matter.
5. He makes extremely limited response and fails to produce any original matter.

Creativity is typical in being an important but unmeasurable quality. One complaint about attempts to produce assessments that have some degree of objectivity is that they are restricted to a limited range of subject areas. It is difficult to get beyond the stage of considering objectives when the majority of school activities are considered for assessment because they have no easily identifiable product, or the objectives themselves are intangible, subject to rapid change, or disturbed by the very act of assessing. Inevitably therefore the criteria specified will become broader in definition once curricular areas not concerned with measurable skills are evaluated. But these criteria can still reflect the views of the teachers responsible for organizing the work and can still indicate achievement and clarify the expected outcomes.

The need to invest in continuous assessment has increased with the attempt to adjust learning situations to individuals rather than to school classes as a whole. It is easy to exaggerate the changes, but there has been a shift in the secondary schools following earlier developments in the primary sector. The response to the need to develop recording and assessments that will ensure continuity of learning has been delayed because it takes time that has tended to be devoted to the developments themselves. In the examples of new forms of assessment that follow there are obvious dangers. Pupils do not necessarily learn in the same sequence. They forget a lot after apparently attaining mastery. But in each of the examples given here there has been an awareness of these and other problems. The solution is to leave the teachers responsible to select and use techniques flexibly in the context of particular schools. The points at which progress is checked can be spaced out. The assessments can be made at a few stages where staff agree that an important skill should have been mastered. These examples are attempts to reduce the labour involved in producing tailor-made schemes in each school. But they still assume that teachers will use them with discrimination.

The spread of learner-centred and mixed-ability learning situations in secondary schools has stimulated many new developments in assessment and record keeping. The way to support curriculum developments with assessment techniques and records that were an integral part of the curriculum package was pioneered in some early Schools Council projects. This unity of curriculum and assessment has long been appreciated in primary schooling where individualized learning was developed. For example, the Inner London Education Authority's mathematics inspectors have developed Guidelines and Checkpoints. The former indicate the basic mathematical concepts and skills that pupils of different ages can be expected to master. The Checkpoints provide a resource for teachers to develop their own assessment and recording to match their own curriculum. Jo Stephens, writing on these Checkpoints likens them to checkpoints in a car rally or cross-country race.[1] It is a standard port-of-call, necessary to ensure that vital connecting ideas are mastered and that mathematically fatal discontinuity is not masked.

In Inner London secondary schools the Secondary Mathematics Individualized Learning Experiment (SMILE) is one of many authority-wide projects being developed by working parties of inspectors, advisors, and teachers. SMILE is designed for use in mixed ability groups in the lower forms of secondary schools. Teachers play an active part in adding new materials so that the experiment remains open-ended. The key feature is that pupils are given a series of matrices to guide them through a series of planned mathematical tasks. The matrices provide a framework for the orderly development of mathematical principles. The pupils work from cards and can check their success on each matrix before proceding to the next. The completion of each section is tested and the teacher records the progress made.

These developments are examples of an upsurge of interest in new methods of assessment as the organization of learning has been changed. The common characteristics of all this activity is that it starts with an appraisal of the objectives of the teachers involved and includes working parties to ensure that some agreement is obtained over the anticipated learning outcomes before the curriculum with its accompanying assessment techniques is consolidated. The cycle of planning is that recommended here for evaluating the work of the school. This is not accidental. Because evaluation is an integral part of the organization of learning, and because new developments in that organization depend on adequate recording and assessment, there has had to be a more systematic approach based on the assumptions and priorities of the teachers concerned. But these developments also create uncertainty and anxiety over both ends and means. Consequently new forms of evaluation are at a premium.

All this activity arises from concern with new curricula and

[1] Stephens, J. (1977), 'Checkpoints in Primary Maths'. *Contact*, issue 27, pp. 27-8.

teaching methods rather than with pressure for accountability exerted from outside the school. Older forms of assessment were based on tests designed to differentiate between pupils being taught as a class. Newer forms of assessment need to be designed to give information on the levels of attainment being reached by pupils to enable planning for continuity in individualized learning situations. Comprehensive schooling and developments inside the secondary schools have produced a need for assessment techniques that will help pupils and teachers once groups of pupils are not taught as if they were homogeneous. In the sciences and technical subjects where individual methods have always been common there have always been methods of planning and of checking the steps towards mastery. Such techniques are increasingly central to mixed ability groups and their advantages have been seen to extend to conventional class teaching.

These developments call for a lot of hard work and a lot of expertise from the teachers involved. Curriculum development of any sort is hard work, but when it is in the direction of individualizing learning there has to be the extra strain of designing adequate recording and assessment. However, the growing number of teachers with in-service, diploma, and post-graduate qualifications is increasing. In addition, there are increasing numbers involved in CSE validation and moderation. These teachers are used to examining objectives, syllabi, methods of examination, continuous assessment, and marking. There are also large numbers of teachers who have been involved in curriculum projects associated with the Nuffield Foundation or Schools Council. The nature of Schools Council Projects has also changed as secondary schooling has become comprehensive, and methods and organization first introduced in the primary schools have spread. The directors of the early projects in the 1960s helped these new developments along and were overtaken by them. In the 1970s more attention is being given to supporting teachers in the changed situation. But the sophistication of the teaching force has increased with participation in all kinds of project.

A significant development is the *Progress in Learning Science* project organized under Wynne Harlen for the Schools Council at the University of Reading.[1] Dr. Harlen has been concerned with the evaluation of earlier Schools Council science projects. Her concern at Reading was to help teachers to collect reliable information for planning classroom activities. Since pupils were seen to have particular aptitudes, abilities, and attainments, learning situations were seen as necessarily individual. There was a need to help pupils and teachers

[1] Harlen, W. (1976), *Progress in Learning Science, Check List for Later Development*. Schools Council Project at the University of Reading. This project has been published as: Harlen, W. (1977), *Match and Mismatch*. Edinburgh, Oliver and Boyd.

to handle the sequences of learning experiences. The objective was to produce an assessment and recording system that would enable activities to be matched to the characteristics of the pupils and to their previous stage of development. While the project is called *Progress in Learning Science*, Dr. Harlen sees it as having more general application to individualized learning situations.

Part of the exercise of matching pupils at particular stages of development to appropriate learning situations consists of the production of checklists. These were designed by working parties of teachers. The checklists were to serve two purposes. First, they were to guide teacher observations of pupils so that the development of abilities and attitudes could be assessed. Second, the checklists were to serve as a record of development. Such recording would take place two or three times a year. They would show the individual strengths and weaknesses of pupils and serve as a guide to longer-term planning by teachers. The teachers involved in the working parties tried out different forms of record. Illustrated opposite is a method that they favoured.[1] It is a combination of boxes to be shaded in and statements describing patterns of behaviour observed in the pupils along a number of dimensions important in science. The similarity to the Scottish *Profile Assessment System* is obvious. In both cases the statements of attainments were agreed on after consideration by working parties of professionals. But where the Scottish system uses assessments based on performance relative to the age group in the school, the system developed at Reading refers assessments direct to the graduated statements.

The emphasis laid on continuous records, on checklists, and criterion-referenced tests in this book follows from the need to build assessment into changing learning situations. If there is to be mixed-ability grouping, individualized learning, and learner-centred education there has to be systematic recording and assessment. There was little need to record and assess individual progress when a class was taught as a group. The teacher had only to remember where the whole class had got to. This is a parody of the actual situation, but clearly, once pupils are in individualized learning situations the teacher has a difficult job ensuring that all know where they go next, whether they are ready to move on, and how well they have mastered previous work. If pupils are to learn as individuals there has to be a lot of planning. Assessment has to play a central role in this. Unfortunately the vanguard for mixed-ability teaching and individualized methods are often in the van for the abolition of testing and record-keeping as well. In an attempt to avoid labelling and to give all pupils a fair chance of attainment new methods have often been introduced without the additional assessment and recording that could ensure their success.

[1] Harlen, W. (1976), *op. cit.*

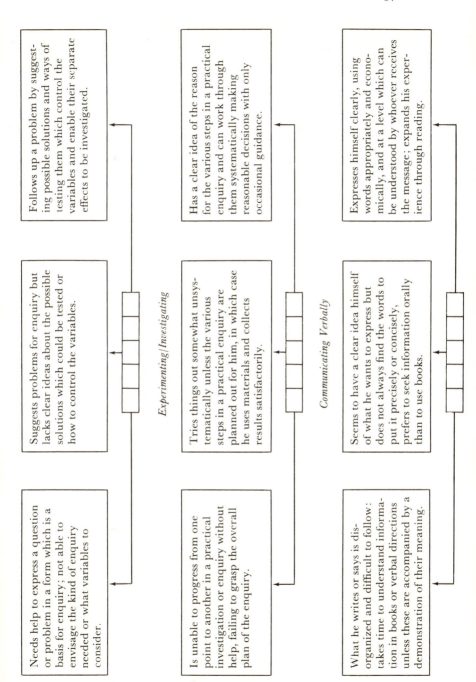

Follows up a problem by suggesting possible solutions and ways of testing them which control the variables and enable their separate effects to be investigated.

Has a clear idea of the reason for the various steps in a practical enquiry and can work through them systematically making reasonable decisions with only occasional guidance.

Expresses himself clearly, using words appropriately and economically, and at a level which can be understood by whoever receives the message; expands his experience through reading.

Suggests problems for enquiry but lacks clear ideas about the possible solutions which could be tested or how to control the variables.

Experimenting/Investigating

Tries things out somewhat unsystematically unless the various steps in a practical enquiry are planned out for him, in which case he uses materials and collects results satisfactorily.

Communicating Verbally

Seems to have a clear idea himself of what he wants to express but does not always find the words to put it precisely or concisely, prefers to seek information orally than to use books.

Needs help to express a question or problem in a form which is a basis for enquiry; not able to envisage the kind of enquiry needed or what variables to consider.

Is unable to progress from one point to another in a practical investigation or enquiry without help, failing to grasp the overall plan of the enquiry.

What he writes or says is disorganized and difficult to follow: takes time to understand information in books or verbal directions unless these are accompanied by a demonstration of their meaning.

Pupil assessment and school evaluation

The use of a systematic record-keeping and assessment system in the school is an important teaching technique. It is also the main way of accumulating information for evaluating the success of the school. There will still be a need to look at the wider objectives of teachers, at the school in context, and these are dealt with in later chapters. Similarly there will be a need to produce not only results based on internal assessments using the standards agreed among teachers, but assessments obtained from external sources such as examination boards, or referenced against national norms, such as standardized tests or the opinions of experts and the public of the school. But as an assessment and record-keeping system is devised, there should be consideration of the way the data accumulated can be used to reflect on the performance of the school as a whole.

This need to accumulate information for school evaluation from the performance of pupils is more easily met when assessments can be made in terms of the mastery of skills rather than of comparisons between pupils. It is more meaningful to know that 56 per cent of pupils can swim 50 yards than to know that the average swimming attainment in the school lies at the 61st percentile nationally. Once pupils are assessed against standards of attainment it is possible to specify a level that is to be considered as 'mastery'. But caution has to be exercised. In the examples of referencing grades against standards above, and in the suggestions for prior agreement on the proportions to be allocated to different grades, the top 10 per cent, the next 20 per cent and so on are fixed arbitrarily. They can not then be used to assess mastery of a skill. The prior decision has already determined how many will fall into each category. But it is useful to select a few basic areas of the curriculum and to test, using a cut-off to assess those who have mastered the skill involved.

This was the information sought by the teachers consulted in advance of writing this book. They also tended to agree on the important areas. Reading, writing, and basic mathematics were quoted by all. Here are some of the basic objectives shared among this group.

'Pupils should be able to read books in everyday use throughout the range of subjects offered before the end of the second year.'

'Pupils should be able to write legibly and coherently by the end of the second year.'

'Pupils should have mastered the basic mathematical skills by the end of the second year, particularly so that they will experience little trouble in subjects requiring such mathematics.'

'Pupils should be able to employ a scientific approach to the solution of problems by the end of the fourth year.'

'Pupils should have gained a perspective of historical time before the end of the fourth year.'

'Pupils should have gained a working knowledge of the geography of Britain and of the major regions of the world by the end of the fourth year.'

Many teachers will object to the rather conservative nature of these objectives. Obviously there were many others quoted, but this core recurred. There will also be objections to the idea of a threshold of reading or mathematics, rather than a developmental view. But these teachers were recognizing the demand for information from parents and from other teachers and the dogmatic way in which these were expressed. The selection also omits cultural and social objectives which were strongly expressed. These are dealt with in Chapters 5 and 6. There may also be the objection that the selection here contains the more easily measured objectives. But they are those that most worry parents, pupils, employers, and teachers. They are usually easy to test because there are tests available. But these exist because these are the curriculum areas over which there has been most concern.

The first step is to define the objectives. This can be done either from scratch or by looking at what is currently taught. The latter is more realistic and short-circuits lengthy theoretical arguments about the worth of different curriculum areas. Take the mastery of mathematical skills at the end of the second year as an example. It should be easy to look over the mathematics syllabus for years one and two and to agree on a few essential skills. Second, it should be possible to discuss the need for these and other skills with staff responsible for teaching mathematics in senior forms or for teaching science where mathematics is needed. Out of such discussions there will be a list of basic skills such as:

Ability to Handle Numbers
Place value
Division, multiplication, addition, subtraction
Approximation
Use of decimals and fractions, ratio, proportion, and scale
Collection, ordering, and interpretation of data

Ability to Measure
Lines, solids, containers
Standard units of measurement
Approximation
Compound measures
Use of calculating aids

The third step is to produce items which will test each of these agreed skills. Item writing requires skill and experience, particularly when the more profound intellectual skills are to be tested. But where the concern is with more basic skills it should be possible to build up a number of items which all pupils who have taken the course in mathematics should be able to answer.

Take the skill of 'approximation' under the *Ability to Measure* objective above. Items would range from approximations of simple lengths such as the height of a door or the weight of a bucket of water, to complicated approximations such as the effect of changing wind speed on the time an aircraft will take on a journey or the relation between the volume of a gas, the pressure on it, and the temperature. Each question could be given a level of difficulty from 1 to 10 so that in the selection of items for a test, there would not only be coverage of all the skills being assessed, but a range of items from easy to difficult. These levels of difficulty should be determined by trials on samples of pupils, but teacher judgement can be used as a first approximation.

The final step in organizing for the evaluation of these basic areas is for the staff to decide on the standard which they are aiming at. If each item is graded 1 to 10 and the selection of items for a test is arranged to give a test containing items of similar total difficulty for each objective being tested, the overall standard could be stated in numerical form. But there will always be two criteria that have to be established:

1 The level of performance that is to be set to indicate mastery of the skill.
2 The proportion of pupils who are expected to reach this level.

Obviously not every pupil who has mastered a skill will get every item right. Some level around 8 items correct out of 10 will usually be appropriate as indicating mastery. Similarly there will always be some pupils who will not achieve the level of mastery of even the most basic skill. Once again staff have to set this level and can set intermediate grades as well. The crucial point is that the setting of objectives must be accompanied by setting the levels of expected performance. Once these are set they act as the criterion against which later performance will be evaluated. For example, one commercially available criterion-referenced test in mathematics defines 'mastery' as 90 per cent correct answers. [1]

Table 2:2 shows how the information collected through the specification of criteria of mastery could be used. The example chosen includes a measure of the mathematical attainment of the children two years before when they entered the secondary school and a space for any curricular changes to be noted.

Obviously such an evaluation of the proportion attaining a level of mathematical skill enabling them to benefit from work in senior forms without further remedial help can be used as a basis for, and assessment of, curricular changes. It can also be used as information for negotiations with the staff of feeder primary to raise levels of

---

[1] *Yardsticks: Criterion-Referenced Tests in Mathematics*. London, Nelson.

Table 2:2   Basic mathematical skills at end of second year

Year	No. in 2nd year	No. achieving mastery level	Per cent reaching mastery level	Maths* grade at entry 2 years before	Curricular changes over 2 years
1971	172	137	79.7	81	—
1972	170	135	79.4	80	—
1973	182	148	81.3	76	new remedial arrangements
1974	172	148	81.3	84	—
1975	164	146	89.0	86	—
1976	166	149	89.8	86	change to mixed ability grouping
1977	167	154	92.2	88	—

*5 grades given on class tests at entry to secondary school. Figure given is per cent in top 4 grades.

attainment before transfer. Similar tests of mastery can be organized for pupils leaving school particularly where they will not be taking public examinations. This would provide evidence to use when applying for jobs and would provide staff with a guide on the terminal attainment of leavers.

Peer evaluation

This chapter has so far concentrated on the quantitative aspects of evaluation. But many objectives can not be stated in terms of numbers. Furthermore, these unmeasurable objectives often turn out to be the most important. Figures often reflect the trivial. Very often it is necessary to organize evaluation through the judgement by teachers of their own work, or, more usefully, that of their colleagues.

The overwhelming advantage of peer evaluation is its ubiquity. Attainments, aptitudes, behaviour, creativity and the whole alphabet of important yet difficult to define, and impossible to measure attributes are open to observation and question, and hence to judgement by fellow professionals. This is the way of probing into the effectiveness of those profound areas of schooling that lie beneath those open to testing. Yet this flexibility is a danger. It can lead to judgement without frame of reference. The evidence may not be interpretable against any specified or identifiable criteria. Peer evaluation requires decisions in advance about what is to be observed and which criteria are to be used in judging, if it is to attain and retain credibility.

Evaluation by peers is a common feature of professions. It is the way standards of conduct are established. It is the way scientific evidence is accepted. It is the way teachers are informally assessed by other teachers. Sometimes peer evaluation is formalized in education. Teachers in training are evaluated by their tutors and by senior staff in the schools used for teaching practice. Teachers in their first year of teaching are evaluated by inspectors, and by senior staff in their first school. References for experienced teachers are written on the basis of knowledge obtained about them by senior colleagues. Head-teachers are evaluated by their staff in every common room.

In secondary schools there are many opportunities for staff to organize peer evaluation and to monitor and improve standards. Senior staff can be formed into an evaluation panel. This is the arrangement in one inner city girls' comprehensive school where annual inspections of selected forms are made. The work of the form in key curriculum areas is inspected by the panel, usually over a period of four or five days. Afterwards, each girl receives a report on her work and is involved in follow-up sessions to advise on strengths and weaknesses. The inspections also provide the basis of a report to parents and they are invited to come to the school to discuss the work of their daughters. Standards of work between classes, the homework set, the usefulness of marking schemes and written comments on work, the standards of presentation are discussed with the teachers responsible after the inspection. Through careful consultation these arrangements were accepted by staff and have become part of the annual routine of the school.

There are other opportunities for formal and informal peer evaluation. It can be confined within subject departments. One department such as science can inspect mathematics on which their own teaching depends. Departments can agree to mutually inspect. Assistant teachers can arrange to provide each other with objective assessments. In one North London secondary school the Heads of Houses encourage new staff to pair up and visit each other's class-rooms.

The advantages of peer evaluation can be seen where team teaching has brought teachers into planning and evaluation groups. The historian has to defend the right to include brass rubbing against the claim of the geographer to take the group for orientation exercises. Afterwards the team assesses the value of both against other possibilities. Claims for time are discussed by peers as part of the organization of team teaching. In one West Midlands junior high school the work of the team responsible for integrated studies in the first and second year as evaluated by a visiting team of the senior staff responsible for the third-year subjects into which integrated studies fed. Once again, the peer evaluation gave the evaluated an idea of their standards and ensured the evaluators that they would have a secure foundation for their work.

In later chapters the use of teachers and other professionals and laymen from outside the school will be discussed. Obviously peer evaluation confined within a school may lack objectivity. But it is the easiest way of ensuring that each teacher receives some feed-back from the colleagues on whom he or she depends or who depend on him or her. Peer evaluation is also a way of assessing areas of the curriculum which are beyond measurement, which would be disturbed by the attempt to measure, or which would exhaust too much energy in the organization of tests. But the procedures for observing and the criteria for evaluating must be determined in advance. The evaluating and evaluated group must know what is being aimed at. They must be clear what aspects of work are to be examined, what levels are expected, and who is to receive any report. Even more important than with test construction and quantitative evaluation, the sequence recommended in Chapter 1 needs to be followed.

The steps outlined below help ensure the quality of evaluation:

1 State the objectives of the exercise in a form that enables their achievement to be verified. This means spelling out the details of what is being aimed at. It is essential that those involved realize what is being evaluated and over what period of time.
2 Spell out the actions that are seen to be necessary for the objectives to be attained. This is equivalent to the establishment of indicators in quantitative evaluation.
3 Spell out the criteria for the attainment of the objectives. These tell the audience what has been observed in order to judge success or failure. The question to ask is, 'How will we know when this objective has been achieved?' If this question is asked by the teachers, their judgement of the end-product will be more convincing to those who use the evaluation evidence.
4 Spell out whose judgements are to be involved.
5 State in advance the form of any report to be made and who is to receive it.

These steps are guides to specifying the criteria that will be used in the evaluation. The aim is to select objectives that are verifiable and to state the criteria for that verification. This qualitative evaluation is already a responsibility accepted by teachers. It is a suitable instrument for in-school evaluation, as that is where objectives are determined and is where they can be clarified. It involves taking trouble over judgements where these are for public consumption or for use in making important decisions. It is the responsibility that is the companion of teacher autonomy.

3. The School Assessment Programme: externally referenced by tests and evaluation panels

It would be possible for all teachers in a school to be using the same yardstick for assessing, yet to be using very different standards from those in use in other schools. Many parents will have experienced a dramatic change in the marks received by a child on moving from one school to another and before any real change could have taken place in attainment. The 'outstanding' work at Winchester will differ markedly from the same category in a non-selective school in an area with generous grammar school provision. Standards inside a school tend to be gauged against previous performance. The yardstick used may be unique. Each school develops its own yardstick. But not only other teachers in other schools, but inspectors, examiners, and moderators may be using very different standards. When we ask the question 'how are we doing in this school?' a reference outside the school is needed.

The teachers' questions in Chapter 2 arose from a shared awareness that the key questions about evaluation were about the school compared with other schools in like circumstances, and with similar intakes. When the teachers consulted talked about evaluation they explicitly or implicitly referred to standards in their schools compared with all schools in their local authority or in the nation. When a first draft of this book was shown to teachers they unanimously pointed to its weakness in not providing more ways of making these tough, often uncomfortable, yet crucial comparisons. This was realistic. The public for education also wants this detached information in order to make choices between schools, to reassure themselves, or to confirm a doubt as a first step to trying to get things changed. This is hard on teachers who are in the best position to see problems of context, or intake, or staff and pupil turnover. But teachers are also professional enough to face this if these statements are representative objectives:

That standards in the basic skills should compare with other schools with similar intakes.

That all school leavers should be able to compete successfully for jobs and not be handicapped by low attainment.

That standards of reading should not fall below the national average for genuinely comprehensive schools.

That attainments should not fall below those of schools in similar areas and with similar types of pupil.

Most of the suggestions that follow in this and later chapters deal with ways of obtaining some degree of external reference, whether by comparing performance with that of other representative groups of children or schools, or by using experts to give their independent judgements of levels of attainment. Externally-referenced measures are difficult to design within a school. Teachers usually depend on ready-made standardized tests, public examinations, or the opinions of some group of experts for such a reference. Once again, the choice should be made after considering the use that is to be made of the assessments. But at some stage of a pupil's career, at some point in the management of a school, attainment has to be laid alongside that of other pupils in other schools. Teachers do not rely exclusively on their running assessments or even their scaled assessments. They need to know whether the standards they are setting in their school measure up to those expected and achieved elsewhere. In this chapter we deal with standardized tests and external evaluation panels. Public examinations will be covered in Chapter 4.

Standardized tests

Standardized tests are dealt with first because they are designed to be reliable. Used with the same children under similar conditions at different times by different teachers, the results should be the same within small and known limits. Technically this is the measure of reliability. Such tests can be used if the results are related to the content of the particular test or to an area of the curriculum that is similar. Standardized tests should be reliable, and therefore good models, because of the care taken to specify the objectives of the test (and hence its content), the way it should be administered, and the way it should be marked. These tests are also designed for pupils of specific age ranges and usually give scores for both boys and girls.

The National Foundation for Educational Research publishes a catalogue showing available tests and others can be found in the catalogues of commercial publishers.[1] There is also an excellent guide to tests which is regularly brought up to date.[2] Some tests are not made available to teachers as they require special skills in adminis-

[1] A full list of test publishers can be found in Vincent, D. and Cresswell, M. *op. cit.* The address of the NFER Publishing Company is 2 Jennings Buildings, Thames Street, Windsor, Berks.

[2] Jackson, S. (1974), *A Teacher's Guide to Tests and Testing*, 3rd edition. London, Longman, Green.

tration, but catalogues indicate the availability of tests as well as details of their content and suitability for children of various ages.

A standardized test is objective in being administered and scored in ways that eliminate the judgement of the tester. This is achieved through trials of questions on large samples at the design stage. This thorough preparation ensures that the questions asked are suitable for the age range for whom the test is designed and that the scores of pupils taking it can be related to those of a sample representative of his or her age group. The teacher can see how any one pupil compares with this sample and can arrange his class in order of performance as the score of each is related to the same set of scores determined externally. Alternatively a standardized test can yield information on the attainment of a pupil or a group of pupils in relation to some pre-determined level.

As long as standardized tests are administered according to instructions they should give consistent results if the same pupils were soon tested again. They are also designed to assess a specific skill, knowledge, aptitude, ability, or attitude. They are designed to be valid measures of this limited range of performances. A test of word-recognition does not test all aspects of reading and a test of arithmetical skills is not a test of mathematics. Tests may be valid when used for assessing what they were designed to assess but may be invalid or irrelevant if used indiscriminately. This is another reason for care over their use.

There are two places where standardized tests having established consistency are invaluable in school evaluation programmes:

1. To compare the attainment of pupils, or groups of pupils with those in different schools, or in the same school over a period of time.
2. To measure progress across a course on a before and after basis.

Both these uses rest on the reliability of standardized tests. Because each score is referred to the same yardstick, the same set of norms on each occasion, and because these scores are given on the basis of prescribed procedures for administering the test, comparisons are possible. But caution is still necessary. First, however reliable the test, problems can arise from often unconsidered differences between the schools being compared. Non-attenders in a school may be given the test when they return until the whole group has been tested. But in another school they may be left out. But non-attenders tend to be low attainers. The attendance rate at the time of testing can alter the average score. Similarly not all tests take into account differences between the performance of boys and girls in some subject areas and the sex balance in a school may invalidate comparisons.

There are similar difficulties in using standardized tests to measure progress over time. If a test is used twice with the same pupils, **practice in** doing the test may account for any improvement in attainment. The same test used year after year may become redundant and increasingly difficult thus depressing scores. National standards may change, but test norms stay related to out-of-date standards. Practice effects can be avoided by using equivalent forms of a test. Here similar versions are deliberately produced to overcome this problem. The statistical characteristics of a test can help avoid unwarranted conclusions about progress. There are usually statistical measures of the tolerance that should be allowed a test score because reliability is never perfect. But a rough guide is firstly that the larger the group tested the greater can be the confidence that differences between groups or between the same pupils at different times are genuine, not due to the unreliability of the test. Secondly, do not assume progress or regress on the basis of small differences after a single repeat of a test. If two different tests are used and each shows a similar movement on re-test confidence increases. But a trend requires three or more scores for confidence that attainment is going up or down. It is always safest to err on the side of caution. Thirdly, look for other evidence to confirm or refute any detected trend. This responsibility to collect together confirmatory evidence should be taken on by a senior member of staff. This organization of evaluation is discussed in Chapter 8.

Here are the results attained by pupils in a comprehensive school at the end of their second year, on a standardized test of reading comprehension. There were some 150 in the year-group excluding pupils in a remedial form.

Year	1973	1974	1975	1976	1977
Reading score average	98.5	98.7	98.5	98.4	98.3

This series of scores does not indicate any trend. Because the same test was used each year, because it was a standardized test, and because it is likely that small variations in score could be the result of different numbers of absences, small unreliabilities in the test or in its administration, it is safest to assume that reading comprehension standards have not changed. However, standards outside the school may have changed. If national standards had changed, the test might progressively give lower or higher scores for this age group compared with their national peers in each year compared with scores when the test was standardized. Trends in reading standards are published occasionally and national standards can apparently change quickly. More can be done about the possibility that other schools in the same local education authority have had changed reading scores, particularly if that authority itself organizes the testing and this covers all schools. The scores of any one school can now be placed alongside the scores of the remaining schools, or the scores of all schools, if the scores of individual schools can not be withdrawn to enable their staffs to make a comparison with their neighbours. The reading scores above now appear in a new light.

Year	1973	1974	1975	1976	1977
School score	98.5	98.7	98.5	98.4	98.3
LEA score	97.5	97.4	97.9	98.8	98.9

It now appears that the school reading comprehension scores have remained the same, but that scores in surrounding schools seem to have improved. Given the large numbers tested across all schools this seems likely to have happened, though it could still be a reflection of a national trend. But the step from assessing the evidence to planning action requires still further information. What if the ability of the intake into the school has gone down, while that to other schools has gone up or remained stable? Let us suppose that verbal reasoning (V.R.) scores measured on a standardized test were also available in each school and for all schools for these second-year pupils when they entered the school 21 months previously. The addition of this new evidence now suggests a different interpretation of the reading performance in the school when compared with other schools in the same authority.

Year	1973	1974	1975	1976	1977	
School score on						
Reading	98.5	98.7	98.5	98.4	98.3	
LEA score on						
Reading	97.5	97.4	97.9	98.8	98.9	

Year	1971	1972	1973	1974	1975	1976
School score V.R.	100.7	100.4	99.1	98.8	99.1	99.3
LEA score V.R.	97.7	97.4	98.0	98.1	98.7	99.1

While the reading standards in the school may be getting relatively worse when looked at alongside other schools in the same local education authority, the school seems to have had a slight deterioration in the measured verbal reasoning of its intake, while this has slightly improved in the surrounding schools. The staff of the school could conclude that they had succeeded in the face of a deteriorating intake. Alternatively they could conclude that they must plan action to improve reading comprehension to match the apparent improvement in other schools.

The researcher's solution to the problem of evidence that is difficult to interpret is to ask for time and resources to do more research. Teachers too might like more evidence. For example, in Chapter 7, the possibilities of using information on eligibility for free meals is discussed as a way of getting information on the social background of the intake into the school, compared with that of other schools. It might be useful to have reading test scores at intake as well as at the end of the second year. It would be interesting to have reading scores as pupils leave school to see if there is improvement or deterioration once pupils move towards employment. It would certainly be valuable to have separate scores for the able and less able. But decisions have to be made on evidence that is always incomplete. In a school they are also made on educational grounds. The test evidence is important. It indicates that a trend may be developing. It can confirm or deny hunches by the staff, parents, inspectors, employers, and so on. It serves as an important part of the information considered before action is taken. But the actual decision is made through professional judgements of alternative courses of action, and of the comparative costs in time, energy, and resources that will be involved.

Intelligence tests, or verbal reasoning tests as they are now more commonly called, went out of favour because of their misuse in selection procedures for secondary schooling. However they still have an important use in an evaluation programme. When examination results or tests of attainment are used to measure output, it is convenient to evaluate the results against the verbal reasoning scores of the pupils at intake to the course. It is by no means agreed what verbal reasoning or intelligence tests actually measure. But they do indicate the ability of children to solve problems on written tests. As these problems are not purely mathematical or solely related to the use of words, the test score is an indication of something more than attainment. Practice can raise the score on these tests, but there are limits to practice effects that suggest that the tests are indeed measuring ability to reason. In Chapter 4, for example, V.R. scores have been used to help in the interpretation of the examination results of a school.

Standardized tests are often used to check on the comparability of standards of marking on different examinations. Thus a verbal reasoning test can be used to arrange a comparison of the performance of pupils in examinations that are supposed to be of equal difficulty. Verbal reasoning tests are also used to check if a pupil's attainment is above or below that expected given his verbal reasoning score. Great caution is needed in interpreting such evidence. Over- and under-performance can result from many factors besides verbal reasoning as measured on a test. The evidence should be treated as an indicator only. This is stressed for all marks, test scores, and assessments listed in this book. But it is especially important here. It is too easy to slip from verbal reasoning to talk of potential or intelligence and then to adjust expectation of the pupil in the light of that assessment. Indicators indicate. They alert teachers to possible ways of improving a situation. They need cautious interpretation in the light of the many other factors in education.

Standardized tests rarely cover even the more obvious parts of a subject curriculum. There are a wide range of tests of reading and of mathematics, but beyond this the choice is small. Even with a basic skill such as reading, the available tests do not cover all the objectives that a teacher might consider important when deciding how to improve literacy. For example a reading test is unlikely to indicate whether a child is enthusiastic to read, yet this may be a basic aim of the teacher. Mathematics teachers not only have a choice between modern and traditional approaches to the subject, but may also lay different emphases on the need to master basic skills, prepare for later learning, or understand underlying concepts. No test, designed outside the school, is likely to fit the curriculum resulting from any two such approaches. Standardized tests also exclude that which can not be measured. This is an obvious weakness that conceals a more profound one. The test designer has to restrict the scope of answers to increase reliability. In doing so he restricts the opportunities for the pupil to answer in extended, original ways. This may not only be unfair to some children who are used to looking for the unusual or the unanticipated solution to problems, but may handicap children from cultural backgrounds different from those on which the test was standardized. This applies to different social class, different ethnic origin, and to children taking a test designed some years before. It has always to be remembered that standardized tests contain questions, instructions, and norms that have been included because of trials with samples who may differ from those on whom the test is ultimately used.

Standardized tests provide a ready-made means of assessing against an external reference. They must be used with caution. This caution is needed, not only because such tests may not be measuring the skills that are built into the curriculum, but because they can become redundant. Tests stay in the catalogues for a long time after the date when they were first standardized and standards of performance can change. Thus a reading test standardized in the early 1960s might be a misleading reference for scores twenty years later, as national standards may have changed. Thus, apart from the unsuitability of tests, their norms can be out of date.

There is another use of standardized tests which is rarely discussed. Because they are designed, administered, and scored without adjustment by teachers, they can serve as a yardstick of what can be expected of pupils of a particular age, in a particular subject area. They serve as a target for teachers who are often forced to rely on their own judgement of attainable standards. The tests are not designed to fix levels of work or expected levels of performance, but where these are not set for schools, or where clear advice is not provided by advisors or inspectors, standardized tests tend to get used instead. They are externally referenced in the same way as public examinations, and just as the examination board syllabus can determine the work in the senior forms of a secondary school, so a standardized test can be used as a check on internal standards. The popularity of test programmes in the United States is only partly due to the promise that tests give a reliable measure of standards in key curriculum areas. It is also their promise as checks on the attainment of targets easily recognized as important by the public for education, as well as by teachers.

There are technical and educational dangers in the use of standardized tests as a check on the curriculum and on standards achieved. They do give a valuable external reference, but for test scores to be used as a base for planning there has to be confidence in the test. Some doubts have already been expressed. Redundancy, unsuitable samples used for standardizing, minor unreliabilities, and titles suggesting they are tests of reading or mathematics when only specific areas within these broad subjects are being tested are common. But the existence of poor tests is difficult to detect. The accompanying test manuals often contain too little information for even experienced psychologists to assess reliability or suitability for a particular group of pupils, or for a particular subject area. It is always safest to obtain advice from the schools' psychological service or inspectorate before adopting a test for school evaluation.

The educational objections spring first from the danger of the test determining the curriculum. Once evaluation is taken seriously, high performance can be achieved by teaching to the test. Few teachers would consciously do this, but it is easy to slip towards the test content once the results are available to other teachers or the public. Probably even more difficult to resist is the temptation to use the average on the test as the target, whereas what really matters is that each pupil is stretched and motivated to aim high.

Criterion-referenced tests

The external reference of the usual standardized test is the sample on whom it has been standardized. The score of any one pupil taking the test is being referred to the range of scores of that sample used in the test's design. There is a similar reference when public examination results are used in evaluation. The examiner's skill is in marking papers so that they can be ranked in order of attainment, which means that any one pupil's work is compared with that of all those taking the examination. These are norm-referenced. In each case there is checking by other examiners, other test constructors, or psychologists, and the results of the test are open to scrutiny by fellow professionals. In both these cases, the external reference can be obtained by the teachers in a school wanting to use the reference for evaluation at the cost of having to adjust the curriculum. It might be more useful for school evaluation to have figures on how many pupils had achieved various levels of performance in a number of subject areas, rather than on how much better or worse results were when compared with the sample used to construct the test or which took the examination.

Take, for example, study skills. There are a series of tests available which are standardized and give a norm-referenced score.[1] But it

[1] Brimer, A. *et al.*, *Bristol Achievement Tests. Study Skills.* London, Nelson.

would be more useful if, in any subject area, a list of skills could be agreed among staff, levels of mastery specified, and ways of testing the levels attained by pupils developed. Clearly this is the content of most impressionistic assessment by teachers. They are continually checking who, and how many, in the class have mastered regular verbs ending in 'er' before deciding to go on to verbs ending in 'ir'. In this judgement teachers are using some measure of mastery across the class, not only in terms of defining the knowledge or skill to be mastered, but in fixing some level of mastery above which it is profitable to proceed. By a few questions, a written test, a show of hands, and a look at a few books the proportion who seem to have got it is assessed and the decision to move on is made.

This specification of a skill, or an inventory of skills, the determination of levels of their mastery and of ways of assessing this mastery are the steps used in constructing criterion-referenced tests. Obviously the term is being used loosely here. But a range of methods are available from standardized criterion-referenced tests to checklists that can give some measure of the proportion of pupils that have mastered particular parts of the curriculum and which retain some degree of external reference. The common feature is that performance is referenced to some objective or criterion.

It is significant that public examinations and standardized testing in schools proliferated when education was organized as a succession of gates through which progressively fewer pupils passed as they went from primary to selective secondary school and on to higher education. Within schools this progressive selection encouraged streaming. Tests and examinations were needed to ensure that the selection and sorting out was done fairly and did not handicap the pupils from poor social backgrounds. The objectivity ensured some degree of fairness in the competition. With the ending of selection, the accompanying diminution in streaming, and the broadening of opportunities in further and higher education, the need for tests to compare one pupil against others decreased. Ironically tests developed to promote equality of opportunity are less needed in what superficially seems to be a more open system but which appears still to handicap the poorer pupil. In comprehensive secondary schools there is an urgent need to be able to check that pupils of all ability are attaining to the best of their ability, but less need to know their position relative to each other. For both teaching and evaluation, referencing against criteria of performance seems to be essential.

The use of criterion-referenced materials for teaching purposes enables learning sequences to be followed without leaving pupils stranded because stages have not been mastered before the class has moved on to the next topic. There is a clear connection here with diagnostic testing. In areas such as reading there are many diagnostic tests designed to uncover individual strengths and weaknesses as a first step to taking remedial action. Here too the objective of testing is to ensure that each sequence has been mastered sufficiently for progress to be made. It is necessary to check this before moving on and occasionally necessary to trace back to find out what has not been mastered to account for the learning problems. In diagnostic testing the relative performance of the pupil is of little interest. What matters is to discover where there is an important step that is proving troublesome.

The available tests stretch from those designed to provide national monitoring information to those that are for screening purposes only, indicating whether pupils will need extra help before being able to benefit in normal classroom learning. An example of the first is the Secondary Mathematics Item Bank developed by the National Foundation for Educational Research.[1] This consists of a large number of questions covering the secondary school mathematics curriculum for 12- to 14-year-olds. These questions cover ten areas of mathematics, and in each area the questions are designed to yield information on the achievement of different types of objectives such as the accumulation of knowledge, the acquisition of techniques or skills, comprehension, application, concrete operations, and formal operations. The questions are stored in a 'bank'. This has the advantage that from the large number of items stored, a school or a number of schools can use those items that fit their curriculum. As the statistical characteristics of each item are known, a total score can be worked out for performance on the items selected. This work by the NFER has been developed to prepare for national monitoring through the DES Assessment of Performance Unit.

At the other end of the spectrum, the NFER have developed tests for measuring proficiency in English.[2] These have been designed to help teachers establish the levels of difficulty experienced by immigrant children. Three levels of proficiency dealing with single words, phrases, sentences or questions, and extended passages or productive language are included. At each level proficiency is indicated by success rates of 90, 80 and 70 per cent respectively, while 'not proficient' is indicated by a 30 per cent or less success rate. This is primarily designed for younger pupils. While it is a screening device, the separation into proficient or not proficient still gives information on the level of proficiency in the school. This information is important for bringing help to individual pupils; it is also a guide to the problems facing the teachers throughout the school.

[1] Sumner, R. and Robertson, T. S. (1977), *Criterion Referenced Measurement and Criterion Referenced Tests*. Slough, NFER; and Sumner, R. (1975), *Tests of Attainment in Mathematics in Schools*. Slough, NFER.

[2] National Foundation for Educational Research (1973), *Proficiency in English Tests*. Slough, NFER.

Checkpoints and mastery checks

Many structured learning packs such as the SRA reading scheme have tests built into them so that the pupil or teacher can test whether enough has been learned for progress to the next step. Programmed machines and books contain the same checkpoints, guiding the learner back to supplementary learning or guiding to the next sequence. At this level checkpoints are more an aid to effective learning than a source of data for evaluation. Nevertheless, the completion of a structured course that contains checkpoints, which, if successfully negotiated, indicate some mastery of the skill, is an important piece of information for other teachers, parents, and employers. It is common practice to set standards in sporting activities and encourage pupils to get as far as they can. The technique is used in home economics and craft subjects. Where the mastery of a skill is essential as a guarantee that a person is competent to do a job, whether this be making a dovetail joint or using a compass, the number reaching competence is an important indicator.

There are many subject areas where the test of competence is established externally to the school or college and assessed externally. The City and Guilds examinations are examples, where craft skills are graded to indicate competence. The music examinations of the Royal Schools are others. Many schools encourage pupils to enter for the Duke of Edinburgh's Award scheme. Voluntary schools often have similar tests in religious knowledge and it is common practice before confirmation into the Church of England. Later in this chapter the extension of such tests of mastery will be recommended as a way of evaluating the success of the school in attaining objectives set by the staff, through using teachers in other schools, and, where relevant, other members of the public.

There are other examples where the standards are laid down externally, but their attainment assessed internally by the teachers. The structured learning packages are examples. The Scottish Council for Research in Education's *Profile Assessment System* is another.[1] Many local education authorities are developing model curricula in the basic skills which have levels of competence built into them for different ages of children. The advantage of these schemes is that they structure learning experiences, ensure that the curriculum is thought through systematically, usually by a working party of inspectors, advisors, and experienced teachers, and that they provide some indication of the levels being attained by the pupils. Because the actual grading is done by the teachers the results are not immediately useable for assessing the performance of the school in relation to others, but it is an easy task to organize the external moderation that

[1] SCRE, *Profile Assessment System: Manual, op. cit.*

would serve as a check on too lenient or too harsh grading in any schools. All this activity in producing checklists, records of progress, ratings, and progress charts produces criterion-referenced information. Yet very little use is made of this approach to assessment in informing the public. It would be more meaningful than many of the more common indicators in use, even though these remain essential. A parent might find the fact that the reading age of the first form in July was 103.2 somewhat difficult to interpret, for there would not be the accompanying information on the characteristics of the test and the sample on which it was standardized to enable even the most informed parent to make the real comparison. But the information that 82 per cent had mastered a defined level of reading comprehension would be easier to interpret. Similarly an employer might find it difficult to use the information that a pupil was on the 79th percentile in practical electricity tests. He would be more pleased with the information that the applicant had mastered the skills involved in wiring electrical circuits and that this had been confirmed by a local electrical contractor or lecturer in the local college of further education.

The use of external referees, moderators, experts, and laymen

It is frustrating for teachers to hold a broad set of objectives for the school, yet be judged on the narrow evidence from public examinations and standardized tests. This test and examination evidence is very important because it is focussed on the heart of the curriculum. It is important because it is of such concern to parents and employers. But if teachers want to present evidence on other aspects of school life that they hold dear, they must organize the collection of convincing evidence. This has to involve externally-referenced assessments.

In higher education there is a well-developed system for bringing the experience and knowledge of each specialism to bear on the standards of courses and examinations. The external referee sits with the internal to assess a thesis. The external examiner approves questions for examinations, sees students, and comments on the standards of answer and those of marking. His report goes before the senate of the university or academic board, where other academics can comment on his summary of the work done. The setting-up of the Council for National Academic Awards has added another moderating body. Applications to start new courses have to be presented in detail from objectives through to assessment procedures and the organization of reviewing and revising courses. The applying institution is visited by a panel of experts who look at staff qualifications and experience, ask questions about the course and the division of labour on it, look at the library provision, and other necessary facilities, and then report back to CNAA. This is a very thorough proceeding and often leads to developments in the college concerned before a course is approved. The CNAA then arranges for external examining in the conventional way and asks for reviews and, if necessary, new submissions for revisions once a course has run.

Similar arrangements have spread rapidly through secondary schools. Furthermore, there has always been inspection, whether from DES or the Local Education Authority. The work of CSE subject panels is similar to that of CNAA. The staff concerned in a CSE submission draw up a proposal with aims and objectives, the organization of learning, and methods of assessment. The panel receiving the proposal is made up of teachers who examine it as peers, helping the staff in the school in the preparation and presentation, but finally judging whether it meets their standards as an examination syllabus. The modes of assessing encouraged by the CSE boards makes this peer assessment very important. The teachers concerned sit as watchdogs of the standards of their subject and of standards generally.

The principle of external moderation is now firmly established in school examinations. Mode 3 CSE rests on external moderation after examinations and coursework have been set and marked by the school staff who designed the syllabus. There are also schemes under which a group of schools shares a syllabus and assessment procedures. But these are also subject to external moderation. The result of this activity in designing, assessing, and approving courses and moderating assessments has been to accumulate more skill among the teaching profession. The teachers are now experienced in organizing assessment; an extension to involve other teachers from other schools and other outsiders in the evaluation programme of a school would not be an impossible task.

All teachers are internal assessors. From interpreting the light or lack-lustre in the eyes of the pupils in order to decide on the next step in a lesson, to designing end-of-year examinations, teaching is about assessment. But this assessment tends to be exclusive. Teachers tend to assess their own courses and objectivity can be low. Team teaching tends to break down this exclusiveness and facilitates collective assessments or multiple assessments of each pupil's work. Some teachers also assess each other's work, some subject departments organize mutual checking of standards, and senior staff will sometimes check on standards being used. But evaluation still requires external reference to guarantee credibility. It would be easy to establish evaluation panels of volunteers who could offer a variety of different perspectives and skills to be used by the staff of the school for an external reference. The organization of such panels could be facilitated by consultations between the local education authority and the staff of local academic institutions. The establishment of a pool of volunteers by the local education authority's advisory staff would enable the staffs of schools readily to recruit experts with a variety of skills. Colleges and departments of education could offer not only staff, but diploma and higher degree students, often from the local areas and usually experienced teachers. The exercise would be mutually beneficial, improving communications between schools and higher education, spreading ideas, and providing the school staff with an external reference.

However, the most profitable source of external referees would usually be teachers from nearby schools. The sharing of experience is commonplace on an informal basis between teachers, through the efforts of inspectors and advisory staff and on in-service courses. But it could be extended to bring outside moderation to bear in evaluation. There are also a number of other sources of possible members of evaluation panels who might be appropriate for helping in the evaluation of some aspects of the work of a school. Parents and employers are often vocal in criticizing schools, and the challenge could be accepted by staff by involving them in evaluation. In the community around any school there are persons whose judgement would be valuable. This may rarely be the case in academic matters, but if evaluation is to cover those wider aspects of schooling valued by teachers, the accumulation of contrasting external views of how well things are going could be valuable. It would help teachers obtain a second opinion on the success of their efforts. But it would also provide a source of evidence on standards, underwritten by members of the public that is asking for evidence. This externally referenced evidence would not only carry weight through the involvement of outsiders but would be educative. Too often the public is guessing because it lacks information and assumes the worst. This would be difficult if members of that public were involved in the production of the necessary evidence.

One panel formed to help in the evaluation of the introduction of integrated studies in a comprehensive school consisted of a local authority researcher, a professor of education, and a college of education lecturer. Reserves were a local authority inspector, a head of integrated studies in a nearby school, and a local resident who had written widely on the curriculum. The evaluation was mainly concerned to share information with the staff of the school. The team was acting as consultants, asking questions and making suggestions based on their experiences in other schools. An annual report was produced for the teachers and, through them, for the governors. This raised problems of confidentiality. In this case the decision about publication and of informing governors was left to the teachers in the school.

Peer evaluation introduces a new dimension into existing arrangements for evaluation in a school. For example, inspectors play a part, but their role is confused with administration, particularly in relation to resources for the school, the promotion of teaching staff, and the probation of new teachers. Their evaluation is related to the need to influence the staff of a school in a direction desired by the inspector. Advisory teachers can adopt a more detached position, but are still likely to be trying to influence the curriculum in some previously agreed direction. Similarly inspectors and advisors are in business to effect changes not to evaluate.

The evaluation of specific subject areas requires a panel with specialized experience. This can be found among governors, parents, and employers, but the staff of a school will probably feel that most benefit will come from using other teachers, advisors or academics. But there are areas of the work of a school that staff will see as having high priority for evaluation which nevertheless are not the concern of particular specialists. Where the social, cultural, and sporting activities are being evaluated it may seem sensible to ask interested laymen to help. A small panel to help evaluate behaviour in the school, or of the pupils in the community around the school, might be useful. Such a panel could usefully look at such areas as the relations with the community, the destination of school leavers, the problems of transfer from primary to secondary school, parent-teacher relations, and so on. The determination of objectives, the method of evaluation, and the direction of the exercise would remain in the hands of the teachers in the school. But their internal efforts would be supplemented by the judgement of outsiders. Approaches to the evaluation of these more general aspects are covered in Chapter 5.

It is misleading to see even general matters in a school as distinct from the concern of specialists. All the areas listed in the previous paragraph are the immediate concern, not only of staff in the school, but of support services for the school. The careers service, the educational welfare service, the schools' psychological service, and above all the local education authority's advisory services are available for advice. The teachers' centres are often in a position both to advise and to provide a member of an evaluation panel. Above all, the schools themselves could combine to provide external references. A consortium of schools agreeing to exchange information would provide each with data for comparison. It would provide a means of acquiring local moderation. Many secondary schools now share sixth-form teaching. Many have intimate co-operative arrangements with primary schools to ensure continuity at transfer. A number of these schemes already contain informal arrangements for evaluating the success of the scheme. They could also provide the kernel of externally referenced evaluation through visits, exchanges of staff, involvement in examination marking, and agreement on common ways of accumulating evaluative data.

Many teachers will not consider that the help of outsiders in evaluation is appropriate. The problem then is to devise some method of making staff's judgements of their own efforts more systematic than just an overall impression or an addition of marks lacking an external reference. The use of assessment techniques outlined in Chapter 2 will help. But in the end the absence of a standard outside the school that can be used for comparison will reduce the value of this purely internal evaluation. In the examples that follow internal and external assessments are combined. The object is not to replace testing and examinations but to use the flexibility of peer evaluation and the utility of criterion-referencing. Once it is decided that a panel is necessary to add external reference, the easiest approach is to form a group of schools who will share teachers for evaluation and produce comparable results. Later, in Chapter 4, the role of the local education authority in producing a baseline for comparison will be discussed.

The sequence of events should always be to think out the purpose of evaluation, to determine appropriate means of evaluation, and then to organize these to give reinforcing information. The means of evaluation follow from the objective of the exercise. In some cases internal staff judgement may be sufficient. In other cases some external reference will be essential for the evidence to be credible. In many cases, and particularly in mathematics and reading, this can be provided by standardized tests. But the more flexible method of employing panels of relevant outsiders will often be the only way forward.

Evaluating the basic skills

The requisite here is for a form of criterion-referenced test. The performance of pupils in relation to some absolute standard needs to be assessed and recorded. For each skill to be assessed the same procedure will be necessary. The objective of mastery requires the establishment of a level of performance on a specified number of skills, and a test that will enable the attainment of this level of skill to be determined. This is not an activity that can be divorced from curriculum planning. The sequence of stating objectives, determining acceptable levels of performance, and finding methods for their assessment is that used in determining any planned cycle of learning experiences. The sequence of attainments in the basic skills are those that should be recorded on sequential records that follow pupils around and which enable staff to build on previous mastery by the pupil. Here then we are not discussing evaluation for its own sake, but the heart of the learning process. Because of this it is an area that will need frequent reviewing in case the objectives, once established, begin to restrict the curriculum in undesirable directions. The examples below have been chosen because they are of interest to parents and employers, are not open to standardized testing and are of importance to pupils. They have been chosen to illustrate a possible approach to evaluation, not as a model.

Spelling

It may seem strange to include spelling as a subject for systematic evaluation in the secondary school. Yet it can be neglected, and adults who find difficulty with spelling carry a serious handicap. The problem is often that spelling is not the responsibility of any group of teachers. The idea of language across the curriculum applies here.[1] There may be benefits in specifying levels of mastery of spelling at various ages and particularly for school leavers. The first step has to be the acceptance by all staff that mastery of spelling is an objective that they accept and work to achieve.

Spelling is not a simple skill that is fully understood. There is no agreement on whether it is caught or taught. There is however evidence that teachers, in their practices and attitudes, do make a difference. Spelling, while it can be improved by learning strategies that can be taught, is not learned out of context. It is the consistency of teachers in their attitudes towards spelling that seems to matter. Its importance as a skill has to be seen to be appreciated, not in sessions devoted to spelling, but in the whole work of the school. Margaret Peters' work is particularly relevant to this perspective.[2] There are tests of spelling commercially available.[3] One New Zealand test is criterion-referenced and designed to assess mastery at the 90 per cent standard for seven levels of spelling.[4] It is easy for staff to compile lists for regular campaigns to improve performance. Sampling daily newspapers is another way of compiling such lists. But once again, this is an area where the involvement of outsiders with the staff would produce benefits. It would convince the public of the school that spelling is taken seriously. It would be a way of bringing home to parents their own responsibility to support the teachers in their efforts to raise attainment. It could provide evidence for a certificate of basic skills, with levels of mastery specified by the staff and countersigned by the evaluation panel.

In practice, testing of spelling could be carried out at the same time as testing writing. Indeed it is the ability to spell properly in context and while writing that matters. Here there is another benefit from the involvement of outsiders in evaluation. With apparently 'primary school' activities such as spelling, older pupils may resent the emphasis in secondary schools. It is not pleasant still to be learning to read, spell, or write, in one's teens. The presence of an evaluation panel annually would help in underlining the importance attached

[1] See, for example, Marland, M. (1977), *Language across the Curriculum*. London, Heinemann Educational Books.

[2] Peters, M. (1975), *Diagnostic and Remedial Spelling Manual*. London, Macmillan.

[3] For example Schonell, F. J. (1972), *The Essential Spelling List*. London, Macmillan.

[4] Arvidson, G. L. (1960), *Learning to spell*, New Zealand Council for Educational Research.

to these activities. It would add the imprint of the adult world to what are often seen as childish pursuits. The secondary benefits from evaluation may be considerable.

The indicators of success in attaining the objectives of staff need only be simple criteria. They can be related to scores on a test, if one is used. An arbitrary cut-off such as 75 per cent right on average, or a number of cut-offs at 50, 70 and 90 per cent correct would have to be agreed by the staff involved as indicating levels of mastery. Alternatively, if there is not to be any testing, a series of agreed definitions of good, adequate, and poor spelling would be needed for the year-group concerned. The evaluating panel would have to allocate pupils to these categories on the basis of samples of work collected for them. These are crude indicators, but the need is for a running indication of levels of competence. The panel, consisting of teachers and interested and representative persons such as governors, employers, and parents would act as the auditors, reviewing the campaign to improve spelling, being informed of the assessment procedures, receiving and confirming the evidence and disseminating it to the bodies to which they belong. There is no absolute standard bar perfection as a standard of spelling. But it is an area where the public is concerned and capable of judging attainment. Accumulated over the years such indicators as average scores on annual criterion-referenced tests could serve to satisfy the public about standards and to inform the staff about their maintenance.

Spelling is one of those areas of the curriculum where there is liable to be unanimity over importance. Yet specialist teachers may not give good spelling high priority as they drive for high standards in the sciences, mathematics, or history. Similarly, while parents usually complain about weak spelling, they do not often take steps to encourage their own children to take a pride in spelling accurately. It is an area where rhetoric is not matched by action. Here the informative contribution from evaluation is important. Promoting spelling to prominence might initiate a more systematic, common effort among all staff, and would show parents that it was taken seriously in school and that their help was needed.

Writing

The ability to express thoughts clearly on paper is an important skill. It is given high priority by teachers. It remains an area where the public is anxious. Employers complain and parents make comparisons between their children's shoddy writing and some golden age in the past when all was copperplate. Once again the evaluation will be educative, extending the discussion of writing beyond the concentration on appearance on the page to writing as an art and craft. There may be some point in setting up a panel to look at writing in the school. Indeed, any area where there is intense public concern is suitable for an informal assessment. But this would be little more than a public relations exercise. Evaluation needs to provide information that can be used to track standards and plan measures for improvement as well as satisfy public concern. Let us assume that the aim is that by the age of 15, all pupils should be able to write cogently. Obviously this needs breaking down into a number of skills that could serve as bases for assessment. One scheme is to define the objectives as mastery of the following writing abilities.[1]

1 Ideas—the ability to express ideas with clarity.
2 Form—the ability to organize thoughts in writing.
3 Flavour—the ability to write interestingly.
4 Legibility—the ability to write neatly in an easy to read hand.
5 Mechanics—the ability to punctuate and be grammatical.
6 Wording—the ability to choose and arrange words meaningfully.

The stimulus for the writing test can be determined by the panel of experts that will do the marking. For preference this would involve the multiple marking of each script by a panel consisting of interested laymen and professionals. They would each mark the scripts for the abilities listed above. To remove the complication of different length essays, only the first 200 words need be marked. Again, a simple 3- or 5-point scale would be sufficient in each area, with each level defined in advance to indicate the level of attainment. Fine differences are not needed, only the numbers performing to a previously determined level of writing ability. But the consistency and validity of assessment would be increased if each of the six abilities above were translated into clearly defined levels of performance as illustrated in Chapter 2 in the Scottish *Profile Assessment System*.[2]

Regardless of the methods used to look at performance in the basic skills, whether teachers only, teachers supplemented by the second opinion of outsiders, or some variation on the more systematic approach outlined here, the results will serve as a way of evaluating the degree of success in achieving a minimum level of basic skill. Each year it should be possible to state the percentage of pupils who have mastered the basic level set in reading, arithmetic, the mechanics of writing, spelling, and writing style. The staff will have established a number of criteria which need not be limited to those considered here. These criteria will consist of professional judgements of the level of performance which all but a stated ten or so per cent of pupils should have mastered by a specified age. The performances will be in basic skills judged as crucial not only for further education but for employment later.

[1] McColly, W. (1965), 'What does educational research say about the judgement of writing ability?' *Journal of Educational Research*, vol. 4, pp. 148–56.
[2] SCRE, *op. cit.*

Technical competence

It is only possible to give examples of the type of skill that could be included in an externally referenced evaluation of the school using a panel of experts and interested laypeople. The technique, sharpened up by the staff of the school through their definition of objectives, methods and levels of assessment, and determination of criteria, gives only crude indicators. But it is flexible. One set of objectives stressed by the teachers consulted before writing this book was that of competence in doing the jobs facing adults in their everyday life. These skills are learned in a number of subjects such as craft, home economics, and health education, but there may be advantages in pulling them together into a single area for evaluation.

In this case outsiders could play a part not only in providing an external reference for the assessment against criteria, but in setting the objectives. It could be a 'twenty skills that all adults should have mastered' list of objectives. Letter writing, form filling, meter reading, fuse mending, plug wiring, choosing a doctor, using a telephone, filing correspondence, removing stains, mending a tap washer, and stopping an overflowing cistern are useful assets for adults and a list could easily be drawn up and tests of competence devised. The pupils could accumulate credits for learning these skills and the evaluation panel could serve as external assessors to add their authority to the exercise. Among governors, parents, and employers are experts in these and other areas, such as skills needed for work in offices, or shops, or industry. Most of these aspects are covered on the school curriculum. But regular, systematic evaluation involving the establishment of criteria of mastery can provide an annual record of attainment throughout the school as well as providing a useful testimonial for the individual pupil.

The involvement of parents who are skilled craftsmen, technicians, or professionals in evaluation could have many advantages. The pupils would be in contact with a range of experts beyond those available in the school. The parents would have a natural place in the life of the school. Often the skilled outsider visiting the school to give a talk to pupils makes little impact because he or she is a stranger. The continuing involvement of parents would benefit teachers through the added motivation of the pupils.

Once a staff decides to establish such a criterion-referenced evaluation they will have an annual measure of their success in teaching these basic skills. But as with all evaluation, the information should be used not only to reflect on, and improve the curriculum, but to help the pupils. Mastery of the basic skills to the specified level could be rewarded by a Certificate of Basic Skills. This could be given to any pupil achieving mastery in the areas tested. To avoid competition it need only be presented on leaving school and those failing to get to the necessary standard when the tests were first set, probably at the end of the third year, could take it later. This Certificate would be a useful incentive for pupils and an asset for those who at present seek employment without any certificated evidence of their achievements. Being criterion-referenced it would not be a competitive, differentiating examination.

The reports from the panels evaluating the degree of mastery of the basic skills could be collected together to form part of an annual account of the work of the school. But the information should, as usual, be used to meet the three foci of evaluation: to assess and help the work of pupils, to provide data for teachers for reviewing the curriculum, and to provide information for the school's public. If the annual report is the school's equivalent of the director's report to the shareholders of a company, the evaluation by panels plays the part of the auditor, providing an independent check on the accounts.

The questions asked by teachers at the start of the two chapters on the school assessment programme can now be answered. It is possible to evaluate the work of a single teacher, a departmental group of teachers, or a whole school staff by using internal and external references. But at all times the running assessment programme must be separated from the controlled, standardized programme. Furthermore, not only must comparisons be based on scaled marks, but these, or externally referenced assessments, should be the only ones to be made public. Two warnings are worth repeating. Assessment is only the first step to evaluation and the judgements have to be added to marks, grades, and other indicators. But the small part of the total life of a school that can be evaluated on the basis of numerical indicators should not be taken for the whole. Because the largest part cannot be measured, it does not mean that it cannot be evaluated. Statistics have to be selected and evaluated. The judgement is always there. The professional appraisal has to fill the gaps, but is valuable in itself, particularly when there are a number of different appraisals of the same aspect.

The entry of parents, employers, and other members of the public into the working life of a school is still not accepted by many teachers. The suggestion in this chapter that some qualified members of that public should be deliberately co-opted into evaluation panels to help the teachers may be even more unwelcome. Yet this not only makes evaluation more credible, but reinforces the efforts of teachers and is a way of avoiding the misunderstanding and suspicion that can make the work of teachers difficult. It is unlikely that such panels will be used widely by teachers. They are likely to be composed of experts rather than typical parents or employers. But they are a way of bringing another perspective to bear on the work of the school and are a possible aid to teachers in checking whether internally determined objectives are being achieved.

4. The School Assessment Programme: externally referenced by public examination results

The results obtained by pupils in public examinations are the most widely-used criteria of the success of secondary schools. The debate over the merits of comprehensive schooling has been largely confined to comparing such results for selective and non-selective schools. They are often the only hard evidence available. Yet the inconclusive nature of this debate indicates the need to use examination results with caution, and in context. Four weaknesses in examination data need to be overcome:

1. Results can be the product of the attainment of pupils at entry to a school rather than of the quality of schooling.
2. Even if the attainment of pupils at entry to school is taken into account, differences in results when comparisons are made with other schools may still not be the result of different quality schooling. For example, as social background is a powerful factor behind attainment, pupils of similar attainment at intake in two schools may still be expected to achieve different examination results if they came from different social backgrounds.
3. The results of examinations in different subjects of different boards at different times, and between GCE and CSE may not be directly comparable.
4. Examinations only cover a part of the school population, sample only a part of the curriculum, and the results depend on the different examination policies of different schools.

Nevertheless, despite these weaknesses, examination results can be used in a school to check the performance year by year of pupils entering five, six, or seven years before with differing attainments and abilities. They are externally referenced and are accorded priority by parents and employers. The teachers consulted asked for extensive cover of ways in which examination results could be used. In this chapter methods of collecting and tabulating results for internal consideration are discussed first. Then methods of obtaining comparisons with other schools, nationally or locally, are discussed. Many different tables are presented because the teachers consulted came from schools with very different examination policies. Staff with an open-door examination policy will expect different results from a staff operating a restricted policy of entry to examinations. It is easy to obtain 100 per cent passes by restricting entries. It is easy to ensure that all but a few pupils get some sort of grade at CSE examinations by allowing all to enter. In these cases the information required to monitor the effects of the policies will differ.

Examination results are not the only indicators of the academic quality of a school. They indicate the degree to which some implicit or explicit objectives of the staff of the school are being attained. The sequence of actions should not be to decide on the collection of results and then to analyse these to determine the level of success, but to review the school's examination policies as a reflection of wider academic objectives, and then to organize the collection and analysis of results to assess the extent to which these objectives are being attained. Decisions over objectives still take precedence. The examination results are indicators, means to an end, rather than ends in themselves. Thus the methods of organizing public examination results suggested in this chapter should not be taken as a blueprint. Each school staff will want to organize available information in different ways to meet different objectives. Selection among the methods suggested may help.

The tables are presented without division into boys and girls. Yet this is often an important piece of information and in mixed schools this separation is recommended in case there are wide discrepancies in performance when the figures for the school are laid alongside those produced by the DES or examination boards. For example, while girls obtain a higher proportion of grade A, B, or C on GCE O level than do boys, the latter obtain more 'passes' in mathematics, while girls do very much better in modern languages and English. If evaluation is to produce information for decisions about important educational issues in the school, division into boys' and girls' results is advisable.

The objectives that follow were selected from those stated by teachers consulted before writing this book. These were not volunteered readily. Most teachers had implicit objectives for the examination policy they organized, but few had thought through the purpose of the exercise in any thorough way. The objectives can vary widely. Here are four examples:

1. To maximize GCE and CSE entries.
2. To maximize all passes on public examinations.
3. To maximize the number of passes while minimizing the number of failures.
4. To maximize entries and passes in English, mathematics, and science.

Each of these objectives will lead to different results and will require examination information organized in different ways to provide an adequate indication of the success of the policy.

How not to present examination results

It is rare to find published accounts of the examination results of a school that do not give an incomplete or biased picture. Here are the results of one comprehensive school on O level and CSE 1 grades, described by the headteacher as a 'remarkable academic achievement'. [1]

		GCE O level passes	A and B grades	CSE Grade 1 passes	Total GCE O level and CSE 1
1967	3 contributory schools	372	37	—	372
1968	Highbury Grove	290	33	17	307
1969		204	21	19	323
1970		307	43	20	327
1971		343	36	15	358
1972		345	47	23	368

Now it may be that this is a remarkable achievement if the intake into the school changed between 1962, when the 1967 examination group entered, and 1967 when the 1972 examination group entered. But the reader is only given a part of the total examination picture, has not got the size of the last complete age group from which the examination forms were formed, is not given the national trend across the years 1967 and 1972, or the trend in neighbouring schools. This is not necessarily misleading the reader, but it is denying him or her the opportunity to judge the interpretation given in the text.

The three examples that follow are from schools that asked for advice on how to organize their results. These schools were making results public and were concerned to improve their presentation. They were likely to be among the most thorough in preparing examination statistics.

Type 1

This school makes no use of public examination results for internal purposes. For Speech Day it produces the names of pupils with the subjects 'passed' in CSE and GCE although no definition of 'pass' is given. This appears as:

General Certificate of Education O level: A. Adams (Art, English), B. Brown (Maths, Physics, Technical Drawing), etc.

Certificate of Secondary Education: A. Abrahams (English,

[1] Boyson, R. (1974), *Oversubscribed*. London, Ward Lock Educational.

History, Maths), B. Black (French, English, Geography, History, Music, Religious Education), etc.

Type 2
This school produces a simple statistical picture of its results as follows:

Summer Examinations 1978. Number in fifth year = 170.
Number not taking any examination = 40 (23 per cent). Number obtaining over 5 O level Grade A, B or C or CSE grade 1 = 36 (28 per cent).
Number obtaining CSE grades 2 to 5 = 72 (55 per cent).

There are obscure aspects in this collection of figures. If collected each year they would indicate examination success. The public however needs to be mathematically sophisticated. First, the percentages obtaining grades are expressed in relation to those entering examinations not the whole age group. Secondly, there is no information on the numbers taking examinations but failing. Thirdly, there is no information on successes and failures in subjects or of individual pupils. The separate presentation of each examination conceals the tendency for pupils to accumulate grades in different years or in winter as well as summer examinations. Fourthly, it shows nothing of the pattern of success overall, only indicating selected parts of the examination scene. In the programme for Open Day the results were presented only as total numbers passing GCE and CSE with the figures for the preceding year. The number in the year-group was not given.

Type 3
This school prepared its public examination results in a similar form to Table 4:1. These tables also served to produce the number of entrants and the number of pupils obtaining 5 or more O level 'passes' or CSE grade 1. The staff used the number obtaining 5 or more O levels as a way of comparing its success year after year. This school printed a brief summary of examination results annually. This was available for governors and was made available to parents who made enquiries. It consisted of the numbers entering for GCE or CSE summer examinations and the percentage 'passing' each. A pass meant GCE A, B or C and CSE grades 1 to 5. The figures for the year were compared with those from preceding years.

There are many weaknesses in the way the results in these schools were collected together and used for internal purposes. There were no figures on the total, terminal performance of pupils on leaving school. There was no attempt to build up time series showing how examination performance varied year by year. There was information on passes but not on failures. The examination results were not related to the attainment of the pupils at entry to the school five years earlier.

There was no attempt to relate the results to national figures or to figures provided by the examination boards. They were not related to the examination policy of the schools. Yet these schools had taken the trouble to seek advice on the use of their results and were probably in a better position than most. The information presented to parents was even less informative. However, the absence of useful examination data sprang from the absence of an articulated examination policy. In none of the schools was there a clear policy agreed among the staff over the object of the examination exercise. The balance between GCE and CSE, the number being entered for each, the number re-taking by staying on into the sixth form, the levels of failure that could be tolerated, the length of courses leading to examinations, even the balance of subjects to be taken seemed to have been decided without explicit decisions having been made. Insufficient evidence was available to help make such decisions. The form in which results were made public was designed to give parents the one piece of information they already had, the performance of their own child. In addition it gave the performance of peers. But it did not give any idea of the examination policy of the school, or its success in achieving the objectives built into that policy. Curiously, where parents were given some idea of this success, the information was incomplete and gave an unnecessarily bad impression.

Methods of organizing examination results

The three schools described earlier all had members of staff who were keen to make greater use of examination results to help in making decisions about public examination entries and about curriculum. In discussion their problem was about priorities. Was priority to be given to maximizing the number of pupils obtaining five or more O levels or CSE 1 in the more marketable subjects or to ensuring that all pupils had a good general education, with examination results being the by-product not the primary aim? Should they press on with integrated studies, social studies, community studies, or place more time and resources into traditional subjects? Should they extend mixed-ability grouping into third and later years or separate a GCE examination group early in their schooling? Should the A-level pattern offered in the sixth form determine the curriculum lower down the school, even though few would stay on into the traditional sixth form? As soon as the results of public examinations were looked at as a useful source for decision-making over the curriculum, questions about the objectives of that curriculum were asked. The wish to assess was forcing these teachers to consider the purpose of the schooling they were offering.

The outcome of discussions over public examinations was usually a policy of maximum success with minimum failure. The discussions were frustrated by the lack of sufficient information on previous examinations. It is hoped that the act of organizing results systematically will enable objectives to be further clarified. But there was another set of priorities to be decided. The staff were rightly worried about the time and trouble involved in the extraction and organization of examination results. Once again the final decision was pragmatic. A few tabulations would be made and if these were useful they would be extended. This could be wasteful, for the statistics only became useful when collected over time. The tables that follow should help in the selection of data of most use in schools with different objectives.

The most satisfactory method of storing information from examinations is to keep a record of the grades, including unclassified, of all the examinations taken in all subjects by each pupil. But to produce tables from record cards is very time-consuming unless the information is punched on to a special card that can be sorted mechanically or processed by a computer. Methods of using such means of storage can be found in Appendix B. Commercial firms are of course keen to be of service. Once information is stored in this way it can be retrieved for any analyses that are required. Many schools have the facilities to store, retrieve, and analyse in this way, but it would be unrealistic to assume that it will be given a high enough priority in many.

Examination results arrive at the schools from the examination boards on a computer printout or duplicated list showing the name of pupils followed by the subjects they have taken and the grade achieved. The easiest way of producing a basic table from which other information can be obtained is shown in Table 4:1. This merely organizes the information from each examination board in a more convenient form and enables available intake data to be added. Here the reading age and the verbal reasoning score of each pupil obtained five years before have been used to give some idea of the impact of the teaching across these years. Table 4:1 contains information that can be organized to produce most of the tables that follow. In a large school the table is too long to be useful, but it gives an immediate picture of the successes and failures of pupils and a simple indication of ability and attainment at intake to the school. Read down the columns it gives the level of success in individual subjects.

Another start to the collection of examination statistics can be the DES Form 7d, used for the 10 per cent leavers' survey every autumn term. The back of this form contains space for grades obtained by the leaver on CSE, O and A level GCE on some 60 subjects. This form can be used for 100 per cent of leavers, or as a model for a form for collecting results on summer and winter examinations. It can be filled in for each pupil, or a single, expanded form can be used to give an aggregated picture of all results of all pupils. Here is the layout of this form which provides a useful model for the collection of

Table 4:1 Examination results of pupils by subject

	Art		English		Maths		Geography		Social Studies		Biology		Woodwork		French		V.R.	Reading
	GCE	CSE	GCE	CSE	GCE	CSE	GCE	CSE	GCE	CSE	GCE	CSE	GCE	CSE	GCE	CSE		
A. Adams	E	2	B	3	U		C	5	1		C			3	D		98	10 yrs 2 mths
B. Brown	B	4	B	4	A		C				C			3	A		119	Absent
C. Cook																	92	9 yrs 8 mths
Z. Zavier																	126	12 yrs

statistics. Only the first three of 60 subjects listed are shown (Table 4:2).

The number of passes and failures

It is impossible to present all the many ways in which public examination results might be organized. Different school staffs will have different objectives in entering pupils for examinations and will require different data from the results to check how well their objectives are being achieved. Another complication is that the same results can be used to indicate different levels of success. For example, the A, B and C grades on GCE O level cover the older 'pass' grade. CSE grade 1 corresponds to a GCE pass. But there the clarity ends. The DES presents CSE figures using both grade 4 and grade 5 as a pass. Five passes at grades A, B, or C on GCE or CSE grade 1 is frequently used as an indication of a significant level of success among employers and teachers. But GCE grades D and E, while failures, cannot be compared with CSE grades 2 to 5, as each set of grades is the result of different criteria. Particularly where school policy is to enter the same pupils for both GCE and CSE there has to be some arbitrary decision on how results are to be presented. Once the decision is made, it should be continued to give comparable data year after year.

The entry policy of a school staff determines the success and failure rates. This is why public examination results have to be presented not only within the context of the other work of the school and its environment, but also in relation to the examination policy of the school, or even of subject departments. Maximizing entries may increase both passes and failures. But parents will be pressing for their children to be entered, particularly for GCE. A few CSE grades 4, 5, or unclassified are not a marketable qualification, but may reflect a far more rewarding education than GCE grades D, E, and certainly U, the unclassified GCE category. The presentation and internal use of examination results must be educative. They should show parents, employers, and the staff of the school what is being attempted and why, as well as the results of that policy.

To illustrate the possibilities of organizing public examination results, the policies of secondary schools were examined and questions asked about the objectives incorporated in those policies. A selection of those objectives has been made and suggested treatments of public examination results presented.

Objective—to maximize the number in each successive year-group getting five or more O levels or CSE grade 1. However, this success should not be at the cost of excessive numbers failing.

Table 4:2 The DES Form 7d

Subject (2)	CSE (4) Please use grades 1, 2, 3, 4 or 5; 6 = ungraded		GCE 'O' level papers (4) Please use Grades A, B, C, D, E or U = ungraded or P = pass, F = fail as appropriate (3)							GCE 'A' level papers (5) In columns J to N please enter A, B, C, D, E, O or F to indicate grades					
	1974/5 or earlier	1975/6	1972/3 or earlier	1973/4 Winter	1973/4 Summer	1974/5 Winter	1974/5 Summer	1975/6 Winter	1975/6 Summer	1973/4 or earlier	1974/5 Winter	1974/5 Summer	1975/6 Winter	1975/6 Summer	
	A	B	C	D	E	F	G	H	I	J	K	L	M	N	
Pure Mathematics (6)	501														501
Applied Maths and/or Mechanics (6)	502														502
Pure & Applied Maths (single subj.)	503														503

The most widely recognized level of success in public examinations is five GCE grades A, B, or C, or CSE grade 1, which is the equivalent of a GCE pass. This number of passes is the entry requirement for many courses in further education and for entry to professions. The number of pupils gaining this basic five subjects is a useful single indicator. It can be balanced by the number obtaining U grade on GCE, or grades 5 or U, or U only in CSE. The former is a fail and the latter is the lowest CSE result. There are, however, other considerations in the use of these simple indicators. The subjects included in the 'passes' and 'failures' are important. Five 'passes' including maths, English, a science, and a modern language are more marketable than one including subjects less respected by employers and not accepted for entry to some further education courses. Table 4:3 shows one way of presenting this information. It is limited in scope but it is easy to accumulate and gives staff an indicator of the extent of success and failure.

Table 4:3   Success and failure on GCE and CSE examinations

		Number of pupils obtaining			
		5 'passes'	*Grade U*		
	5 O level	*inc. maths*	*GCE*	*CSE U*	*Number in*
Year	*or CSE 1*	*+ English*	*1 2 3 +*	*1 2 3 +*	*age group*
1975	29 (18%)	18 (11%)	13 8 4	23 9 2	160
1976	24 (16%)	18 (12%)	11 8 1	22 18 7	150
1977	22 (14%)	16 (10%)	9 6 4	22 14 9	152

Table 4:3 indicates the tendency for the number obtaining five 'passes' to fall although there is some compensation in the fall in numbers 'failing' GCE. Again, such tables can only be interpreted in the light of events in the school, the characteristics of the intake five plus years before, and against the objectives of the staff.

Objective—to attain an entry to examinations that will keep pass rates (GCE A, B, and C, CSE grade 5 or better) high, and failure rates low, for all pupils regardless of how many subjects they take.

This objective is similar to the last objective. But this staff was worried as much by the pupil who took eight or more subjects as the pupil who took only a single CSE. To them, failure could be damaging across the whole range of ability, and success as rewarding. Tables 4:4 and 4:5 opposite are not in a form that is suitable for release to the public, although the percentages calculated from them could be. They are in the form used by the DES in their annual statistics on leavers. Read across, these tables give the number of entries of pupils; read down the columns they give the numbers getting a Grade 5 or better CSE or Grade C or better in GCE. The grades specified can be decided by the staff of the school. The DES also

Table 4:4   GCE O level—pupils gaining grade C or better

Number of subjects attempted by pupils	0	1	2	3	4	5	6	7	8+	Pupil total	Total attempts
0	104									104	
1	2	2								4	4
2	1	2	2							5	10
3			1	1						2	6
4	2		1	2						5	20
5		1	2	2	2	4				11	55
6		1	2	3	2	2				10	60
7							4	3		7	49
8+						1		1	2	4	32
Pupil total	109	6	8	8	4	7	4	4	2	152	236
Total of grades		6	16	24	16	35	24	28	16	165	

Table 4:5   CSE—pupils gaining grade 5 (or better) results

Number of subjects attempted by pupils	0	1	2	3	4	5	6	7	8+	Pupil total	Total attempts
0	27									27	
1	9	14								23	23
2	9	5	8							22	44
3	4	1	3	3						11	33
4	2	1	1	4	2					10	40
5			2	2	5	8				15	75
6			2		6	8	9			25	150
7	1						13	5		19	133
8+											
Pupil total	52	21	14	9	13	16	22	5		152	498
Total grades		21	28	27	52	80	132	35		375	

provides a table giving CSE grade 4 or better. As the number of entries and number of grades of each pupil is entered into each table it is easy to calculate the total number of subjects attempted and the total number of the specified grades achieved. These have been used to calculate pass, failure, and entry rates. This is probably the most useful information for monitoring the success of the examination policy of a school in detail.

Tables 4:4 and 4:5 do not give any information on separate subjects. Neither do they give information on the total examination attainment of individual pupils, for some pupils will take both CSE and GCE. However, any of the five pieces of information extracted from the tables can be used to build up a useful year-by-year picture. Further, the juxtaposition of entries and passes shows up the cases where failures seem excessive. Clearly in this school there were some pupils who were entered for GCE in particular when their chances of obtaining an A, B or C grade were slight.

From Table 4:4 the following can be extracted:

1. GCE O level (grades A, B, C) pass rate $= \dfrac{165}{236} = 70\%$

2. GCE O level (grades D, E, U) failure rate $= \dfrac{71}{236} = 30\%$

3. GCE O level entry rate $= \dfrac{48}{152} = 32\%$

4. GCE O level average entries (year-group) $= \dfrac{236}{152} = 1.55$

5. GCE O level, average entries (GCE group) $= \dfrac{236}{48} = 4.91$

Some national figures on the results of examinations taken in summer and winter are published annually by the DES. These appear some two years after the dates of the examinations. The national percentages getting A–C grades on GCE for summer 1975 were 58.1 per cent for boys and 60.8 per cent for girls.

From Table 4:5 the following can be extracted:

1. CSE (grades 1–5) pass rate $= \dfrac{375}{498} = 75\%$

2. CSE unclassified, failure rate $= \dfrac{123}{498} = 25\%$

3. CSE entry rate $= \dfrac{125}{152} = 82\%$

4. CSE average entries (year-group) $= \dfrac{498}{152} = 3.27$

5. CSE average entries (CSE group) $= \dfrac{498}{125} = 3.98$

The DES figures for the 1975 summer CSE examinations show

that 90.8 per cent of boys and 91.7 per cent of girls entering obtained grade 5 or better.

The objectives considered so far have concentrated on the need to ensure that success is not balanced by excessive failure. Statistics produced for each year's examinations might not be sufficient to check on the success of this policy, unless staff can agree on some acceptable levels of success and failure after looking at the rates achieved by all candidates for the relevant examination boards. In any case, staff will want to look at results year by year to see how successful their policy and their teaching is, but also to detect any trends that may need action. Tables 4:4 and 4:5, for example, yielded summary information for comparison across years. Table 4:6 shows the percentage pass and fail rates for a school across three years. Such a table can serve to alert staff to any trends towards excessive failure and can monitor the effects of changes in entry policies to examinations. In this school there had been a gradual increase in the numbers being entered for both GCE and CSE, and this did seem to be raising failure rates. However, not too much should be read into such trends. Changes in the ability of the fifth year could easily account for such fluctuations. The collection of such information across the years would ensure that staff were aware of the consequence of such combinations of changes.

Teachers may prefer a simple indicator of success in GCE and CSE for internal planning purposes. This is straightforward for CSE as the grades run from 1 to 5 and U, which can count as 6. To produce a parallel GCE numerical scale it is convenient to count GCE A grade as a 1, B as 2, down to grade U as 6. Table 4:7 shows these averages where a low score indicates a high success rate. These could easily be reversed so that the high scores more conventionally indicated the better performance.

Obviously the choice between preparing one table and the next will depend on the audience in view as well as the examination objectives under review. The tables reproduced from Rowe below, and Tables 4:3 and 4:6, are suitable for release to the public. But

Table 4:6 Pupils obtaining pass or fail grades in GCE and CSE

	Year					
	1975		*1976*		*1977*	
Grades	Subject entries	% obtaining	Subject entries	% obtaining	Subject entries	% obtaining
GCE	186		208		236	
A, B, C		68		73		70
U		6		8		9
CSE	408		414		498	
1		19		21		22
U		22		22		25

**Table 4:7   Average grade on GCE
and CSE on a 1–6 scale for all subjects
entered**

Year	GCE	CSE
1975	2.91	2.60
1976	3.24	2.40
1977	3.08	2.71

Tables 4:4 and 4:5, while probably the most informative, may be too complicated for release. They, and some of the tables that follow, give details necessary to make decisions among staff, but are not in a form that is suitable for parents as they need too much interpretation.

None of the tables presented so far has been specially designed to give information to the public. Yet this demand is persistent and justified. The difficulty lies in the absence of any detectable agreement among parents or employers about the indications they require. The factors involved—the total numbers in age groups, the numbers entering public examinations, entries to GCE or CSE, the definition of pass or fail, the subject mix required, the level of pass compared with the ability of the pupil are manifold and no single set of figures is going to satisfy all audiences. A good example of time series used to illustrate changes as a comprehensive school built up its examination entries is found in Albert Rowe's personal, informative account of the organization of David Lister School, Hull.[1] It has to be remembered that the switch to GCE grades only occurred in 1975 and that the pass grades 1 to 6 presented are now A, B, or C. The definition of 'pass' for CSE is a grade 5 or better.

Tables 4:8a and 4:8b have many useful features. They give previous years as a basis for comparison. They indicate subject range and level of success. They would not answer questions about the proportion of pupils in an age group taking examinations. Rowe deals with the attainment of the intake to the school over the years elsewhere in his book, and in the early years of a school this is important planning information. The average number of subjects passed column for GCE, which is omitted, rises slowly from 1.1 to 1.8 between 1965 and 1970, with, as in CSE, a peak in 1969. No questions can be answered about the attainment of pupils as the mix of CSE and GCE is unknown. These and other questions that could not be answered are not criticisms of Rowe. To answer all possible questions would require a large number of tables and without a clear expression of the public's interests in advance, they would still not be complete. For example, a favourite question is 'how well does the average

[1] Rowe, A. (1971), *The School as a Guidance Community*. Hull, Pearson Press.

Table 4:8a Yorkshire Regional Examinations Board Certificate of Secondary Education Examinations

Year	Candidates	Subjects offered	Total subjects taken	Av. no. subjects taken	1*	2	3	4	5	U	Total no. of passes	Av. no. of subjects passed
1965	7	1	7	1.0	1	2	3	1			7	1.0
1966	45	10	79	1.8	14	23	11	17	9	5	74	1.6
1967	67	19	313	4.7	32	53	72	90	50	16	297	4.4
1968	103	20	471	4.6	70	74	125	141	53	8	463	4.5
1969	177	21	883	5	160	211	198	193	83	38	845	4.8
1970	210	22	998	4.7	180	227	240	222	105	24	974	4.6

* GCE equivalent

Table 4:8b Joint Matriculation Board. GCE O Level Examinations

Year	Candidates	Subjects offered	Total subjects taken	Av. no. of subjects taken	1	2	3	4	5	6	Total no. of passes
1965	46	13	132	2.9	4	3	8	7	15	15	52
1966	48	16	153	3.2	8	6	13	11	25	25	88
1967	55	18	204	3.7	6	3	17	16	21	24	87
1968	115	21	286	2.5	11	9	43	24	57	35	179
1969	159	25	707	4.4	11	18	94	58	103	94	378
1970	221	26	810	3.2	5	15	98	73	115	101	405

pupil do on examinations'. The real answer to this question would come only from a sophisticated exercise to identify this average pupil and his or her results. Even then the definition of 'average pupil' would have to be very carefully spelled out. With the size of each year's age group and a definition of 'passes', these tables for David Lister school would give most teachers and the public of the school sufficient information to judge the success of examination policies.

Here is a selection of results presented by a headteacher of a comprehensive school to his governors. The report on examinations was extensive and each year one examination was analysed in detail. Table 4:9 dealt with A levels. These were presented as a time series as follows, for summer examinations only. This school kept a record of the pupils' grades on a seven-point scale based on a verbal reasoning score at entry seven years before. There were pupils who joined after entry at 11 years, but a table was included in the report to governors showing the relation between ability at intake and A level results (Table 4:10). These were designed to show how few pupils would have normally gone to a grammar school and how many of

Table 4:9   Percentage entries and passes

Year	No. of candidates A	4th year 3 years before B	$\frac{A}{B}$ %	Subject entries	Passes	Passes per candidate	% Passes	% Passes national
1972	36	168	21	81	53	1.5	65	68.3
1973	48	164	29	111	76	1.6	68	68.7
1974	62	169	37	141	93	1.5	66	68.3
1975	59	176	34.5	130	85	1.4	65	67.6
1976	67	167	40	159	105	1.6	66	—
1977	79	181	44	190	122	1.5	64	—

Table 4:10   A level results and entry grade seven years before

		Grade at entry 7 years earlier							Total candidates with known entry grades
		1	2	3	4	5	6	7	
A level	1	—	2	6	4	2	1	—	15
passes	2	4	4	6	4	2	—	—	20
	3	2	3	2	—	—	—	—	7
	4	2	—	—	—	—	—	—	2
									44

those obtaining A levels were from grades at entry not often considered to have academic potential. Results are for 1976 only.

This school laid its CSE results out in a similar way to that used by Albert Rowe at David Lister. The GCE O level results were, however, designed to show the number of subject passes of those pupils obtaining three or more O level passes or CSE 1 grades. They were tabulated as shown in Table 4:11.

These tables have been extracted from a longer report on the examination results of this comprehensive school. There are still important pieces of information missing. While A level results are related to grading at entry, this is only done selectively to show that selection is a dubious procedure at 11 years. There is no evidence on whether the school was receiving a more or less able intake across the years. But these were the most complete set of examination statistics found while preparing this book. At the end of the period the local education authority concerned finally stopped selection for its secondary schools, and the school in question was receiving an intake that was drawn from a representative sample of the population for the first time. The results stored would be a most useful basis for watching the effect of this changed intake and for planning new curricula to take account of these changed conditions.

There is another missing piece of evidence that illustrates the difficulty in covering all the important questions in a few tables. Clearly from the A level Table 4:9 the proportion of the last complete year (in this case taken as fourth year to avoid the problem of the raising of the school leaving age) taking A levels is high for a comprehensive school. But a look at the supplementary evidence on the numbers for whom grades at entry to the school were known gives a clue to this high proportion. For 1976, only 44 were known out of an A level group of 67. Many of the sixth form had joined from other maintained and independent schools.

**Table 4:11 Number of candidates with more than 3 GCE grades
A, B, or C or CSE 1 grade**

	Pupils Passing:						Total 3 or more A	No. in previous 4th yr B	$\frac{A}{B}$ %
Year	8	7	6	5	4	3			
1972	2	4	4	5	4	7	26	169	15
1973	2	7	4	10	6	7	36	176	20
1974	3	5	11	9	8	8	44	167	26
1975	3	9	15	12	12	10	61	181	34
1976	2	8	14	13	11	15	63	174	36
1977	4	8	14	7	13	17	63	174	36

Success and failure within subjects

The staff of a school will often want to know the pattern of examination policies across departments. They may also want to know how successful such policies are. This is not mere nosey-parkering. It is essential for decision-making. Resources have to be allocated between subject departments on some basis, preferably rational. Examination policies and successes are one possible basis. For example, teachers in one department may decide that they have a claim, based on more entrants to GCE or superior examination performance, for available resources. Staff may want to counter criticism from outside the school, directed at one or more subject departments. Headteachers or inspectors might be concerned about the efficiency of a department, or wish to spread a form of examination policy used by a successful department to other schools, or to have information prior to inspection. The difficulty in collecting together meaningful statistics is that there are often few departments entering enough candidates for comparisons to be made. English and mathematics are usually big enough, but caution has to be exercised when using small numbers from small departments. There are other factors that can confuse results. Girls tend to attain a lower level than boys of equivalent ability in mathematics, but are superior in English. The level of severity of marking tends to differ between subjects. For example, mathematics seems to be marked more severely than English in both GCE and CSE examinations. Only when differences are large and persistent should they be assumed to be a reflection of real differences.

Objective—to ensure that the examination policies of subject departments do not result in excessive failure rates.

Subject departments in a school will want their own data on public examinations. Table 4:12 shows information extracted from an examination board printout for all pupils in a school taking mathematics. The information on this table can be treated further to give average grades and percentages passing, although with small numbers the layout in Table 4:12 will probably be safer. Table 4:13 shows the results from several subject departments gathered together to give a time series which can guide staff in making decisions not only about examinations, but about the curriculum. The numbering of grades is given in Table 4:13, the higher grades being given smaller numbers. It has to be remembered however that there is not strict comparability between the grades obtained between subjects. It is probably safest to look at the results of each subject across time rather than at the results of different subjects in the same year.

Tables 4:12 and 4:13 are suitable for discussion within and between subject departments, but unsuitable for publication. Table 4:12 would need repeating for all departments and some subjects would

Table 4:12 Average GCE and CSE grades obtained by pupils in mathematics

| Year | GCE | | | | | | | | | CSE | | | | | | | | |
	A (1)	B (2)	C (3)	D (4)	E (5)	U (6)	Ab.	Total	Average	1	2	3	4	5	6(U)	Ab.	Total	Average
1975	2	4	1	3	4	2	3	19	3.0	12	4	14	6	5	9	2	52	2.7
1976	5	3	4	2	1	4	4	23	2.6	2	11	9	14	12	7	7	62	2.2
1977	2	2	4	4	7	6	2	27	3.9	3	13	12	5	11	4	6	54	2.6

Table 4:13 Average GCE and CSE grades obtained by pupils on selected subjects (grades translated into numbers as in Table 4:7)

| Year | Maths | | English | | French | | Physics | | History | | Geography | | Art | |
	GCE	CSE	GCE	CSE	GCE	CSE	GCE	CSE	GCE	CSE	GCE	CSE	GCE	CSE
1975	3.0	2.7	2.2	2.0	3.1	3.2	3.7	2.9	2.4	2.3	2.5	2.5	2.1	2.0
1976	2.6	2.2	2.1	2.2	2.6	2.9	3.5	3.1	2.4	2.5	2.9	2.7	2.6	2.0
1977	3.9	2.6	2.2	2.0	2.4	3.6	3.6	2.8	2.3	2.1	2.9	2.7	2.8	2.2

Table 4:14   Entries and passes in GCE and CSE in selected subjects

Subject	Pupils in year	GCE entrants	GCE A, B, or C	% pass	CSE entrants	CSE 1–5	% grades 1–5
English	152	31	24	77	75	60	90
Maths	152	22	14	64	67	61	91
Art	152	22	18	82	64	52	81
History	152	24	20	83	40	34	85
Geography	152	26	20 .	77	64	56	88
Physics	152	18	14	78	50	44	88
French	152	15	12	80	14	13	93

be too small to give meaningful figures. Table 4:13 is convenient for internal discussion but is indicative only, and open to misinterpretation if the basis of the figures is not understood. The public usually wants to know how many enter and pass different subjects. Table 4:14 is an attempt to give the information required to the public. Again the need to place tables like this in the context of the total examination policy and the attainment of pupils at intake to the school is obvious. Parents often assume that it is usual for pupils to take GCE, and the release of results will inevitably lead to further questions about examination policy.

Once again, such a table will not satisfy all parents, employers, and so on. It will give the public a picture of the examination entries and results, but most parents will go on to ask how this compares with other schools. Even if such comparative information were available it would need to be put into the context of the school and the nature of its intake compared with the other schools. This raises the problem of the release of statistics by local education authorities on a school by school basis. The statistics might reflect very different situations, not the results of teaching similar intakes. When results are prepared within the school they can be placed within context and changes over the years can be included.

Total pupil performance

So far only separate GCE and CSE entries and grades have been considered. But each pupil can take a combination of subjects from these two examinations. Staff may find it useful to tabulate these total examination achievements. Read across, Table 4:15 gives the subject grades above 5 on CSE; read down the columns it gives GCE subjects 'passed' (pre-1975). Only the results from summer examinations have been included. The DES produces results in this form, but for leavers in one school year; these can include

Table 4:15   CSE and GCE achievements

Number of subjects with A, B, or C grade on O level papers

Number of			1	2	3	4	5	6	7	8+	Total
subjects at	0	27	2	3	5	2	4	4	3	2	52
grade 5 or	1–2	22	2	4	1	2	3		1		35
better on	3–4	17	2	1	2						22
CSE papers	5–7	38									38
	7+	5									5
	Total	109	6	8	8	4	7	4	4	2	152

achievements accumulated by pupils over one, two, or three years.[1] Comparisons are unwise unless made for all annual leavers. These problems of comparison with national statistics are expanded at the end of this chapter.

Table 4:15 shows a school still running one GCE group which tends not to take CSE subjects, and another that takes subjects from both examinations. Comparison with the DES tables is not possible unless the total achievements of all leavers are used. Those staying on into the sixth form having taken CSE in the fifth are likely to pick up GCE grades, while a few who have taken GCE in the fifth will pick up CSE grades.

The tables presented so far suffer from not showing the achievement of pupils in a simple, single measure. This makes it impossible to tabulate change across the years in a simple way. What is needed is a single scale that will give a picture of the performance of pupils in all their public examinations. This should provide an indicator of performance that will show staff whether their policies in relation to examinations are successful. The indicator need have little meaning by itself, nor is it suitable for public consumption. It can however serve as the examination litmus paper for staff.

There are various ways of combining all public examination results into a single scale. All are arbitrary. Different methods should be used in schools where staff have different examination policies. Fortunately CSE grade 1 is supposed to be the equivalent of GCE grade C, and this helps to produce a single scale from the different examinations. For example, CSE grades 1 to 5 and U can be given scores so that grade 1 counts as 6, grade 2 as 5 and so on. GCE grade A can then be given 8, grade B 7, and grade C given 6, the same as CSE grade 1. From there on it becomes more arbitrary and the results are not suitable for publication. GCE unclassified grade U could count as 1 or zero, while grades D and E on GCE can count as 5 and 4 or as 3 and 2, or as 2 and 1. Whatever scale is chosen, it

[1] Department of Education and Science (1976), *Statistics of Education, Volume 2, School Leavers, CSE and GCE*. London, HMSO.

should be adhered to year by year, as it is annual results collected across the years that give the indicator meaning and enable staff to assess the success of their work.

This scoring from 8 for GCE grade A down to 1 or zero for unclassified results gives a total positive score for all candidates that can be summed to give an annual indicator of examination success. However, some school staffs may prefer to use a scale that gives less emphasis to higher grades and which indicates successes alongside failures. A method of achieving such an indicator is to give positive and negative scores for grades and keep these separate in the summing of results. For example:

GCE grades A, B, and C, and CSE 1 can count as + 2.
CSE grades 2 to 5 can count as + 1.
GCE grades D and E can count as − 1.
GCE and CSE unclassified can count as − 2.

This scale reveals failures but compared with the previous method over-emphasizes lower CSE grades while under-rating GCE grades D and E. For example, on the first scale, a GCE D or E grade count as 5 and 4 respectively. On the second they both count as − 1. This illustrates the problem with indicators. They will be chosen to illuminate policies agreed among the staffs of schools. But different policies will be illuminated best by different indicators. The first method of producing a single scale would suit a staff interested in maximizing success. The second would suit a staff interested in minimizing failure. It is difficult to design an indicator that combines both. In any case such single indicators, referred to an arbitrary scale, are for internal use only. It is useful to have a single measure of examination results incorporating both GCE and CSE on a single scale. But it has meaning only in relation to that scale and could easily be misinterpreted. The method of keeping positive and negative scores separate is valuable as a check on failure as well as success, and teachers can stretch the scale beyond + 2 to − 2 to suit their own priorities.

In Table 4:16 the positive and negative scores have been presented as a time series. A ratio of total positive to total negative results has also been calculated for each year.

Table 4:16 Total positive and negative results on public examinations

	1970	1971	1972	1973	1974	1975	1976	1977
Total + ve	860	940	940	1060	998	1006	980	961
Total − ve	210	266	270	266	294	333	324	316
Ratio $\frac{+ve}{-ve}$	4.09	3.53	3.48	3.98	3.39	3.02	3.02	3.04

Table 4:16 suggests that the efforts of the staff to raise examination performance succeeded, but at the cost of raising failure rates. Remedial action could be taken by altering the balance between entry to GCE and CSE examinations, and by ensuring that fewer pupils who were unlikely to pass were entered. But these were policies being discussed by the teachers. The actual action taken in any one case would depend on the examination policy, the curriculum of the school, and the ability of the pupils. The figures serve as indicators only, showing that policies are working or failing. If figures are to serve as a basis for action the results will need to be related at least to the attainment of pupils to see if any particular group of pupils is doing unexpectedly well or badly.

Examination results and attainment at entry to school

The valid interpretation of examination results depends on allowing for factors outside actual teaching that might account for changes across the years or between subjects, or between a school and others. Most schools collect some measures of attainment at intake and these are some check on the possibility that results may be due more to the characteristics of the pupils than to any policy of the school.

Objective—to secure the maximum number of examination passes for pupils of all ability.

This objective needs further specification to be useful as a guide to preparing statistics. One school might be interested in ensuring that the brightest pupils were obtaining the public examination results expected of them. They might isolate this group by looking at the results of the top 10 per cent V.R. group. Another school might be particularly concerned about lower ability boys and would want to isolate the bottom quarter V.R. group and look at their results. It cannot be stressed frequently enough that any decisions made on such tables must be educational. The statistics help staff in coming to such decisions. They do not lead directly to action.

Tables 4:17 and 4:18 show some relation between examination results and verbal reasoning scores five years before, at entry to the school. Any attainment score, whether obtained by testing at the end of primary schooling or at the start in the secondary school, could be used. So could the grades passed on by primary school staff. It is illuminating to tabulate the results separately for boys and girls. The tables serve as a check that some groups are not being entered for examinations where they have little chance of success. They show if some groups are getting better results over time, while others may be deteriorating.

Table 4:17 Performance on public examinations compared with V.R. score 5 years earlier

V.R. score 5 years earlier	Average no. of GCE A, B, C + CSE 1	All GCE + CSE (see Table 4 : 16)
120 +	4.37	+ 10.2, — 1.2
100–119	1.06	+ 3.8, — 1.4
80–99	0.21	+ 2.8, — 1.4
79	—	+ 0.6, — 0.4

Table 4:18 Verbal reasoning and average number of GCE A, B, C and CSE 1 grades per pupil

	V.R.			
	120 +	100–119	80–99	79
1975	4.91	1.21	0.13	—
1976	4.71	1.10	0.19	—
1977	4.37	1.06	0.21	—

The school in question was aware that there could have been a deterioration in the examination attainment of the most able pupils while that of less able groups was improving. There was also a possibility that GCE results may have started to deteriorate while CSE results were holding up. There is no necessity to wait for trends to develop. One advantage of monitoring results over time is that possible trends can be used to introduce slight adjustments that rectify adverse developments before they become serious.

Neither Table 4:17 nor 4:18 would give much information to parents. Yet it is essential to release results related to input. This is usually achieved through selecting the pupils who have low measured attainment at entry yet achieve good examination results five years later. This selection can be made from Table 4:1 which is the basic collection of examination data. This is one aspect of the reporting of public examination results where it is safer technically to rely on examples, providing they are put into context. The difficulty is in finding any comparable statistics. Unless a single school has access to the results of other school staffs who are releasing their statistics in the same form, no comparison is possible. It is very doubtful whether the comparison would be valid anyway as numbers are likely to be small. It would be possible to organize input-output statistics over a large number of schools, but a single school staff will usually be advised to compare only with their own performance in previous years, unless the local education authority organize results for use by schools for comparative purposes as suggested at the end of this chapter.

Table 4:19   Average number of subjects passed by pupils in different ability groups

		Ability level (V.R. test at entry to school)		*Bottom $\frac{1}{3}$ pupils*	
	Top $\frac{1}{3}$ pupils		*Middle $\frac{1}{3}$ pupils*	*Pass or*	
	Pass or		*Pass or*		
Year	*GCE A, B, C*	*CSE 1–5*	*GCE A, B, C*	*CSE 1–5*	*GCE A, B, C*	*CSE 1–5*
1970	4.3	2.7	2.0	4.1	0	1.4
1971	4.3	2.9	2.1	4.7	0.2	1.2
1972	4.9	2.9	2.1	4.7	0	1.5
1973	4.9	2.6	2.1	4.5	0.1	1.4
1974	4.7	2.4	2.0	4.8	0.4	1.7
1975	4.7	2.4	2.3	4.8	0.4	1.9
1976	4.7	2.2	2.5	4.9	0.2	2.2
1977	4.5	2.0	2.0	5.6	0.2	2.3

Table 4:19 was prepared as suitable for release to the parents of a school. Pupils were allocated to one of three groups of equal size, defined by score on a verbal reasoning test taken at entry to the school. The CSE results were available from 1972. GCE results were available from 1972 as passes and from 1975 when grading was introduced. The table is useful as a picture of changes in examination results, but there is no external reference that can be used to check whether this school is obtaining results comparable with those of other schools. Furthermore, the table has to be presented in context. The balance between GCE and CSE entries has to be explained. The unreliability of the verbal reasoning test as a predictor of later attainment has also to be explained and related to the balance between entry to the two examinations at the lower end of the top one third and the top end of the middle third. There should also be an explanation related to the low predictive power of the test at entry, of the few pupils in the lowest category obtaining A, B, or C grades at the GCE. The table is indeed a useful vehicle for explaining some of the weakness of public examination results as indicators of attainment in school, and of the weaknesses of standardized tests as predictors.

The attainment of different social and cultural groups

So far the body of pupils in the school has been treated as homogeneous. But the available research evidence suggests that the same educational treatment of children of equal ability from different social and cultural groups can have very different effects. A school staff may be doing well or badly when evaluation is confined to overall pupil performance. But there may still be some groups who are over- or under-performing. If evaluation is to lead to informed decisions it seems sensible to produce evidence on the way different groups attain. The two most usual categories for looking at differential attainment are social class and ethnic origin. The research evidence showing that unskilled and semi-skilled workers' children were not attaining at the level predicted by their measured ability lies behind the drive to lessen selection and to introduce comprehensive secondary schooling. There is a danger that having attained the target of educating all children under the same roof, we are assuming that the problem is solved. Yet the evidence continues to be produced that some social groups are still losing out. The position of children of different ethnic groups is similar. Some groups are not attaining at the level of their peers.

The problem of evaluating the performance of different groups of children identified by social class or descent is that it smacks of discrimination. This makes it a sensitive issue for teachers. Despite a feeling that all is not well, teachers are reluctant to identify unskilled workers' children or Asian or West Indian children and measure their attainment. The reasons for this reluctance seem to be mixed. Some teachers take the view that all children are equal and that it is wrong to label them. This attitude is to be respected, but can lead to the persistence of under-attainment by the very children that the teachers are protecting. The second motive is again rooted in an objection to discrimination. But here identification is opposed because the consequent action is positive discrimination wherein the under-performing groups are given preferential treatment compared with the remaining groups. This is another respectable view, but once again leaves the problem untouched. The decision to collect information on the performance of groups that may be being penalized has to take account of the sensitivities of teachers and of parents and pupils. In other countries facing similar problems there appears to be less opposition to the collection of data on which remedial action can be based. The decision to evaluate performance within the student body is usually taken outside the schools. But once again, the teachers are in the best position to place the data in context and to take action upon it.

There are many ways of defining social class or cultural groups. The most usual definition of social class is parental occupation, usually that of the father. A simple unskilled or semi-skilled category and 'others' is sufficient. Unemployed fathers count as unskilled unless previous occupation is otherwise. If the child lives with the mother only, or with a guardian, their occupation is taken. However crude, such definitions are sufficient to obtain indicators of the performance of these groups of children. The identification of children of different

ethnic groups is more complicated. The DES used to identify immigrants on the basis of the birth of the child abroad, or to parents
who were born abroad and who had been in this country less than
ten years. New York City and State use the criterion 'Does the
school or community consider this pupil to be Black, Puerto Rican,
American Indian, Spanish Surnamed American, Oriental, or from
some other ethnic group?' The usual practice is for the teacher to
decide without asking the pupil. All definitions are crude, but even
these crude indicators are sufficient to allow the local authorities
and central government departments to allocate resources and to
allow teachers to assess the dimensions of the problem.

The method of collection and presentation can be the same as for
children from different ability groups as illustrated in Tables 4:17,
4:18, and 4:19. The data once collected will be used to decide on
curricular changes. But there are two issues that have to be faced
once a decision is made to collect. First, the evidence has to be evaluated. It is best to be clear in advance who is to judge what the
evidence means. Parents, employers, local pressure groups, and the
pupils are liable to interpret evidence very differently from teachers. A
second question is therefore whether to release the information
once collected. It is very difficult to maintain the confidentiality of
data that is of intense political interest. A school going it alone in
preparing and presenting such data will be liable to come under the
spotlight of local and possibly national concern. This is an area where
the concerted action of schools, local authorities and central government seems desirable, but there is some reluctance at all levels to be
the first to go ahead.

Comparisons with other schools, locally and nationally

To date, examination statistics produced by the DES, by examination boards, and by local education authorities have not been designed
to provide schools with standards against which staff can judge
performance. The DES produces only limited information on
summer and winter examinations in any one year. It produces very
full data on the attainments of the leavers in a year. But this is unsuitable for comparisons because leavers from the upper sixth having
some two or three A levels will also have a number of O level passes
and these can not be separated into the years in which they were
obtained. Leavers with say five O levels may be a minority leaving
at the end of the fifth year. The difficulty can be seen in Table

Table 4:20   School leavers: by type of school and examination achievement, 1973-74

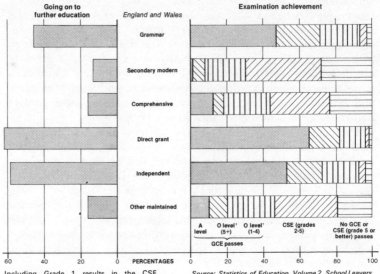

Including Grade 1 results in the CSE examination and O level passes on A level papers.

Source: Statistics of Education, Volume 2, School Leavers. CSE and GCE. Department of Education and Science.

4:20 above, extracted from the DES statistics and published in *Social Trends*.[1]

The right-hand graph shows examination achievements of leavers from different types of school and can serve as a useful comparison for teachers wanting to know what examination performance is found nationally. But the 'GCE passes' part of the graph contains three sets of qualification. A look at the 'Grammar' school line will show the problem clearly. Nearly 50 per cent have A levels on leaving. But obviously, many of these also have five or more O levels and the number of pupils obtaining these is greatly in excess of the 10 per cent shown. Similarly the '1–4 O level' group is likely to be under-represented. There is also a problem with the 'CSE grades 2–5' group, as many of these may have been obtained in the first year of the sixth. The only reliable figures for passes in this year, 1973–4, are likely to be 'A levels' and 'No GCE or CSE (grade 5 or better) passes' as these are likely to be confined to upper sixth and fifth formers respectively.

The DES appreciates the difficulty and is considering ways of extracting the examination attainments of year-groups, but until these are produced, comparisons are difficult. Examination boards tend only to give grades subject by subject of all those who entered

[1] Government Statistical Service (1976), *Social Trends*. London, HMSO, p. 90.

the board's examinations at a particular date. Many schools also enter candidates for more than one GCE board. But the great dis-advantage is that no single board is in a position to produce figures for the total entries and passes in any area. Some local education authorities collect in examination results from schools or direct from the examination boards, but they are used to gauge performance across all schools rather than to provide any one school with an external reference.

If some external yardstick of public examination results could be found it would still be necessary to ensure that the attainment of the pupils entering the school, and their social background, were taken into account before comparisons were made. Nevertheless, some attempt to gauge the examination performance of a school against national, regional, or local standards seems to be wanted by teachers. Those consulted prior to writing this book wanted to be shown how they could tell how well they were doing compared with like schools. Those who saw an early draft suggested I was pussyfooting around and that teachers wanted the objective information, good or bad. The methods that follow are crude. Better data for comparisons may soon become available. It would be possible for local education authorities to provide data for schools. But a warning is necessary. Such information might enable each secondary school to assess its examination performance against those of other schools. It might enable different attainments and different social backgrounds at intake to be taken into account. But this superior data also makes comparisons between schools more meaningful to the public for education. It could produce better quality league tables as well as better quality data for use by teachers in the schools.

The suggestions below are designed to give secondary school staffs some indication of their examination results compared with those achieved in similar types of school nationally, or within the same CSE region. The crudity of the comparisons comes from the impossibility of ensuring that all the differences between any one school and others on the characteristics of the intake and the environ-ment are taken into account. Furthermore, each school is likely to have a distinctive examination policy which will produce a different collection of results. But there is also a technical problem. The DES statistics are not only based on leavers rather than year-groups, but are mainly derived from a ten per cent sample. This means that they are estimates only. For example, for the 1975 school leaver statistics, 79.9 per cent of leavers from maintained grammar schools obtained grades A, B, or C at GCE O level. There is a 95 per cent chance that the true percentage, as distinct from the reported estimate from the 10 per cent sample, lies between 78.8 and 81 per cent. Thus any comparisons have to be made against a figure plus or minus 1.1 per cent. With the information currently available nationally or region-ally, indicators of success on public examinations available to individual schools and referenced against other schools are liable to be misleading and should be confined to internal use, unless intake and social background factors can be taken into account.

Step 1—organize examination statistics for leavers each year as for for Table 4:1. Alternatively use the examination results part of the DES 10 per cent sample of school leavers collected in the autumn term of each year, to accumulate individual entries and passes for all leavers from the school. Both methods require considerable work as it is not usual to organize results under leavers.

Step 2—select levels of examination success that reflect the priorities of the policies decided by staff and which are available in DES statistics, or from the CSE board. GCE board examination statistics are of little use to an individual school as each school is likely to use more than one such board and each examination board is likely to receive candidates from a wide geographical area. CSE boards are regionalized. The two most convenient levels for national comparisons are 2 plus A levels and 'no graded GCE or CSE results.' These levels are not complicated by the accumulation of results in more than one year and can be used without introducing too much error due to the fact that the statistics are based on year-groups rather than leavers. The popular five passes at GCE (A, B, or C) or CSE (1) and similar indicators where results can be accumulated will have to be collected on a leavers' basis.

Step 3—determine whether the school can be compared with available DES statistics by using intake or social background data. Methods are described in the examples that follow. These checks are very crude. The aim is to ensure that the school is roughly comparable with the remaining schools in England and Wales (or Scotland if these statistics are used), or with the schools taking a particular CSE board's examinations. The difficulty of these comparisons underlines the caution needed in this exercise expressed earlier.

Step 4—repeat the comparisons of the school's results with DES statistics, but this time with regional figures of leavers' achievements. The two A level and 'no graded pass' levels can be used to compare with the broad regions at present presented in the DES Annual Statistics. The DES will be producing figures for smaller regions in the future. However, a technical warning is necessary. The smaller the region for which statistics are presented, the greater is the possible margin of error due to the very small samples picked up in small areas. It will be very important to scrutinize the small print in these cases.

Step 5—select subjects which are considered to be especially important such as English, mathematics, a foreign language, the sciences, and tabulate the percentages attaining different grades for the summer examinations in each year. Work out the percentage getting GCE grades A, B, or C at O level, grade 1 at CSE, and passing A level at A, B, or C grades, and D and E grades. Compare these results with those presented in the DES statistics for summer examinations. These are collected by DES from the examination boards. It is useful to compare separately for boys and girls. They are separated in the DES figures.

The examples that follow are included to give some idea of ways in which teachers can obtain a rough idea of how their school's examination results should compare with national or regional figures. The caution over making direct comparisons without considering intake and background factors follows from the approach to evaluation adopted in this book. Later chapters extend the study of factors outside the school as an important context for considering information collected within. Technically these methods are weak, but the demand for such comparisons among those consulted overcame academic objections.

School A
This is a comprehensive school in an area where selection was abandoned over five years ago. On measured verbal reasoning at intake there was a spread of ability close to that which would be expected nationally. Similar results were obtained on a standardized test of reading at intake. This could be checked because the tests used had the usual statistical characteristics of a mean of 100 and a standard deviation of 15. The mean of the intake into the school five years before the public examinations being analysed for the fifth year was close to 100 on both tests, and roughly two-thirds of the intake fell between scores of 85 and 115. This suggested that the intake was similar to the national average and national spread of ability. This check is possible because of the way standardized tests are designed. Their average (mean) and spread (standard deviation) are fixed, usually at 100 and 15 respectively. Because the distribution of abilities such as verbal reasoning and reading tend to be bell-shaped or normal around the mean, the proportions falling within specified ranges of scores can be calculated. Thus on a normal curve, two-thirds will fall within plus or minus 15 of the mean, in this case 100, if the standard deviation is fixed at 15. This is a rough check and depends on the mathematics of sampling. The mathematics department of a school will be able to advise on the theory behind the approximation and on ways of calculating the statistics for the checks.

In 1975–6, this school achieved results which compared as follows with the national figures. Percentages are given based on all leavers for the year, whether they took examinations or not in their years in school. For A level, 14.6 per cent passed 2 or more subjects, compared with 9.7 per cent in all maintained schools for England and Wales.

For 'no graded pass' there were 28.5 per cent in the school compared
with 20.6 per cent for pupils in all maintained schools in England
and Wales. It would be unwise to make judgements on the results
from only one year, given the crudity of the comparison. The choice
of 'maintained' schools for comparison is another choice that has
to be made when using official statistics. Figures are usually given
for maintained, county, and voluntary schools.

School B

This is a comprehensive school in an area where the last selective
intake into secondary schools was in 1976. Thus, until the fifth year
examinations of 1981 and A levels taken in 1983, the year groups
will be from selected intakes. Until these dates comparisons could be
made with the DES examination figures for maintained, county,
or voluntary grammar schools. But once again, there is no certainty
that the school had similar intakes to other selective schools. Thus it
would be wise to carry out checks with any intake figures that are
available, as with School A above.

As selective intakes leave the school the staff would want to know
how their more able pupils were doing in the comprehensive year
groups compared with previous selective intakes. A very crude indicator could be obtained by using the average scores of the last selective
intakes as a basis for comparison. Test scores for unselected intakes
could then be scrutinized and those scoring at or over the previously
selective mean extracted. Their examination results could then be
compared with their predecessors. Once again, time series enable
statistics to be used more profitably.

School C

This school is comprehensive in name only, as it receives an intake
that is below neighbouring schools in the numbers of pupils in the
top band of three on the basis of primary school teachers' assessments
guided by a verbal reasoning test. It is in an area with much poverty.
A quick check on social background could be made by comparing
the proportion of those eligible for free school meals with the figure
for England and Wales. These can be obtained from the Chartered
Institute of Public Finance and Accountancy (see Appendix A).[1]
They should also be available from the local education authority
who can also supply their own figure for comparison. The social
background figures will only show the difficulty of making comparisons with national or local figures. Similarly test figures at intake
will only confirm that the school starts with a disadvantage. DES
figures are available for secondary modern schools, but there is no
way of checking whether such schools are comparable, or how they

[1] Chartered Institute of Public Finance and Accountancy. *Education
Estimates Statistics*. London, 1 Buckingham Palace Rd., SWIE 6HS.

compare with comprehensive schools which are receiving an intake containing few able children. In these cases the need is for statistics to be made available at a local level.

Establishing local standards

The advantage of local initiatives in collecting together examination statistics to help teachers in schools to assess the success of their efforts is that it can be achieved through consultation between the teachers concerned and the officers of the authority who can collect the statistics together. This collection can be direct from the examination boards or from each school. Examination board statistics come as computer printouts and duplicated lists of results school by school. But there is no standard form of presentation. For example, some boards do not give date of birth which makes it difficult to calculate leavers' results. Most boards give some aggregated statistical information on the examination results for summer of each year, but there is no common set of statistics. One board refuses to give results to local education authorities, claiming that it is a 'Schools' examination board.

However, whether results are collected from boards or from schools it is possible to produce tables showing the overall performance in the area. But this is of little use as the schools will vary in their intakes and contexts. The advantage of local tabulation of results is that these factors, which will affect results, can be taken into consideration. The tables produced, with results related to different intakes and different social backgrounds, could be distributed to schools for internal use. Whether the schools then should release their results related to these local figures would need to be decided in advance. Once again, information that is useful within the school would be of great public interest.

There follows a fictitious set of results from a local education authority. They are for comprehensive schools only. They use the 'five O level or equivalent' level that is so difficult to obtain from DES statistics, but which can easily be collected together, at the local level. The comprehensive schools have been divided into two types by verbal reasoning scores at intake. Type A schools, whose results are listed, have below average scores at intake and Type B average or above average scores. Each school would be informed of the type to which it should compare its results. Alternatively, examination results could be related to ranges of verbal reasoning scores, or to more than two types of school, to facilitate more precise comparisons. Clearly the distribution of pupils within verbal reasoning or other categories will differ within schools, but locally provided figures will provide some useful figures for comparing like with like.

**Table 4:21   Examinations, summer 1977. Average entries and
results for Type A schools**

	Percentage obtaining			
Fifth form	5 + O level grades A–C or CSE 1		No graded passes	
	Boys	*Girls*	*Boys*	*Girls*
	19.6	20.2	24.0	27.8
Sixth form	*2 + A levels*		*3 + A levels*	
	6.4	5.2	2.2	2.4

Table 4:21 would also be produced for Type B schools; they are
very easy tables to produce. A staff receiving them could compare
their performance on the same examination and give some idea of
what can be expected. Once again there are dangers that averages
will become maxima and that some schools will not be comparable.
It can also be seen how such figures could be used to measure the
examination performance of one school against the rest as a sole
indicator of its quality. Nevertheless it was the information required
to meet the requests of teachers for information on how they were
doing.

A local education authority could also produce examination results
related to social background by using free meal statistics. This could
also be produced by school type as for intake above. But schools
may prefer more fine distinctions. In this case results could be printed
out related to ranges of verbal reasoning scores. This relating of
factors such as free meals and intake attainment to examination results
can be the basis of sophisticated schemes for detecting under- or
over-performance. For example, there are cities in the USA where
schools are informed as soon as their results are found to be above
or below the level expected given their intakes.[1] The statistical
technique used, regression analysis, is not complicated. The effect
of introducing such schemes is. Co-operation between local education
authorities and their schools as suggested here, using a simple way of
checking results against intakes, is probably more suited to English
conditions and allows teachers to take the initiative in using the
information and planning the action. But if that initiative is not taken
by teachers, the demand for the information will attract a more
detached evaluation.

There is a danger in such locally produced statistics that schools
might be comparing their results with local results that are below
those to be found in comparable areas. This is a warning that is worth
repeating. Once norms are established they can become levels to be

[1] White, B. F. (1977), *The Atlanta Project: How one large school system res-
ponded to performance information.* Washington, D.C., The Urban Institute.

achieved. They may however be far below what can be accomplished. There is always a tendency to regress to the mean, once that mean is made available.

The emphasis placed on examination results by the teachers consulted before the writing of this book, and those who looked at early drafts, stressed the weight they placed on being able to compare their results with those of other schools. It may be that teachers will not want to wait for the DES or their local education authorities to produce statistics against which they can compare their own performance. In this case it is an easy job for a group of school staffs in an area to agree to collect examination results on the same basis and to prepare collective results against which any one school can evaluate its own entries, passes and failures. The first step is to agree on some arbitrary ways of scoring examination results. Any of the ways suggested in this chapter will do. It can be a decision to count five O level or equivalents, various combinations of passes per pupil and so on. Let us take as an example the combination of GCE and CSE results into a single scale. All staffs would send their results to the teacher organizing the exercise after summer, or summer and winter examinations had been taken. The teacher responsible would work out an average score for all the schools combined by dividing total positive and total negative scores by the total fifth-form age group in all schools. The ratio of positive to negative results could also be calculated and distributed. Each school staff would then calculate their own school scores. It is also an easy task to calculate the percentage difference between each school and the average.

Two points should be noted. First, this choice of an arbitrary score secures the results to the staffs of the school. They have little meaning to the public. Other scores or levels of performance on GCE or CSE separately would be immediately interpretable. Second, the average scores of neighbouring schools may not be comparable. They may still differ widely in their intakes. However, the chances are that neighbouring schools in the same local education authority will have common intake information in the form of test scores or bands of ability based on test scores or primary school assessments. These can be used to obtain examination results for each of the bands or ranges of test score as in the local authority exercise already described. Once again, the averages of all schools in the separate groups can be used for comparison by each school.

This local co-operation will still leave a lot of questions unanswered. More data could be shared between schools, but the easier solution is for the local education authority to co-operate. The questions that will inevitably be asked by teachers, or by parents are as follows: What was the examination policy in these schools? Which subjects were included in these passes? What were the failure rates accompanying these successes? The way forward is for the local education authority to consult the staffs of schools and decide on the information that is needed for comparisons that will serve as a basis for decisions. The possibilities have been spelled out in the tables in this chapter. The form of the statistics will ultimately depend on the objectives of the exercise.

Statistics from examination boards

It is difficult to extract information for evaluation from GCE statistics from individual boards, as pupils tend to take subjects from more than one of them in many schools. As CSE boards are regional this is not a problem. In both cases the results circulated can be used to gauge the level of success in different subjects. Subject departments can compare their results with those of all the schools contributing pupils to the examination. Most boards either spell out all the grades per subject or pick indicators such as number and percentage awarded at least grade E or at least grade C on GCE O level. This percentage should be used with caution if used for success rates of different subjects. Each department may accept pupils with very different attainments. A choosy department, just like a school with a very restrictive examination policy, may appear to be getting near 100 per cent passes, while a department, or school, with an open access policy may get results that compare badly with those of other departments and with the results of the examination board schools. Once again examination results must be related to the intake before comparisons are made.

A possible way around the problem of obtaining comparable statistics would be for the examination boards, or the DES, to produce full, aggregated statistics of the examination results of any year. Given the small number of winter examination entries this could be confined to the summer. The DES may be able to extract such year-based figures from the leavers' survey statistics. But this is still based on a sample. A co-operative venture by the boards, or an initiative from the Schools Council which is responsible for advising on examination policy, could give schools very useful figures for comparative purposes. At a time when there has been rapid secondary school reorganization, and school staffs may have difficulty in fixing targets for pupils covering ranges of ability that are new to some schools, this would serve as a useful guide.

5. Evaluating the Wider Aspects of School Life

A look at the priorities of teachers reported in a survey such as the Schools Council *Enquiry Number One* shows a breadth of concern beyond the academic into the moral, the social, the cultural, and the sporting. [1] One legitimate objection that teachers raise to evaluation is that it tends to narrow the focus of a school. Because parents and pupils seem to have a narrower, more instrumental view of schooling, an evaluation that is concentrated on the purely academic would reinforce those pressing for a restriction of the curriculum to a preparation for occupation. Evaluation might prove to be providing ammunition for those wanting to limit the scope of education. But evaluation is also a powerful instrument for educating the public. The scope of evaluation should indicate the scope of education and the total priorities of teachers.

The solution to the dilemma of having to evaluate, yet fearing to provide ammunition to the enemies of a liberal education, is therefore to widen the scope of that evaluation. If an activity is important it should be stressed as an aim worth breaking down into objectives, and worth evaluating. That evaluation can remain, and often has to remain, impressionistic. But it is still important. One reason for this is that evaluation is an important way of educating the audience for education. It is no use fearing that evaluation will arm the enemy or that evaluation is inevitably concentrated on the academic alone. The task is to inform the public by stressing via the evaluation those aspects that teachers feel are important. If it is important it should be evaluated. Once again the sequence is first to decide on priorities and then on evaluation, not to decide the content of evaluation on the basis of the assessable and then complain that the result is misleading. Evaluation has to reflect what is considered important by the staff and has to educate the public to give them a chance of recognizing that importance.

The same questions about references have to be decided here as with the evaluation of more academic activities. It still has to be decided whether to reference internally or externally, whether to norm- or criterion-reference, whether to reference against current norms or past performance, and whether to assess attainments or efforts. Furthermore, the information has to be presented so that the

[1] Schools Council (1968), *Enquiry 1, Young School Leavers*. London, HMSO.

audience for the evaluation can see where the assessments refer. Evaluation of non-academic activity has to be as systematic as more conventional approaches. If it is not, the public may not accept it as credible. Once again in this chapter the focus is on quantitative indicators. But here, as the focus widens, most evaluation will be in the form of judgements by the staff. From judging the physical appearance of the school to looking at staff consultation procedures, there has to be a reliance on judgement by staff. But the criteria already outlined for systematizing this qualitative evaluation have to be taken seriously. Whether the indicators finally chosen are quantitative or qualitative, the planning of the evaluation should be systematic.

To illustrate this point, let us assume that the staff of a school decide that an important objective is that every pupil, by the end of the first year in the school, should have mastered the reference skills that will enable him or her to find information in all subjects without having to ask for further help over ways of finding and retrieving information stored in the school library, resource centre, and departmental collections. First, the precise nature of the skills involved in finding, retrieving, and using stored information would have to be spelled out. Then a programme would have to be organized, synchronized, and implemented by all staff. Then there would have to be agreement on what would constitute success for such a programme. Then indicators with these definitions established in advance would have to be selected. For example, there are Library User tests.[1] These may be considered as appropriate indicators and a level of performance could be specified for pupils of different ability levels. But few staff would want to depend on a test designed for the more limited library use as an indicator covering all reference skills. There could then be agreement on further objective indicators. The total number of visits to the library, the number of visits per pupil, per form, per year-group, per subject, and so on; the number of books consulted or borrowed and voluntary as distinct from time-tabled use are possible indicators to be chosen once objectives have been determined. Similar indicators could be determined once the objectives in relation to resource centres or departmental collections of reference material have been agreed. The view of librarian, media resources officer, teachers, and pupils could be collected on the importance, frequency of use, and level of competence in reference skills in the school. A panel of teachers could evaluate this aspect of work, or some external evaluation could be organized.

In this assessment of a skill not open to direct measurement, figures would have to be supplemented by staff assessments. But these would have to be systematically worked out in accordance with the targets deemed important by staff. The criteria for deciding on levels of

[1] Lubans, J. (1974), *Educating the Library User*. Epping, Bowker.

mastery need to be specified in advance, even if these are no more than statements to which the assessments of staff can be matched. The answers to the evaluation are not likely to be a simple good or bad. Schools are rich, complicated places. Figures are insensitive reflections of that wealth. But behind the figures or behind the impressions there should be an objective, planned approach to evaluation. There has to be some compromise between the insensitivity of the statistic and the blandness of the impression. The key is a map of the means and ends of the exercise being evaluated, and a set of criteria that specify how successfully the former have achieved the latter.

The evaluation of non-academic curricular activity

A look at a school time-table will show that many activities are not examinable or easily assessed. Yet they often rank high as objectives among teachers. The variety of activities that may be involved requires some cumulative record so that a pupil will receive some recognition of his efforts. This record should also provide some guide to the success of the staff in motivating pupils to work hard in areas of the curriculum that do not lead to examination grades.

The Record of Personal Achievement developed by Swindon and Wiltshire teachers provides some guide to the range of activities that are seen as important for the development of personal qualities. [1] Considered to be of special significance were:

Physical fitness	Personal appearance and bearing
The ability to communicate	Courtesy
Reliability	Punctuality
Diligence and perseverance	
Working with other people	Following instructions
Independence	Initiative
Curiosity	Developing new interests
Creativity	Concern for others

This record is not an examination or a substitute for examinations. It does not contain evaluations by teachers and the pupil decides which aspects of his work to include in the record. The record is primarily a means of organizing work, motivating pupils, and of providing a leaving qualification. Record cards are provided for pupil use divided into eight categories, Course Work, General

[1] Swindon Education Committee (1974), *Record of Personal Achievement*. Swindon, Curriculum Study and Development Centre.

Experience, Work Experience, Time-keeping, Helping Others, Skills, Interests, and Physical Fitness.

This Record of Personal Achievement is deliberately not designed as a form of assessment. It provides an incentive for all pupils to work hard in areas that teachers consider central to a genuine education. But it is these central activities that need evaluating. Such an evaluation has to take into account the costs of the exercise to the staff and the pupils, the alternatives that have to be given up to accommodate the activities, and the benefits to the pupils. There is always a dilemma in allocating time and resources in schools. Both are scarce resources. Examinable subject areas put pressure on the non-examinable. Yet if the latter are given high priority in the list of objectives held by staff they should be evaluated, and that evaluation should be available as an answer to critics. Can such an evaluation be made solid enough to stand alongside examination results? In most areas the answer has to be no. In these cases the strength of any evaluation must lie in the emphasis given to the objectives rather than any evidence accorded their attainment. But many teachers have established techniques of assessment in non-examined areas of the curriculum. The example of physical education will be considered here.

Evaluation of physical skills

The attainment of physical fitness and the mastery of physical skills would be high on the list of objectives of all teachers. Physical education has a prominent part on most time-tables. The P.E. department will be able to spell out a number of specific objectives, most of which will be standards of skill that can be mastered. Indeed, P.E. is one area of the curriculum where criterion-referenced testing has always been common. Pupils can or cannot high jump 1.5 metres, do 10 repeated press-ups, or climb 7 metres of rope using only their hands. Given opposite, is a possible Decathlon. Each activity could be given grades according to the particular performance. These norms could be graduated by age. But a simple pass performance achievable by a pre-specified 80 or 90 per cent of pupils would provide a cumulative record of athletic performance across the whole age group chosen for assessment, or eligible to try. The advantage of this procedure over normal competitive sports is that it gives a measure of the fitness of all pupils. It would be a useful additional measure of the success of the staff in promoting that fitness.

The mixture of activities would be decided by the physical education staff. Much of the 'marking' could be done by peers. The standards set would also vary between schools. But such a set of activities, within reach of a majority, would serve a similar purpose to the Swindon Record of Personal Achievement, or the Duke of

Possible Decathlon open and attainable by a majority

1	100 metres sprint	Criterion level = 17 seconds
2	High jump	Criterion level = 1.5 metres
3	Long jump, running start	Criterion level = 4 metres
4	Long jump, standing start	Criterion level = 1.5 metres
5	Rope climbing	Criterion level = 7 metres
6	Throwing cricket ball	Criterion level = 25 metres
7	Run 1 mile	Criterion level = 7 minutes
8	Swimming	Criterion level = 10 metres
9	Press-ups	Criterion level = 6 consecutively
10	Written test on personal hygiene	Criterion level = 15 out of 20

Edinburgh's Award Scheme, or the tests used in the Boy Scouts. It would motivate pupils, provide them with written evidence of achievement to which could be added any other sporting or leisure-time achievements, and it would give some evidence on the success of the school in promoting the attainment of an objective that lists high among most teachers. Finally, it would provide a valuable guide to parents and the public for the school of the type of activities that are valued by the staff. It is varied in many schools by setting different standards of performance, but the principle is the same.

Physical activities are easy to criterion reference. Yet it has been customary to reference even these activities to norms of performance set to differentiate between pupils. This sorting out of the fit, strong, athletic, and sporting will be done anyway as school teams are picked and competitive games are played. Each pupil rapidly assesses his or her ability against his or her peers. There is little that can be done to alleviate this even if it is undesirable. But setting criteria of performance means that the performance of individuals is measured against those standards, not other pupils. If there is competition it can be organized so that individuals strive to improve their own performance across time.

The evaluation of extra-curricular and hidden curricular activity

Any evaluation of a school should take into account the range of activities organized. The objectives held by the staff will stretch from academic to moral, sporting to cultural, social to vocational. The priorities held by teachers are often more moral than vocational. Schooling is seen as a way of ensuring that children grow up to be good citizens. There is a contrast between this essentially moral view and that held by parents and pupils who tend to see schooling as a means of obtaining the skills that are necessary to obtain employment. The broad, liberal view of schooling held by teachers accounts for the emphasis placed on extra-curricular activities. If these activities are organized because they are seen as ways of attaining important objectives then they should be included in any evaluation of the school. If participation is seen as part of the education of each pupil then the concern has not only to be with the level of extra-curricular activity, but with the extent to which all pupils are involved.

Three areas of activity that most school staff would define as important educationally are sporting, cultural, and social. Obviously these categories overlap. Chess is a game, but is certainly cultural. But it is possible to distinguish games and sports from acting, music, and debating. Both of these sets of activities can be separated from social and community activities where the emphasis on caring, consideration, manners, and so on clearly has moral and social outcomes. Whereas sporting and cultural activities are organized, social activities are often an integral part of the ethos, the climate of the school. Quantitative methods can be used to gauge the level of participation in organized activities and the extent to which all pupils are involved. The organization of the school provides a frame-work for social activities, but these are performed as part of the ongoing communal life of the school and are not measurable out of context. Yet this hidden curriculum is often the basis on which a school is judged. When someone says that this is a good school they usually mean first that it seems orderly, civilized, and pleasant. More tangible, assessible aspects are considered later. First, ways of evaluating organized activities will be considered, and then ways of looking at the moral climate, the hidden curriculum.

Evaluating the extra-curriculum

As with all in-school evaluation, the first look has to be at the total pattern of activity. Frequently no one member of staff will know all that is going on. Even the headteacher may have an incomplete picture, and parents and public are likely to be aware only of the more newsworthy activities, or of those involving their own children. Unlike the public schools where the prospectus proudly displays the range of clubs, and frequently the cost of participation, maintained schools seem shy of advertising the very activities which staff see as essential for attaining some of their most valued objectives. The production of two lists, one of sporting activities and one of cultural, is easy and informative. In most cases it should also be possible to give the numbers of pupils who have participated in each during the year. The problem with these figures is that they may be accounted for by a small group of pupils who monopolize all activities or by a wide range of pupils. There is no way of telling. Yet this is a crucial point. If one important objective is to involve pupils so that they will pick up valuable skills, learn to organize and co-operate, socialize and mature, a monopoly by a few will defeat the effort put in by staff. In addition to the number of activities and the frequency of meetings we need the total numbers involved and the level of involvement of individuals and particular groups of pupils.

Information can be collected direct from pupils. This can be done through keeping diaries for a sample of two or more weeks in at least two terms of the year, or to get organizers of activities to note the names and forms of anyone attending, playing, or performing. Another, more simple method is get pupils to fill in a form asking them if they have played in any school teams or taken part in any school activities listed under the question. These can be divided up in a number of ways. For example, school teams can be distinguished from internal teams. A similar list of school clubs and societies can be treated in the same way, with pupils listing those they belong to, or participate in, or ticking off a checklist. In all cases it is important to distinguish boys from girls and to collect the age or form of the pupils. These factors may be important when action is to be taken on the evidence.

This collection of data on involvement can be organized as part of a social studies or social science exercise. Repeated annually it could provide a useful, practical exercise in data handling. There may be particular groups in the school, for example remedial groups, or the 5th form leavers' group, in whom staff have a particular interest and who should be identified in the analysis. The product of the exercise should look something like Table 5:1 on page 108.

There are various ways in which these figures, in Table 5:1, could be tabulated to illuminate the attainment of the various objectives of organizing extra-curricular activities. Clearly from this table the involvement of pupils seems to get progressively less as the pupil gets older. This is concealed when looking at the number of activities which seems to rise year by year. The other striking feature is that about a third of the pupils never seem to get involved at all and that this rises to almost a half in the fifth year. Meanwhile a small proportion of about 1 in 4 or 5 tend to dominate all activities. If one objective of the staff is to achieve maximum involvement there is need for a re-think, although there is no reason to think that the figures above are exceptional.

It is difficult to get any comparative data against which to lay participation figures for a school. The National Foundation for Educational Research found in 1970–71 that in the 12 comprehensive schools they studied, a range of 24 to 59 per cent of boys, and 19 to 47 per cent of girls played for school teams.[1] A range of from 33 to 79

[1] Ross, J. M., Bunton, W. J., Evison, P., and Robertson, T. S. (1972), *A Critical Appraisal of Comprehensive Education*. Slough, NFER.

Table 5:1 Participation in 4th weeks of autumn and summer terms, 1976-7

Activity	Number involved in year			Number of activities per pupil in year								
Year	1	3	5	1			3			5		
				0	1-4	5+	0	1-4	5+	0	1-4	5+
Sport	240	310	370	61	84	12	70	68	16	84	40	28
Cultural	105	274	286	96	60	1	84	66	24	99	31	22
All	345	584	656	48	79	30	47	65	40	71	44	37
Number in year	157	152	152	31%	50%	19%	31%	43%	26%	47%	29%	24%
Number of activities per pupil	2.2	3.8	4.3									

per cent of boys and 20 to 79 per cent of girls played for internal teams. The abler the pupils and the higher their home background level, the higher was the chance of them playing for school or internal teams. In this NFER study participation in all extra-curricular activities was also studied. It was found that one third of pupils took no part in the voluntary programme of clubs and societies. Participation was at its lowest ebb in the fourth- and fifth-year age group. This tends to confirm the trend in Table 5:1. Here is Table 5:2 from the NFER study for girls and boys.[1] Separate tables were also presented, but this combined table gives some idea of the variety found in the 12 schools.

Table 5:2   Percentage participation in sporting and non-sporting extra-curricular activities

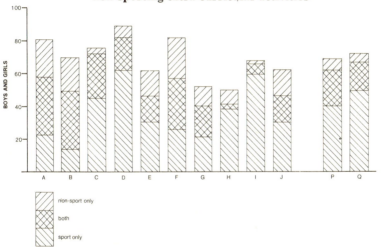

Evaluating the hidden curriculum

When a school is evaluated by its own staff, or by outsiders, it is usually against some undefined notion of the good school. This is often voiced in terms of moral influence, behaviour, interpersonal relations, or some other indicator of the ethos of the school. This communal, social, moral aspect of schooling is stressed by teachers and is very often the centre of parental concern. Research inside schools has shown how powerful the relationships between teachers

[1] *ibid.*, p. 119.

and pupils, pupils and pupils can be in determining not only morale, but in constraining pupils to behave in a particular way. It is difficult to assess this hidden curriculum of rules, customs, relationships, and authority structures. But it is possible to select a few obvious indicators that are generally agreed to point to the success of the school as a social organization, as well as being important factors behind academic success. Here attendance, staying-on, destination of leavers, and parental popularity will be covered. These indicators are also useful sources for detecting trends in the school.

Attendance

Registers are probably the most convenient form of readily available data in a school. This means that even more care than usual should be taken not to start with the indicator and forget that there are objectives behind any policy over attendance and that these can differ widely between schools. Little elaboration on registers is needed. But for a full picture of attendance in a school it is necessary to collect the figures in half-days so that afternoon and morning can be looked at separately. Usually attendance drops after lunch. Similarly, while we will look only at attendance without further elaboration in this section, many staffs will want to take snap registrations or carry out spot checks around the school or its environment to get a picture of the extent of slipping away after registering, staying in the school but not attending classes, and selecting which classes to attend. This extra information can be collected by special surveys.

Pupil absence patterns

Collecting the figures in the simplest way enables a simple attendance rate to be calculated. Here is a table from an inner city comprehensive school for three separate weeks from each of three terms.

		Percentage attending in years			
1	2	3	4	5	1 to 5
90	91	87	88	84	88

Even this simple table can indicate the level of attendance achieved. The figures for all schools on a one-day count in the same local education authority in the same year was:

	Percentage attending in years				
	1	2	3	4	5
Morning	91.6	90.6	88.6	84.5	77.8
Afternoon	91.6	90.2	88.1	83.5	75.3

Here the information on morning and afternoon attendance separately gives extra information on the incidence of attendance. Registers are often called only in the morning when attendance is high. Elaboration by age can be followed by attempts to get to types of absence. In January 1974 the Department of Education and Science surveyed attendance in English and Welsh secondary schools. The overall absence rate was 9.9 per cent.[1] In this survey teachers were asked to distinguish justified from unjustified absences. Of those absent, 22.2 per cent were categorized as unjustified, some 2.2 per cent of those at risk. Among the 15-year-olds this rose to 4.8 per cent of pupils unjustifiably absent. In all studies there does not appear to be great differences in the absence rates of boys and girls. Even the distinction between justified and unjustified absences ignores many forms of truancy which will not show up on register checks. Attending, registering, and then disappearing is one ploy. Registering, but not attending classes is another. Selective attendance at classes is another. The decision on whether such checks are worthwhile depends on the object of the exercise. There is no point in just confirming one's worst fear. There is point if a remedial round-up is planned.

Figure 5:1 shows a time series of absences in a school based on a one-day attendance check carried out by the local education authority every year, with comparable figures for the LEA.

The total figures of attendance are often of less use than the pattern of absence. A pupil with a continuous block of 20 half-days' absence a term is clearly less of a problem than one who has 20 half-days spread out over 40 days. Register checks to search for the pupil settling into a regular pattern of taking Friday afternoons or the odd day off every other week are probably worth more than the collection of elaborate statistics. Probably the best combination is the routine collection and display of attendance statistics, particularly related to ages where there may be sudden improvements and deteriorations that need action, and regular checks on the pattern of absence followed by action through the staff responsible inside

Figure 5:1   Absence rates 1971–2 to 1976–7

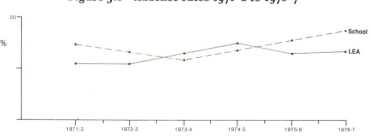

[1] *Hansard.* Written Answers, 25 July 1974.

the school, and if felt necessary, through the Educational Welfare Service.

Shirley Hase at Woodberry Down School carries out checks on attendance in the different age groups, and follows groups through their school career to note changes as they grow older. This alerts staff to the need to focus on particular groups. At the same time pupils with a high number of half-days' absence in a term are signalled to staff for action. In 1976–7 a new statistic was collected giving the number of complete weeks of schooling each pupil had attended. This was introduced because it was suspected that some pupils, without missing many half-days through absence, were nevertheless completing few complete weeks of schooling. In the event, some 47 pupils in the first three years, 6.5 per cent of the total, had completed less than 8 complete weeks out of a possible thirty-two. Three-quarters of them had more than 90 half-days' absence in the year. This systematic approach to absence was coupled with the collection of statistics on lateness. The data was used for combined action by House staff and the Educational Welfare Officer of the school, with a special effort to get quick detection and referral of cases to House staff and EWO. Parents were to be contacted when there was a poor record of complete weeks and where attendance was poor overall.

As with all statistics where a school staff may want to compare results with those in other schools or the nation, some check on the context of the school and the intake is necessary. The research on absence suggests that it is closely related to the socio-economic background of the children entering the school. Factors often associated with absence, such as size of school, tend to be less influential when socio-economic background is controlled. Once again, comparisons should be with like schools or a misleading impression, good or bad, may be given. The importance of socio-economic factors does not mean that the organization of schools is not an important factor in determining rates of absence. Reynolds, Jones, and St. Leger, working in small Welsh secondary modern schools with similar intakes, found attendance rates varying from 89.1 to 77.2 per cent over the years 1966–7 to 1972–3.[1] Furthermore, over the years studied, the schools exhibited a 'remarkable consistency' in relative performance. Tests at intake to these schools suggest that it is the regimes that are responsible for the differences found. This suggests that attendance is an area where the level and perhaps the pattern is related to the way the school is organized. This organization is more than just the attention that is paid to non-attendance.

The implications of looking at the school organization rather than the pupils and their social background when considering

[1] Reynolds, D., Jones, D., and St. Leger, S. (1976), 'Schools do make a difference'. *New Society*, 20 July 1976, pp. 223–5.

'outputs' are that the evaluation is focused where remedial action is possible. But there are costs to any action. If resources are devoted to chasing hard-core fifth-year poor attenders, they will have to be taken from some other activity. Once again the consideration of alternative cost brings attention back to the need to consider objectives and priorities. Many school staffs have given this problem serious thought and decided to concentrate available resources on younger pupils. Others spread their resources more thinly. If members of staff decide that good attendance is an objective worth pursuing through the investment of resources, it is worth using a small part of those resources in collecting together statistics on the level, and particularly on the pattern, of attendance, and probably in organizing some early-warning system. Once set up, the monitoring system can also give evidence on the success of the attempts to reduce the problem.

Lastly, it is possible to use attendance figures as an indicator of organizational problems in the school. Absence rates in different forms, different Houses, different age groups, in single or double periods, under different teachers, in different streams, sets, or bands, and so on can be used to identify strengths and weaknesses. For example, an American study by Cusick, Martin, and Palonsky showed a higher attendance rate in 'structured' when compared with 'unstructured' classes in the same subjects.[1] Pupils attended physics, economics, geometry, and secretarial courses 'with great regularity', but were absent from almost 50 per cent of their life science classes. This seems straightforward. But how is this information to be interpreted? Was absence due to the timing of the subjects, their content, the teaching, the pupils taking them, or some combination of these and other factors? Even more important, attendance is only an indicator. It may indicate boredom or interest among pupils, or laxity or efficiency among staff, or the attraction of a subject, the effectiveness of pastoral care, or the fear of punishment. But it is probably always an incomplete and misleading indicator of anything specific. It is one piece of litmus paper, not a complete chemical analysis.

Staying on

The same cautions about attendance as an indicator apply to staying on at school after the statutory leaving age. Many of the teachers consulted before writing this book listed a high rate as a sign of a successful school. Yet it is a means to an end rather than an end in itself. There is nothing intrinsically good in a high staying-on rate

---

[1] Cusick, P. A., Martin, W., and Palonsky, S. (1976), 'Organizational Structure and Student Behaviour'. *Curriculum Studies*, vol. 8, no. 1, pp. 3–14.

and its popularity as an indicator seems to be based on the belief
that only in a popular school will many stay on. Many other factors
can be at work. However, as falling rolls hit secondary schools, the
staying-on rate does become important, particularly if the school
staff wishes to preserve its own sixth form as numbers fall. In any
case, it is an important piece of information for planning and is of
interest to parents.

The number of pupils staying on beyond the statutory leaving age is
determined by the size of the last complete age group in the fifth
form, and the decisions made by individual pupils. These decisions
are influenced by opportunities available in work or in further
education, but are also the result of the attraction of the school after
an experience of five years and the prospect of staying another one or
two. Providing some check can be made on the other reasons for
staying on, it is a valuable indicator of the way pupils and parents see
the value of the school. The two most useful figures are the numbers in
the lower and upper sixth forms compared with the last complete
year-group from which they came one or two years previously (or two
and three years before the leaving age was raised in 1973). To establish time series the same date should be used in every year. As some
pupils join and leave in the first term, a suitable date to make this
evaluation is in January of each year, at the same time as filling in
DES from 7. Table 5:3 shows the staying-on rates in a comprehensive
school for 1976/7 (at January 1977) and the graph shows the staying-
on rates from 1973 (when the school leaving age was raised) to
1976–7.

Interpretation of this table and graph has to be cautious. National
rates of staying on vary. A rise in the 1960s slowed down in the 70s
and in some areas levelled off. Unemployment can cause a rise un-
connected with the school. Those staying on may be taking a variety
of subjects and may not become part of the traditional A-level sixth.
They may retake CSE or O level, take extra subjects, take a combination of A and O and CSE. They may not take any public examinations. The rise in staying on in the 1960s was partly due to this growth
of the new sixth form. A school staff may decide that it wants to achieve
a particular type of sixth form. In this case information would be
needed year by year to check that this objective, as well as the crude
staying-on rate, was being achieved.

Table 5:3   Staying-on rates 1976–7 in lower and upper sixth forms
(all figures at January)

Fifth form	Fifth form	Lower sixth	Upper sixth.	Lower sixth	Upper sixth
I	2	3	4		
1975–6	1974–5	1976–7	1976–7	$\text{rate} = \dfrac{\text{col. 3}}{\text{col. 1}}$	$\text{rate} = \dfrac{\text{col. 4}}{\text{col. 2}}$
160	152	51	19	32%	12.5%

Figure 5:2   Staying-on rates 1974–7 in lower and upper sixth forms

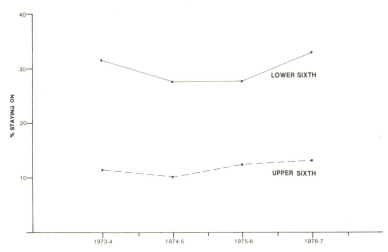

The Department of Education and Science publish annual statistics of the percentage of pupils remaining at school beyond statutory leaving age, broken down by regions and across the previous decade.[1] Before making comparisons the characteristics of these figures have to be remembered. They are by age at the beginning of January. Table 5:4 shows the time series by type of school, 1965 and 1970 to 1976, showing the rise in the sixties and early seventies. If comparisons with national or regional figures are required it is best to use age as at January rather than membership of lower or upper sixth form.

Once again caution should be exercised in making comparisons

Table 5:4   Percentage of pupils remaining at school beyond statutory leaving age

	1965	1970	1971	1972	1973	1974	1975	1975	1976
Age at beginning of January									
All maintained schools*									
Boys and girls									
15	40.2	54.8	56.3	58.0	58.6				
16	22.9	32.1	32.9	34.3	34.0	23.4	23.7	23.7	25.2
17	11.4	17.3	17.8	18.4	18.7	18.0	17.8	17.8	18.6
18	4.1	5.7	6.0	6.1	6.1	6.1	5.8	5.8	6.0
19	0.4	0.5	0.5	0.5	0.5	0.4	0.4	0.4	0.4

* Excluding Special Schools.

[1] DES (1976), *Statistics of Education, vol. 1, op. cit.*, p. 21.

with national figures. One year's sixth form group may not be typical. There are regional variations in staying on and differences between the sexes. Interpretation is also complicated by the growing variety of provision for the 16 to 19 age group. There are sixth-form colleges, A level and other courses in colleges for further education. Employment often includes attractive opportunities for further study. These 'pull' factors may outweigh changes in the 'pull' of the school. Finally, staff might want to keep an eye on the courses within sixth forms. The major growth in many areas in the late sixties and early seventies was in the non A-level sixth. Patterns of resource allocation can often remain the same while trends develop unnoticed. Another trend that has importance for employment and further education prospects is the balance between courses. The DES publishes annual figures on those taking mathematics/science subjects only, other subjects only, and subjects in both groups. Table 5:5 shows the figures for the first year of the sixth form for maintained secondary schools. Full details of pupils following A level courses can be found in DES Statistics of Education, Volume 1, published annually, from which this table has been derived. [1]

A look through this table will show the switch out of mathematics and science across these years and the lack of girls taking these subjects. These figures appear annually and are presented as time series, thus enabling school staffs to compare their own sixth-form balance against that of schools in England and Wales.

Destination of leavers

Table 5:6 shows the national figures for staying on extracted from DES statistics and reproduced in the HMSO publication *Social Trends*. [2] This can be used as a yardstick for a school staff emphasizing particular forms of further education as important.

Table 5:6 is based on the DES leavers' survey. This is a ten per cent sample survey only and does not yield information at local education authority level. Even the category on the leavers' form dealing with going into employment is difficult to interpret at the national level as the unknown category is large. If a school staff wish to keep track of the employment of their leavers, a special form will have to be devised. This tailor-made form would still be useful in completing the DES leavers' form, but would need very careful attention by a careers teacher to prove useful. It is very difficult to get this information on employment from many pupils. But this ignorance is felt by many teachers and a simple categorization might be very enlightening.

---

[1] *ibid.*
[2] Government Statistical Service (1976), *op. cit.*, p. 90.

Table 5:5   Subject groupings taken by pupils following A level courses in the lower sixth forms of maintained schools

	1965			1970			1975		
	Boys	Girls	Total	Boys	Girls	Total	Boys	Girls	Total
Maths/Science subjects only	22,177	6,647	28,824	23,725	7,368	31,093	22,553	7,178	29,731
Percentage	49.3	18.6	35.7	43.4	14.8	29.8	38.4	13.1	26.1
Other subjects only	16,516	23,888	40,404	19,768	33,082	52,850	20,382	35,652	56,034
Percentage	36.7	66.8	50.0	36.2	66.4	50.6	34.7	64.8	49.3
Subjects in both groups	6,279	5,250	11,529	11,123	9,365	20,488	15,772	12,159	27,931
Percentage	14.0	14.7	14.3	20.4	18.8	19.6	26.9	22.1	24.6

Table 5:6   Destination of school leavers: by type of school, 1973-4

| | England and Wales | | | | Percentages and numbers | |
	Universities	Colleges of education	Polytechnics	Other full-time further education	Employment	Total (=100%) (numbers)
Boys (percentages):						
Grammar	21.3	2.5	7.1	8.8	60.3	34,370
Comprehensive	4.3	0.8	1.8	5.2	87.9	195,630
Modern	0.3	0.1	0.2	7.5	91.9	82,530
Other secondary	3.2	1.0	2.3	7.3	86.2	14,130
Direct grant	38.4	2.4	9.9	10.1	39.2	8,070
Independent	31.6	0.7	6.1	17.5	44.1	14,910
Girls (percentages):						
Grammar	14.0	11.6	4.1	20.0	50.3	36,150
Comprehensive	2.6	3.4	1.0	10.6	82.4	184,520
Modern	0.1	0.6	0.3	13.7	85.3	77,870
Other secondary	1.6	3.3	0.6	11.9	82.6	13,300
Direct grant	26.0	12.6	5.2	18.6	37.6	7,970
Independent	14.8	5.5	3.8	36.9	39.0	11,990

The most convenient set of employment categories for young school leavers used to be published in the Department of Employment Gazette using information obtained when National Insurance cards were being issued. Unfortunately the collection of this information ceased when these cards were no longer issued by the Department of Employment in 1974, but the categories will serve for a school's own records. They were:

Apprenticeship to skilled employment.
Employment leading to recognized professional qualifications.
Clerical employment.
Other employment—with planned training
            —without planned training.

A breakdown of school leavers, region by region, can be found in the journal *Social Trends* up to 1972 and in the Department of Employment Gazette (May issue) up to 1974. With the details on leavers going on to more education these employment categories would enable a school staff to accumulate a time series on the post-school career of their pupils and hence evaluate their curriculum through another important criterion.

Popularity with parents

It is a brave staff that decides that parental popularity should have a high priority among a list of objectives for the school. It has already been reported that the available evidence suggests that parents hold more instrumental, vocational expectations of education than do teachers. A school's popularity may be the result of aims that differ from those of parents as well as the efficiency with which staff organize schooling to achieve these aims. Unpopularity can come through being too progressive in a traditional area, too traditional in a progressive area. Trivial accidents can cause popularity or unpopularity. A school with a national reputation can be unpopular locally. Nevertheless there is no future in having a school with high prestige among professionals into which children have to be dragooned. 'Maintaining the reputation of the school among parents', should appear in any list of objectives, particularly in a period of falling school rolls.

Some local education authorities, which allocate secondary school places on a basis of parental choice, produce and publish the proportion of first choices received by schools. In such cases the staff have the figures flourished at them. Even where they are not published they should be obtainable for internal discussion by a school staff, from the local education office. Where parental choice is not taken into account through written choices, the staff have a problem in collecting it in a systematic way. There may be very different results from a request for an expression of a genuine choice for secondary schooling and a request for an expression of parents' perceptions of the school outside the context of selection. Rather than laboriously collecting artificial evidence on parental choice that could not easily include the school's priority in relation to neighbouring schools, it is probably better to rely on more indirect indicators of parental popularity.

The most likely source of this indirect information is the administration, advisors or inspectors of the local education authority. They receive the compliments and complaints about schools. It is their job to discuss the problems causing and arising from any unpopularity of a school. Another source is the governing body of a school who should be sensitive to local attitudes. But the most obvious source is the staff themselves. The articulation of the views of the teachers could serve as a central part of the in-school evaluation. Indeed the commitment to evaluation must involve some consideration of the performance of the school, not against internally determined criteria, but in the light of public opinion as detected by the staff. Assessing the popularity of the school with parents is too important to be left to chance. It may be best organized by allocation to a senior member of staff who will also organize action for improvement. This is also an area where evaluation is intimately connected with the education of the public. External relations has to include giving as well as receiving information.

Unobtrusive measures

Absence and staying-on rates, and pupil destination are convenient indicators. There does not have to be any disturbance to collect such data for evaluation. There is a positive and negative side to the use of such unobtrusive measures. They are frequently convenient indicators but it is difficult to define what they are actually indicating. Absence rates among pupils may indicate ill-health as much as boredom with school. Short absences by teachers may indicate stress but may also suggest low morale, laxity of control, an ill-balanced age structure leading to excessive illness or a lack of ventilation in the staffroom leading to a plethora of colds. On the positive side these unobtrusive measures are not distorted as they are being collected. Test scores may be boosted by teachers arranging for coaching. Questions about discipline in school may promote defensive answers. If you decide to count the cigarette butts in the staffroom at the end of every day you will have a valid measure of something. The problem is that you don't know what is indicated.

There are a number of unobtrusive measures that can be used around schools. An ingenious staff could produce an impressive list. The number of windows repaired per term, the number of chairs smashed, the number of desks defaced, the area of staff notice boards covered with memos, the number of letters congratulating the school compared with those complaining about it, the extent of voluntary social work done by children, the collections for charity, the number of rude words on toilet walls, the list is endless. Some may be useful. All should be used with caution. Another problem is that even if you know what a cigarette-strewn staffroom or a level of participation in sports means, it may be impossible to set a level of disorder or participation that signifies success or failure, unless an objective has been defined in a way that leads to the indicator having specified levels of success or failure. A staff may decide that a staying-on rate of 40 per cent is good, 30–40 per cent fair, and under 30 per cent poor. The indicator can then be used to judge success or failure. The importance of this pre-specification of criteria for judging success or failure has been stressed throughout this book. Collections of indicators can give clues to things that are going well or badly. Their scrutiny is important in the management of a school. But that management finally rests on evaluation as a planned activity producing reliable information on which decisions can be made. This in-school evaluation need not be obtrusive, but it has to be systematic.

6. Evaluating School Organization and Curriculum

Organizations are means to ends. There is a lot written about schools as organizations. But it is often very difficult to detect the ends of any one school. Teachers are often puzzled by questions about objectives as the answers seem self-evident yet difficult to articulate. The chapters in this book are based on assumptions about academic, social, sporting, and cultural ends. Yet evaluation to check how far such ends are being achieved by the teachers would leave important questions about effectiveness unanswered. In this chapter the focus will be on the way resources are organized. There is a duty to account for the use of resources. There is a duty to maintain control over this use. This is not just a response to public scrutiny. It is the way that more informed decisions can be made by teachers about the distribution of scarce material and human resources in the school.

The evaluation of school organization cannot attain the precision of accounting procedures in industry, armed services, or some social services. But there can be objectives specified after discussions between staff, between staff and parents and others outside the school, and after taking into account the views of pupils. These discussions may relate to the scope for teacher or pupil initiative within some framework of rights and responsibilities. They may refer to communications around the school, between the school and its public, within the staff and between headteacher, teachers, pupils, and non-teaching staff. They may be centred on the efficiency with which records are accumulated, maintained and retrieved. They may be concerned with involvement in decision-making, the formulation of objectives, the evaluation of performance. They may be concentrated on the relation between the school and its environment, its responsiveness to changes around it, or its role in effecting changes in that environment. The consideration of objectives, the definition of priorities, the establishment of indicators of success, the whole process of evaluation are themselves parts of school organization. At some time in the year a school staff needs to review this organization. This is not a matter of amassing statistics. It means bringing into the open the various views of what the school stands for, how objectives are supposed to be achieved and how successful the effort has been.

To use resources in the most effective way must be one of the most important aims in a school. Surprisingly few textbooks or induction and in-service courses deal with means of maximizing effectiveness.

One reason lies in the low priority that need be given to husbanding resources as long as education was receiving an increasing share of the Gross National Product year by year. This neglect is unfortunate and has left teachers vulnerable in a cold economic climate. There is a need to state objectives derived from the aim of maximizing cost effectiveness. There is also a need to identify indicators. There is a need to evaluate, not only as a means of accounting for husbandry of resources, but to ensure that the children in the school are getting the most out of the resources that are provided.

Schools are given resources and also receive pupils. It is wrong to conceive of a school as a sausage factory, receiving raw materials that are processed into a product for sale to employers at the exit. But the justification for schooling is that pupils are taught. What is taught depends on the objectives held, implicitly or explicitly, by the staff. The latent assumption behind this book is that the chances of learning occurring in line with those staff objectives are greater where the objectives are explicit and where the degree to which they are attained is regularly evaluated. Thus it is important to treat as an input the abilities, attainments, and expectations of pupils entering the school as well as these enhanced characteristics when these pupils leave. It may be unpopular to think of a school as an organization to develop human capacities, but not to consider effectiveness in this way may lead to a waste of talent. The romantic teacher may be taking too many chances with other people's children.

Evaluation is closely concerned with considering alternative costs within the school. Something has to give, somewhere. With limited resources one person's gain is another's loss. Any resources spent here mean that less is available for spending there. There are always alternative costs. Schools receive money that could go to hospitals, social services, housing, and so on. Resources are allocated between schools. Within schools allocations are made to competing departments. Within departments teachers compete. Each teacher has to allocate scarce funds. If resources are given to buying these video cassettes they are lost to others who wanted to buy those textbooks. A teacher appointed to teach mathematics is lost to the English department. The scope of this concept of alternative costs is limited as long as money is made available to schools in votes for particular types of purchase. Virement of resources widens the competition for scarce resources by allowing transfer between votes. Schemes such as the Inner London Education Authority's Alternative Use of Resources scheme mean that a school staff must plan their expenditure in the open, because resources are allocated to the school, on the basis of its roll and the deprivation it faces, as one sum to be distributed to buy extra teachers, more books, to increase the number of school journeys.[1]

[1] Briault, E. W. H. (1974), 'Alternative Use of Resources'. *Contact*, vol. 2, issue 26, pp. 10–11.

Here there may be competition between those wanting to recruit a teacher to set up an alternative education unit for miscreants, and those wanting some minor works expenditure, new hardware, more secretarial staff, or the financing of some new curriculum development. The more democratic and open the decisions over expenditure, the more important becomes the consideration of alternative costs.

Staffing costs

In education as a whole, salaries account for over 60 per cent of all costs. In schools some 70 per cent of current expenditure is on teachers' salaries and about 15 per cent on non-teaching staff salaries. At the time of writing the average cost of a teacher, including superannuation, was near £5,000 per year. With reduced recruitment making the teaching force more experienced, teaching costs per pupil were rising fast. The annual teaching cost in a 1,500 strong comprehensive school is around £500,000. Education is a labour-intensive industry. The consequences are different in times of rising and falling expenditure. In the good times extra money for education is spent on employing more teachers. In hard times, cuts are made, not in the teaching force, but by pruning the ten per cent left over when teaching salaries and inescapable commitments such as travel have been covered. This ten per cent pays for books, curriculum development, teaching materials and so on. But the extent to which ten per cent can be cut before there is a serious position is limited. At the time of writing the fall in pupil numbers was gaining speed at a time of financial stringency and that ten per cent was under increased pressure.

This economic situation makes it necessary to look at costs, however unpleasant this seems, and however out of tune it seems to be with the spirit of education. Yet this consideration of costs is part of the planning in every school. It is usual to look at teaching group sizes, at teaching loads, at the costs of school journeys, at the claims of technical departments for half classes, at the relative costs of a language laboratory and a computer terminal. Whether recognized or not, running a school involves the consideration of alternative costs. The simplest indicator of teaching costs is teaching group size. Headteachers are used to balancing this indication of cost against the educational benefits of differing sized groups. Remedial groups are claimed to require generous staffing because of the skilled and sensitive nature of the work. Withdrawal groups may have to be staffed generously because of the apparent difficulty of handling troublesome children. Sixth form teaching groups may be small, not only because few opt for particular subjects but because it is claimed that more individual attention is required as the level of work deepens. Technical subjects may use craft rooms designed for half classes. The costs have

to be determined through the consideration of educational requirements.

It is a simple step from knowing teaching group size to calculating
the costs of teaching. Any such figure will be based on arbitrary
assumptions, such as a standard salary for all teachers in the school,
but will serve to illustrate relative costs. If a teacher earns £5,000 a
year and teaches 30 periods per week, the annual cost per period is
£5,000 ÷ 30 = £167. The annual cost per pupil in a group of 20
will be £167 ÷ 20 = £8. It will be £5.5 in a group of 30 and £21 in a
group of 8. This type of costing provides a basis for allocating teaching
resources effectively. The problem in schools is to plan a curriculum
to make the most effective use of staff, and this involves planning
the work of the whole school and evaluating the costs of staffing year-
groups, subject departments, remedial groups, withdrawal groups
in the most effective way. The need is for a simple way of calculating
teaching costs to help in this planning and to evaluate the costs of an
ongoing curriculum to ensure that some groups of pupils are not
being over-generously staffed, or starved of teacher support.

There are a number of ways of costing various time-tabling arrangements. They are all useful in calculating the costs of additions to the
basic structure of a time-table which rests on the number of forms
in each year and the number of periods in the week. The two best
known systems use the concepts of basic, actual, and bonus teaching
periods.[1] The basic number of periods is the number of forms in
each year times the number of periods in the week. There has to be
some arbitrary assumption about the sixth form. Thus for a five form
entry school with a 35 period week the basic for the first year will be
5 times 35 = 175. The actual is the number of teaching periods on the
time-table. This will usually be in excess of the basic as it includes the
arrangements to reduce sizes of groups, provide special help, to set,
and so on. The bonus is the difference between the basic and the
actual. Thus if the first form with a basic of 175 teaching periods was
actually using up 225 groups, its bonus would be 225 − 175 = 50.
This bonus could be compared with that of other year-groups to
check on the distribution of teaching staff. It is once again a simple
step from calculating the basic, actual, and bonus to costing them.
The cost figures can then be used for deciding priorities on educational
grounds.

The use of basic, actual, and bonus teaching groups is a technique
for analysing a curriculum and making more informed choices. But
evaluation often requires a quick method of checking the teaching
costs of a year-group, a subject department, lower, middle and upper
school, sixth form, remedial groups, withdrawal groups, and so on
against some common standard. The difficulty is to obtain a figure,

[1] Davies, T. I. (1969), *School Organization*. Oxford, Pergamon Press. *See also*
Inner London Education Authority (1975), *Curriculum Analysis and Planning*.
London, ILEA.

a baseline, for comparing the costs of various teaching arrangements. The most convenient is pupil-teacher ratio. This ratio is easily calculated by dividing the total number of pupils on roll by the total number of teachers. The latter should include part-time teachers as full-time equivalents, so that three half-timers count as one and a half and so on. Non-teaching senior staff can be excluded and those with reduced teaching loads converted into full-time equivalents. There is no need to go into fine detail. All that is needed is a figure against which the ratio in various grups can be compared.

The number of pupils per teacher can be compared directly with overall school pupil-teacher ratio for any year or subject group. The pupil-teacher ratio of a group can be calculated by dividing the total number of pupils involved by the number of full-time equivalent teachers taking them. The latter can be calculated by first working out the number of periods taught on average by teachers. This may be 30 out of 35 periods per week. Therefore, for every 30 periods taken by a group, regardless of its size, one teacher is involved. The number of teachers involved will be the number of periods in which the group is taught per week divided by 30. If a year-group of 180 pupils took 10 periods per week in groups of 30 this would involve $180 \div 30 \times 10 = 60$ teaching periods. If another 12 periods on the time-table were taken in groups of 20 this would involve $180 \div 20 \times 12 = 108$ teaching periods. Another 8 periods taken in groups of 15 would add $180 \div 15 \times 8 = 96$ teaching periods. There may be 20 other teaching periods where individual pupils are withdrawn for remedial help. This makes $60 + 108 + 96 + 20 = 284$ teaching periods. This involves $284 \div 30 = 9.5$ full-time equivalent staff. The pupil-teacher ratio for the year-group is $180 \div 9.5 = 19$. This can be compared with the ratio in the whole school, in other year-groups and so on. Within subject groups the calculations are easier, but in every case a comparison can be made with the school pupil-teacher ratio or that of comparable groups.

If the use of basic, actual, and bonus is too time-consuming, pupil-teacher ratio is often too crude. In the examples that follow from Woodberry Down School, Michael Marland has developed the concepts of pupil-period load, pupil-teacher claim and percentage of norm. Pupil-period load is the product of the number of pupils taught in a subject department and the number of periods they are taught per week. Thus a mathematics department teaching 180 pupils for 4 periods a week in the first year, 180 for 5 periods a week in the second year, and so on will have a pupil-period load of $180 \times 4 + 180 \times 5$ and so on. This concept enables the investment of resources throughout the school to be compared with the pupil-period load carried. Pupil-teacher claim is another, subtler way of looking at teaching group sizes. If all pupils were sent home and the teachers worked as time-tabled you could call pupils in for individual tuition. The pupil-teacher claim is the amount of tuition that each pupil would receive, expressed in school periods. It indicates the amount of contact that each pupil is receiving from teachers. The percentage of norm is calculated as the ratio between the proportion of the pupil-period load carried by a department and the proportion of the school allowance it receives. The use of these concepts will become clearer when two 1976–7 exercises from Woodberry Down are examined. The first exercise is from a retrospective analysis of the way resources were allocated in the school, to serve as a basis for discussions over the next year's allocation. The second is from an exercise comparing departmental shares of the school allowance with the pupil-period load carried by departments.

To guide discussions over the following year's allocation of resources, Marland calculates the number of time-tabled periods in the current year projected into next. He then calculates the staff who will be available, multiplies this number by the number of periods they each teach and comes to the number of periods that can be covered. This may be less than, greater than, or equal to the number projected to be covered if there are to be no adjustments. Thus the surplus or deficit is known and discussion can centre on how it is to be met. As a guide to this discussion the following are presented to staff:

Staff and money available to the school.
Number of time-tabled periods.
Teaching-period loads carried by Heads of Departments and Houses, deputy heads, assistant staff, and senior staff.
Teaching group sizes in lower school, middle school, and sixth form.
Pupil-teacher claim as follows:
    Overall   1.8
    Lower school   1.8
    Middle school 1.7
    Sixth form   2.6
Overall teaching costs as follows:
    Cost of a teacher-period
        at load of 35 periods £104.55
        at average load   £132.45
    Cost of teacher per pupil-period for a year
    Overall average   £6.97
    Ordinary 'chalk-and-talk'
    group of 25   £5.30
    (and a number of special units showing very much higher teaching costs per period).
School allowance investment per pupil-period.
Absence cover.

Obviously staff will argue the case for their department or their special facility on educational grounds. But if the cost of a pupil-period is ten times as high in one activity compared with another there must

be a very good case to be made. But even this information may not
be enough to settle the competing claims of subject departments to
the resources that are available. Marland produces a separate paper
to help in these negotiations. Twenty-one subjects were listed for
1976–7. Only four are listed here (Table 6:1). PPL, the pupil-period
load is calculated as above for the second column. The PPL of each
department is then converted into a percentage of the total PPL of
44,098 (3rd column). The allocation of the school allowance (capita-
tion) is then treated in the same way to produce columns four and five.
The percentage of norm is then calculated as above for the year in
question and the previous year. The norm here is 100 if the percentage
of school allowance received equals the percentage of pupil-period
load. For mathematics the norm for 1976–7 is 7.28 as a percentage of
12.87 which equals 57. Similarly for English the percentage of norm
is 11.28 as a percentage of 14.76 which equals 76. Once again, there
may be very good educational reasons why one department is well
over a hundred and another well under. But in this list of twenty-one
subjects made for Woodberry Down the range in 1976–7 was from
26 to 429 for normal subject departments, and to 717 when special
centres were included.

These Woodberry Down examples point to the determination of
staffing as probably the most important curricular decision that has
to be made in a school. But this decision has to be made alongside
others about the availability of time-table time, rooms, learning
support services, streaming, setting, and selection. If the modern
language department decide that they should only take the more able
children, other departments will have to cater for the less able for
more of their time. If the sciences claim teaching in double periods
it can reduce the chance of integrated studies getting anything but
single periods. If geography teachers always claim rooms with
blackout, other subject departments may not be able to show films.
Evaluating costs is not a sinister intrusion of economics into educational planning. It is always the stuff of that planning. Nevertheless,
decisions about costing different forms of curriculum should always
be educational. A remedial department may be given generous
pupil-teacher ratios because these are educationally essential. Pastoral
care staff may be released from teaching duties because their work

Table 6:1   Departmental allowances

Dept.	PPL =	% of total PPL	SA = £	% of Dept. SA	= % of Norm	% of Norm 1975–6
Maths	5676	12.87	1550	7.28	57	61
English	6509	14.76	2400	11.28	76	93
History, etc.	3092	7.01	1100	5.17	74	56
Geog./Geol.	1626	3.69	1250	5.88	159	135

benefits children who might otherwise be handicapped. Senior staff may carry out administrative tasks instead of teaching, but the justification has to be that the educational performance of the school improves as a result. The evaluation of organization in a school has to be referred to objectives that are concerned with education, not organization for its own sake.

Non-teaching staff and learning support services

A feature of the extended education now received by all children has been the proliferation of activities outside the classroom which are organized to support learning. These are indications of the breadth of objectives now implicit or explicit in schooling. Each of these activities, whether involving teachers, non-teaching staff, or services provided for the school, needs to be looked at in the same way as the employment of teachers. Each activity should be evaluated against objectives, against the costs due to organizing this activity rather than another, against the need to ensure that rewards are proportional to responsibilities, and that a few members of staff are not carrying most of the extra-curricular burden.

The spread of pastoral care as a specific service in the school can be traced to the realization that learning depends on the motivation of the child and hence on his or her social and emotional wellbeing. But expansion of pastoral care was possible because extra resources were being given to education. In a tighter economic climate the alternative costs become more apparent. Because there is an emotional appeal to counselling and guidance it should not exclude them from evaluation. Furthermore, the effectiveness of the organization of pastoral services in the school should be open to scrutiny. This is especially important as a handful of children seen to need special attention can take up a disproportionate amount of teacher time. Sometimes it is necessary to balance the benefits to a minority against the costs to the majority.

The same argument for reviewing pastoral care against objectives can be used to include careers guidance, home-school relations, community service, school visits, and any other services using teacher time. Such a review can ensure that resources do not automatically go to existing activities through inertia. The easiest way to allocate resources is to start by giving last year's claimants their share and then deciding between the new. Regular, routine reviews remove the embarrassment of seeming suddenly to pick on some established practice. The Speech Day that takes up weeks of work by staff and pupils, the printing chapel that takes a major share of available

resources for a favoured few, and the annual visit to Paris that delights
the staff who go year after year with fewer and fewer pupils while
exhausting the teachers left behind are too common in schools for
evaluation not to range over extra-curricular activities that may
become fringe benefits.

Even though the cost of non-teaching staff and material resources is
peanuts compared with the money that has to go to teachers, the
need to extend evaluation across them is important. In stringent
times it is the books, the materials, the part-time secretaries, and so
on that are liable to be cut. Support services for teachers, such as
secretaries, laboratory technicians, media resources officers, librarians,
and auxiliaries can be used wastefully. They can remain on a job
long after its value has diminished. They can be bringing support
to the members of staff who least need it. This is an important managerial problem in a school, yet responsibility is often vague. Access
to the secretaries is often by personal charm. Reprographic services
seem to be monopolized by a few until the demands of the rest come
to be resented. New teachers can exhaust themselves preparing
materials that already exist in the resources centre. Experienced
teachers set up rival empires. The solution to these managerial
problems lies in including these services in regular reviews. It means
that the personnel involved must appreciate the reason for the
organization of their job and they must know the expectations of the
staff. Their involvement in making decisions is not a gesture to
democracy, but a means of increasing their effectiveness. There is
always one perennial problem in organizing resources. Some staff,
usually those who feel cheated of resources, will press for centraliza-
tion, while others, usually those holding most of the soft and hardware,
will support departmental storage. Once again, there is no absolute
answer. The most efficient system will depend on the objectives of the
teachers and the way the school is, as a consequence, organized. Apart
from the problem of who is to make tea and coffee in the staffroom,
access to the stockroom, secretaries and duplicators take up the
major part of the planning time of many school staffs. The inclusion
of these problems in the evaluative procedure can ensure that no
monopolists or property sharks or robber barons take over.

It is useful to measure the use made of a service as part of any
evaluation. This is a check on any tendency for the essential of one
year to persist as the peripheral in the next. Duplicators may be left
unused once a superior machine is hired. Technicians may be serving
the wrong laboratories when a curriculum has been changed. This
kind of check can result either in a re-allocation of resources, or an
effort to ensure that a valuable service is fully used. For example,
it is simple to check the amount of use of a school library because
books have in any case to be checked in and out. Too many libraries
are more ornament than facility and there is a tendency for some
teachers, and hence some groups of pupils, to make little use of an

important resource. Including resources in evaluation can check on possible waste and increase use.

The professional development of staff

The major part of this book so far has been concerned with evaluating the school, and the work of the teachers, through the performance of its pupils. This concern was appropriate because evaluation has been treated as the source of information for making decisions in the school. But decisions are also made on the basis of information about school staff. It is important that this information is reliable. Hence the evaluation of the roles played by teachers and non-teaching staff should also be systematic. Judgements are going to be made prior to decisions about appointment, probation, teaching load, allocation to particular parts of the curriculum, scaled posts, in-service training, applications for jobs, and so on. These judgements should be as fair and as reliable as possible.

There is suspicion about evaluation when it is suggested that it should cover teachers. That it happens anyway may not be a convincing reason for making it systematic. But there are powerful, positive reasons as well. Evaluation is a way of ensuring that teachers know where their responsibilities lie. Someone has to be responsible for keeping records, or pastoral care, or remedial work, or examination entries and so on, and a regular check on the roles being played is a way of ensuring that the jobs are being done and that staff know the part they should be playing. Cyril Poster puts it this way—'The teacher's role *is* capable of definition. In the complex structures of our secondary schools that definition is necessary, if each of us is ever to walk his way through the maze of priorities'.[1] Once again evaluation turns out to be what most school staffs have been doing all along, but is a valuable check that this is really the case. Further, it ensures that the procedures for evaluation are thoroughly planned.

Teachers in their induction year are one group where there is agreement among DES, LEAs, and professional associations that there should be systematic role definition and evaluation. However, although there is agreement on the need for guidance, support, and evaluation for this group of teachers, there is often a gap between ideal and reality. New teachers may not receive advance information on their role, may have a heavy time-table load, and may be confused about the way evaluation occurs. Here, where role definition should be clear there is often obscurity. Frequently the need for definition among other staff may be even greater.

There are other reasons for organizing the review of staff roles

[1] Poster, C., *op. cit.*, p. 36.

in the school. Teachers engaged in team teaching usually say that they realized for the first time how little they knew previously about the quality of their own work, its importance relative to that of other teachers, or how the work of other teachers compared with their own. Teaching can be a lonely job. It can lack encouragement and support. Evaluation not only removes the suspicion that nobody knows or cares yet is going to make important decisions about you, but can bring good news with the bad. Both can serve as bases for improvement and any reluctance to evaluate the work of teachers should be balanced against the need to ensure that staff do not feel isolated and unsupported, particularly in those schools where teaching is a tough job. Evaluating staff roles ensures not only that decisions about staff will be made on a reliable basis, but that senior staff and particularly headteachers are doing the important job of supporting, and being seen to be supporting, assistant staff where it matters, in the classroom and around the school.

The approach to the evaluation of staff roles and effectiveness should be the same as that to pupil performance. There is no point in evaluating the work of a teacher unless it is clear to that teacher as well as to those doing the evaluating what he or she is supposed to be achieving. The sequence of events has to be the same as in any evaluation. First decide what you are trying to achieve, then break these aims down into concrete activities or, in this case, role definitions, and then decide the criteria for assessment. The assessment can be against interior or exterior yardsticks. It can be for achievement or effort or both, or some other quality that should be specified. The assessment can be against the performance of other teachers doing similar jobs, against some specified level of competence, or against the previous performance of the teacher concerned. The assessment procedure can be completely confidential to headteacher and the teacher concerned, or shared with some other staff. This sounds formidable. It is however the current practice in all schools albeit in an unsystematic way. Making it systematic and open to scrutiny also means making it fair. As the evaluation is essentially a way of checking performance against the responsibilities of the specific job done by the teacher, nobody should be excluded. This includes headteachers. But again, this is only to substitute formal, defined, negotiated procedures for the current informal gossip that often serves for an unofficial yet potent evaluation of fellow staff. Evaluation is again making the implicit explicit.

A very full description of the jobs defined for staff in Sydney Stringer School, and Community College has been detailed by Geoffrey Holroyde the first headteacher of the school. [1] These are guides to the responsibilities that are to be carried by the Head, Deputy Head, and Director of Personnel Development, Deputy Head and Director of Resources and Services, Head of Community Activities, House Heads, and House Staff and the staff of the school generally.

[1] Open University, *op. cit.*

For example, the first and last of the 13 duties of the House Heads were, 'Organizing, conducting and supervising a planned programme of meetings and activities in House periods', and 'Continually encouraging pupils to set and maintain high standards of attendance, punctuality, appearance and deportment, care of property and fabric, consideration for others, and school work in all subjects and activities'. Seven key activities are listed for the Head, the first and last being 'The determination of Policy and Objectives and Success Criteria for Sydney Stringer which are acceptable to the LEA and Governors, the parents and pupils, the community it serves, and the staff' and 'The injection of ideas to stimulate the organization's development'.

This sounds a formidable list and it is rare for a headteacher to spell out responsibilities in a school in such minute detail. But this is a consistent element in the management of Sydney Stringer School and Community College. Once a decision has been taken to make objectives explicit, it is a straightforward task to decide on detailed job descriptions, just as it is to detail methods of evaluation once there is a clear set of targets for the staff of a school. Such a blueprint for a school runs the risk of listing aims of the school, organization for the school, the potential of the school as if the school existed apart from the teachers and pupils. In practice it is very difficult to get agreement on targets and hence on job descriptions because staff have different objectives, different perspectives, and these in turn differ from the views of pupils and others inside and outside the school. But the inevitability of difference among staff is a reason for, not against, definition and evaluation. Obtaining some minimal agreement on ends and regularly reviewing the degree to which they are attainable and have been attained at least brings a chance of obtaining unity of purpose.

The first step is to define the teaching roles. This really means looking at the organization of the school and the responsibilities of the teachers. Job description has been curiously neglected in many schools where teachers just fit into existing practices. Teachers are appointed to a school to fill a specified role. As the curriculum is determined every year these roles are redistributed. Internal promotions are made to ensure that crucial jobs are done and that those qualified and accepting the responsibilities are rewarded. This applies particularly to senior staff, whether headteachers, deputies, senior assistants, directors of curriculum, heads of houses, heads of subject departments, heads of years, directors of pastoral care, or others who have recently acquired specialized roles. But it also applies to the many teachers on scaled posts. These are usually awarded for responsibilities accepted even though these tend to change over time. Finally it applies to the assistant staff who not only do their job in the classroom but are often involved in unrewarded even unrecognized activity. Secondary schools are now too complicated for a regular review of role definition not to be instituted.

Obviously a regular review has to be organized by the headteacher and his or her senior staff. That is part of their responsibility. But in such a sensitive area consultation is essential. That consultation will also ensure that the review covers all staff. The staffroom is usually as rife with gossip about the way senior staff fix the time-table to their advantage as it is about the incompetence of some probationary teacher. The organization of the prior consultation is usually inseparable from the arrangements that are necessary for the efficient running of the school. Defining roles and evaluating the effectiveness with which they are performed is part of the management structure of the well-managed school. There may already be staff management, curricular or pastoral committees who can organize the review as part of their routine work. There is no need for a heavy-handed crisis approach. Evaluation need be only a re-definition of existing procedures. The form of evaluation will consist of regular, probably annual reviews of the role definitions of all staff, given changes in the organization of the school to meet changed circumstances or innovations. The assessment of the success of staff in filling these roles will usually consist of discussion with the headteacher, relevant heads of department, deputies or the committees set up to review aspects of organization. Once again, discussions of such reviews with headteachers usually produce the response that they already interview each head of department annually to discuss the curriculum, the attainment of pupils on internal tests and public examinations, and to talk about the assistant staff in the subject department. There are usually parallel discussions with pastoral care staff. But there are often gaps in these reviews. There is some reluctance to look closely at possible changes in the roles of senior colleagues. The balance between responsibilities and rewards can quickly be distorted. The result is often discontent and lack of co-operation. Schools are not business firms. But they are prone to the same worries about rewards for skill and effort, about differentials, and about management structures that do not keep up with actual changes in the working of the enterprise.

One tricky decision that has to be made is whether staff evaluation is to include an assessment of competence in the classroom. This is an accepted part of teacher education and is also part of the assessment of teachers in the probationary year. But it is a very sensitive issue in many schools. Nevertheless, if evaluation is to be taken seriously, it has to occur at the business end, in the classroom. It is difficult to see how there could be meaningful evaluation or indeed any guarantee of efficiency unless there is some supervision of classroom performance. It is also a means of ensuring that effort is recognized and serves as a basis for staff development. There is no definition of a good teacher that is backed by reliable research. But it is possible to go beyond overall impression by spelling out the aspects of teaching to be examined and the criteria of assessment. The components of good teaching have been categorized as gaining and maintaining the attention of learners, informing learners of the objectives of the lesson, causing recall of what has previously been learned, providing clear instructions, sufficient practice and feedback, and providing opportunities for the learners to transfer learning to new situations.[1] These categories can provide a framework for headteacher or head of department or senior teacher to discuss problems with teachers and to help in overcoming them.

Evaluation of staff is not only a way of ensuring useful role definition and a basis for decisions about career development; it can also serve as an early-warning system in cases where a teacher may be under strain. Another available indicator is the pattern of teacher absences. Just as it is the pattern of pupil absences that is the most useful indicator of a problem, so it is the short absences that matter among staff rather than the total numbers of days off, which can be due to ill-health. This indicator is used impressionistically in most schools. The headteacher is alert to the teacher who seems to be taking a large number of days off. The collection of teacher absences is required for administrative purposes and its collection in a form that can give an indication of possible problems is a simple and humane step.

There will be occasions when the internal evaluations organized by the staff of the school will be supplemented by inspections or visits by advisory staff. There will be routine visits to teachers in their probationary year. Whether these external evaluations are rare general inspections in which the entire organization of the school will be assessed or more frequent visits to see a particular subject department or teacher, the existence of internal evaluations will smooth the way. Much of the difficulty of externally organized inspections arises from the lack of documentation within the school. The job is half done where in-school evaluation is already organized.

The evaluation of staff performance is only one part of any programme of staff development. The continuing task is to keep the various teaching roles under review. Are teaching responsibilities clearly defined? Do teachers know the responsibilities that they are assumed to accept? Is there a fair balance between rewards and responsibilities? Are the teaching role definitions appropriate given the organization of the school, its clientele, and context? Are teachers well-informed about the way their roles relate to those of other teachers? Are the teaching roles too tightly defined to allow for initiatives to be taken? The evaluation of the definitions and allocations of roles is an important management task. Once again this evaluation is made by all headteachers, but often in a casual, unsystematic fashion. There may be advantages in regular discussion, in an exchange of views among staff on the way roles are defined, perceived, and related. There

[1] Gagné, R. M. (1970), *The Conditions of Learning*. New York, Holt, Rinehart and Winston.

can be no figures produced on the extent to which roles mesh smoothly or conflict. But there are advantages in bringing this aspect of school organization into the open. There may also be benefits from organizing perspectives from professionals outside the school. There is no need for a school to wait for inspections. If evaluation is accepted as an integral part of school management, and internally and externally referenced assessments are accepted as useful, there is a lot to gain from the regular use of panels of professionals from outside the school. One of the ways in which advisory staff can be most effective is to guide school staffs in techniques of evaluation and to help set up external supports. They can help link schools so that experience can be shared. They can establish a pool of experienced volunteer teachers, willing and qualified to help in evaluation. This pool could be drawn on by school staffs looking for evaluators with particular skills or interests, or could be organized by advisory, inspectorial staff into evaluation teams. School staffs could ask for the services of a team, or teams could be allocated by advisory staff. The objective in all cases is to provide an external reference and to increase perspectives in evaluation.

The ILEA inspectorate has produced a self-assessment exercise to help school staffs in Inner London schools to evaluate their work.[1] The secondary school exercise consists of suggestions for the collection of a number of simple statistics and about 130 questions on the way the school is working. These questions refer to the school environment, resources, decision-making and communications, staff, pupils, parental and community links, arrangements for learning, departmental or faculty self-assessment, questions for the headteacher, for individual teachers, and on action that should have priority. This self-assessment exercise, which has a parallel primary school counterpart, is a form of *aide-mémoire*, reminding teachers of the areas in which questions can be asked about the running of the school. The questions are each designed to suggest further questions that could be asked. The exercise is similar to that suggested here as the start of the process of in-school evaluation, as it is a spur to deciding priorities. Evaluation can never start with a finished set of aims neatly broken down into objectives with sets of indicators attached to each. School life does not lend itself to neat, academic evaluation. That is why most books about evaluation or school management appear to lack relevance from the staffroom and have had so little impact. The ILEA inspectorate was being realistic in suggesting questions rather than giving answers. Evaluation must come first from within the school as that is where the objectives should be decided. That is really what is meant by teacher autonomy. Finally, evaluation is a means to an end not an end in itself. Staff evaluation

[1] Inner London Education Authority (1977), *Keeping the School under Review*. London, ILEA.

should provide the information for decision-making about staff development. The tendency is to concentrate on in-service courses. Valuable as these can be, the meat of staff development must be a planned sequence of experiences that prepare teachers for more responsibilities as their careers develop. Little thought has been given to this largely because of the ease with which promotion was gained in a period of rapid expansion up to the mid-1970s. But the block on promotion in a contracting system and the growing complexity of schooling in a comprehensive secondary sector has increased the need to plan careers. This will only be possible if evaluation has produced the information on the aptitudes and interests of the teacher, the content of the role he or she is playing, and the strengths and weaknesses displayed in playing that role.

The step from collecting information on staff strengths and weaknesses to in-service training for promoting career development is rarely systematic in schools or local education authorities. Courses are organized, but usually without much thought of the gaps to be filled either in schools or for individual teachers. This is partly the result of the number for disconnected agencies in the academic world, the local authorities, their teachers' centres and the DES. Furthermore, the rewards of obtaining a diploma or higher degree may be unrelated to needs in the school, while the in-service course tailored to the situation in schools may provide little personal reward to the teacher taking it. A senior member of staff in the school, or a group of staff should have the responsibility of reviewing career development and in-service opportunities. He or she should talk over the future with staff, find out about opportunities and feed this advice through to the advisory or inspectorial staff responsible for in-service training. Furthermore, the training itself should be evaluated. Increasingly the in-service training provided is including programmes for the whole staff of a school. The conventional course rarely allows a teacher to develop the idea presented when he or she returns to the rush of school life. But a development programme involving the whole staff of a school can begin to be effective. Significantly these development programmes start with discussion of objectives. They are really the start of evaluation of the school, hence their promise.

Grouping pupils in the school

The teachers consulted about this book objected strongly to any model of the school as a factory, processing children through a series of learning experiences. Yet they were all concerned about allocating pupils to groups with different characteristics, in helping over option choices, entry to examination streams, in setting, providing remedial help, extra work for the gifted and careers guidance.

Pupils are sorted out, guided and given very different learning experiences. This applies whether the staff embrace streaming, banding, or mixed ability grouping. Furthermore, teaching resources are rarely allocated equally. A check on this has already been provided in the staff costing exercises. In all these areas the same principle applies. Schools are not sausage machines, but pupils make choices and have choices made for them. The consequences of these choices are important. Evaluation should include a check on whether staff intentions are actually implemented. Only too often researchers find that assumptions bear little relation to reality.

Whether the decision of the staff is to stream, band, stream and set, band and set, have mixed ability groups with or without setting and exceptions, remedial groups, withdrawal for remedial teaching, special centres for helping the badly behaved, the new arrivals, those with English as a second language and so on, there is a need to evaluate. There can be faulty allocation, there can be uneven or unfair allocation of resources to different groups, temporary withdrawal can lengthen into permanence, a flexible system can congeal. It is also difficult to detect this if evaluation is not made systematic. One of the strongest attacks on streaming followed the accumulation of evidence that teachers always over-estimated the extent of the movement of pupils between different streams. [1]

The first question that should guide evaluation is, as usual, what is the purpose of the differentiation between pupils. It should be possible to spell out why mixed ability grouping is preferred to streaming or banding. Evaluation follows from this, for very different criteria of success would apply if the objective was to maximize attainment, than if the object was to promote social mixing or equality of opportunity. The act of evaluating is once again a reminder that it is necessary to know why something is being done before it can be shown to be done effectively.

There are a few questions that can be asked of any method of organizing pupils into groups having distinctive purposes. Are the groups really what is intended? Streaming by ability often turns out to leave many pupils wrongly placed. The basis of the differentiation often turns out to have little to do with ability or attainment and a lot to do with teachers' perceptions of the pupils. Table 6:2 gives figures produced in a study of nine streamed comprehensive schools by the National Foundation for Educational Research, showing placement errors by social class, calculated after testing for attainment. [2] Ford, in another study of a comprehensive school found that

---

[1] Daniels, J. C. (1961), 'The Effects of Streaming in the Primary School', *British Journal of Educational Psychology*, vol. 31, pp. 69–78. *See also* Douglas, J. W. B. (1964), *The Home and the School*. London, MacGibbon and Kee.
[2] Ross, J. M. *et al.*, *op. cit.*

Table 6:2   Percentages of pupils incorrectly and correctly placed in streams or bands

Social class	Overplaced	Underplaced	Correctly placed	No. of pupils† (100%)
Middle	11	8*	81	288
Working	12	13*	76	858
Unknown	16	14	71	185
Total	12	12	76	1,331

† Number of pupils with first-year NF68 scores.
* Proportions are significantly different $p < .05$.

68 per cent of high scoring middle-class pupils were in the top band, but only 35 per cent of high scoring working-class pupils.[1]

However, this problem of incorrect placement also occurs in mixed ability grouping. Unless groups are carefully formed on the basis of objective testing they are liable to contain pupils who are far from mixed, particularly if pupils are allowed to make choices. Furthermore, within the mixed groups there can be voluntary or organized differentiation. The same problem arises with remedial groups, or other groups formed to solve particular problems. It is necessary to have regular checks to see that allocation has been correct. For example, a group set up to help those who can not cope in the ordinary classroom should not always be full of extroverted behaviour problems, unless that is the objective for such special provision.

The next question to include in any evaluation of special groups is 'how long do pupils stay compared with expected length of time?' An accompanying statistic to collect is the time that pupils spend in the special group on average. The tendency of teachers to over-estimate the mobility of pupils between streams, the movement in and out of remedial groups, through withdrawal units and so on, results from concentrating on the prominent individual case and not looking at the whole picture. As secondary schools develop more special units and individualize education, the chances of temporary stays becoming permanent increase. The very act of withdrawal to give special attention leads towards long stays. The pupil in the remedial group for reading soon feels more at home there than among the good readers. If he fails to improve he has to stay. If he improves there is every reason to continue the good work. The pupil in the withdrawal group is not disturbing his old class. He gets used to the intimate atmosphere of the specially equipped unit. He responds to the friendly teacher who is skilled at making him feel secure. Everyone

[1] Ford, J. (1969), *Social Class and the Comprehensive School*. London, Routledge and Kegan Paul.

concerned has every incentive to leave him where he is. A DES survey
in 1976 showed how common this form of special group has become. [1]
The danger is that without systematic evaluation, they could produce
a new form of selection within schools. The basis of that selection and
the success in achieving the objective of improvement followed by
return to the ordinary classroom should be looked at regularly.

The allocation of teachers

The calculation of pupil-teacher ratios for different subjects, for
lower and upper school and so on, and the calculation of similar
statistics such as the pupil-teacher claim used in Woodberry Down
are means of checking that teaching resources are not being used in too
unbalanced a way. This imbalance can occur between sixth forms
and below, between the able and less able, between different subjects
and so on. In four of the 11 comprehensive schools studied by the
National Foundation for Educational Research, the most able
pupils received markedly more resources than other boys and girls. [2]
Five more allocated teaching resources in this direction. However,
this is offset by teaching the less able in smaller groups. In some of
these schools teachers on scaled posts tended to be allocated to the
least able and the most able. In general the NFER found that there
was a more equable distribution of resources in comprehensive
schools than in grammar or secondary moderns. Furthermore, there
is no right or wrong balance. The decisions about allocation of staff
are made after consideration of objectives. Most staffs try to secure
an equitable balance. But it is worthwhile reviewing these arrangements in the light of these objectives.

Staff-pupil relations

Most schools are organized to harmonize, as far as possible, the
relations between staff and pupils. This is one of the reasons for
houses and house staff, tutors and tutor groups and pastoral care
arrangements, whether organized by counsellors or as a supplementary responsibility of teachers. These arrangements are expensive
of time and energy. They can become ends in themselves, insulated
from any policies agreed among all staff. The maintenance of a balance
between the obvious need to ensure that pupils can receive help over
personal or inter-personal problems and the equally pressing need to
get on with the teaching programme is not easy to manage. But it is a

[1] DES (1976), *Statistics of Education*, vol. 1.
[2] Ross, J. M. *et al.*, *op. cit.*, pp. 55–8.

management task and somebody has to accept the responsibility to assess how well the arrangements are working. This is not an easy task. Priorities are sure to clash as there will be many contrasting opinions on the value of pastoral as compared with academic work.

This is also an area of the work of the school where external services are important. The school psychological service, the Education Welfare Service, and the various social services all play a part. These services are the target of many complaints by teachers. They move too slowly when asked for help. Their advice is difficult to put into practice in the school. They may appear to be undermining the authority of the teacher. This discontent makes the extension of the review of teacher-pupil relations to include external support services essential. The school in this area stretches far beyond its boundaries. So therefore should evaluation.

One repetitive theme in recommending ways of improving the quality of judgements made in evaluation has been that the same aspect should be viewed from more than one position. A mix can consist of internally and externally referenced judgements, of panels of experts from different schools or colleges, of teachers at different levels in the school. There are some areas of school organization where the views of pupils would add to this triangulation of judgements. Pupils make important decisions. In many cases they are not only affected by decisions but are in the best position to judge their effects. This is not a plea for pupil power, but for pupil evaluations to be added to the pool where they are relevant and informed. There is also an educative function in the involvement of pupils. Pupils often seem to drift through school with little idea of what they are aiming at or why the school curriculum is organized in a particular way. Yet choices have to be made and involvement in evaluation is a way of informing the decisions. Some of these choices, for example over subject options, will determine the future of the pupil beyond school. Other decisions, such as the content of school meals, the choice of games on the time-table, and the organization of the sixth form, can be guided by the opinions of pupils because they are often in the best position to judge. As usual, the responses of the pupils are taken into consideration when such decisions are made. There may be some point in systematically collecting such views to ensure that the interpretation is correct.

Many teachers will have organized surveys to find the views of pupils on school matters. A small-scale survey of fourth-year subject choices in one comprehensive school for example found that over half the pupils who believed that they had made wrong subject choices thought that their own pre-conceptions were wrong. This was seen as a reflection of the quality of information given to pupils. One in five pupils thought that they had been wrongly advised by the staff. The survey also identified which source of advice proved to be most and least helpful to pupils. Such modest evaluations can serve as a guide to decisions about guidance over subject choices.

Repeated in the same form annually they could tell staff whether new methods were seen as any more effective by pupils. This particular report wisely concluded that it was perhaps encouraging that over 80 per cent of the pupils were not desperately unhappy. Evaluation often appears to be a way of deepening the gloom through a focus on the twenty per cent with problems. It is refreshing to look at the satisfied majority at the same time. Evaluation is a means to making more informed decisions. Deciding to carry on with the successful is as important as deciding to remedy the failures. Both rest on evaluation.

External relations

'This is a community school. We try to provide services that benefit the community and in turn benefit from the support of that community.' Many school staffs would endorse this statement by the headteacher of a new secondary school built to provide cultural and recreational services for a small East Midlands town. It may be difficult to define the aims of community schooling, but in sentiment at least, many teachers are in favour of it. There is, therefore, an advantage in looking systematically at the relations between the school and the various agents in its environment, particularly parents, employers, schools and colleges, where pupil attainment may be at stake.

Relations with the many groups who have contacts with the school are open to few quantitative evaluations. Nevertheless the effort to review the communal links of the school can be valuable. Few teaching staff find it easy to spare time to go through their relations with parents, employers, teachers in other schools, lecturers, the welfare and psychological services, social workers, police, youth leaders, local politicians, pressure groups, residents' associations, shopkeepers, clergymen, and the many agencies that form a community. There may be advantages in a working party of staff with this responsibility to review relations annually. There are often members of staff who have special responsibilities for building up and maintaining links. But the many groups who influence the school can never be covered by teachers having such specialist responsibilities. There may also be advantages in regularly looking across the groups, to see where gaps have arisen. Pastoral care staff may have established many useful links, but careers guidance, links with primary schools, co-operation with the local library services, and so on are often the responsibility of someone else or not specifically allocated.

As an example, the links with local pressure groups are often overlooked. Many schools now serve communities comprising people from very different cultures. Some of these groups may feel that the schools are not catering for the special circumstances faced by their

children. It is rare for all the groups to be asking for the same programme, but this makes regular consideration of the situation desirable. It may also be better to seek views on the education of children
from minority cultures in order to evaluate. The alternative may be to
overlook anxiety and to let tension build up. The evaluation of
relations has to be concerned with two questions. First, are those
relations achieving the intended benefits to both the school and the
community? Is the message that the school wants to be at the centre
of communal life understood in the community? The answers will
have to come mainly from discussions with groups in the community.
It can also come from written enquiries and offers to discuss from the
staff of the school. It may be possible for the teaching staff to foster
contacts with community organizations to ensure feedback. The
evaluation will come from the consideration of the different perspectives of the groups and individuals involved. The information may be
impressionistic, but bringing it together will uncover contrasting
views and any groups who feel frustrated. Once again, where objectivity cannot be obtained through the use of assessment techniques, it
can be approximated by triangulating the views of those in different
positions around the school.

Evaluating the structure of the curriculum

There are many informative texts on curriculum innovation, varying
from those that recommend a rigidly measuring approach to those
that prefer illumination through observation. But whether these
specify the microscope or flashlight as tools, they deal with particular
courses, usually innovations. This is to be expected as the academic
study of the curriculum expanded as curriculum innovation picked up
momentum in the 1960s, particularly in the early days of the Schools
Council. In practice attempts to develop a theory of evaluation never
helped teachers responsible for the major part of the curriculum.
They also gave a false impression that education had been suddenly
propelled into experimentation. All attention was focused on the
froth and little on the beer. Most teachers want to know how to
evaluate the bulk of their work that remains unchanged, not the
fringes where they innovate.

Most of this book has been about ways of setting about evaluation.
While the sequence of specifying aims, objectives, and indicators is
near that recommended by early curriculum theorists it has been
repeatedly stressed that the indicators of success or failure need often
be the judgement of professionals not measurements. Indeed, measurements are themselves indicative only and need judgement to be
translated into evaluations. Hence the search recommended has been
for tangible, specific objectives regardless of whether they can be

reduced to acts of behaviour that can be measured. Furthermore, this book is concerned with the total work in a school, not just those parts where innovation occurs.

The curriculum is a means to ends defined, implicitly or explicitly, by teachers. The act of evaluation has to start by considering these ends. One curious aspect of the attack on curriculum theorists who recommended the specification of measurable objectives has been the implication that the curriculum just occurs. It may be possible for a grammar school or a secondary modern school to carry on without any deliberations over objectives because these are implicit in the organization of such schools. A comprehensive school has no obvious, externally defined curricular rationale. Objectives have to be worked out for pupils of very different talents, backgrounds and hopes. If the curriculum is not planned in the light of this diverse clientele it is liable to satisfy none. The need to review the curriculum as the means of attaining definable objectives, however vague these turn out to be, also results from the difficulty that any single teacher has in comprehending the whole rather than that part for which he or she is responsible. Similarly, teachers in a subject department may have little idea of the way their work relates to that in other departments. Usually the headteacher or his senior staff carry out a brief review of the curriculum when the time has come to think about next year's time-table. The demands of subject departments are collected together. Innovations are suggested, facilities are reviewed. The final decisions fed into the time-tabling exercise will be based on last year's arrangements. The simplest way forward is to do it the same next year. There is nothing against this sensible approach. But it does mean that the curriculum can continue unchanged year after year without review or evaluation. The stability this brings is an asset. Innovation should never be an end in itself. But this continuity, while desirable, can be organized without meeting the objectives of the staff. Once a school staff has a look at its own priorities, the curriculum needs reviewing as it is the means of attaining the objectives that will be specified.

The review of the curriculum follows from the decision to evaluate the work of the school. The responsibility for the review can lie with the whole staff, but a small working party can produce recommendations in advance to focus the discussion. The job is not to evaluate parts of the curriculum. That can be done by subject departments or by consideration of results collected as part of routine assessments. The need is for a global look at the curriculum, at the way the parts cohere, at the way groups of pupils are tracked through courses that have a clear sequence of learning experiences built into them, at the way the sequence of learning in one part prepares not only for the next part in the same subject, but for other parallel subject areas. Any review of the curriculum will have to involve consultation across subject departments. Does a lack of mathematics hold up pupils in physics at particular stages? Are modern language teachers in difficulty because the teaching of English does not give pupils a knowledge of grammar? Does integrated studies provide sufficient geographical or historical skills? The answers to these and other questions can also be obtained direct from pupils as well as from analysis of their work. In this review the evaluators are close to the key to planned learning. The curriculum is made up of different subjects. But the knowledge has to cohere in the mind of the pupil. The task of evaluation is to provide evidence on which an effective, synchronized sequence of learning experiences can be planned.

If the first aspect of curricular evaluation is coherence, the second is the relation between subjects. This is not just concerned with securing continuity between the parts in one subject that are necessary for learning in another. It is a review of the often competing claims of subject departments for time-table time with particular groups of pupils. How many periods of English per week are desirable for all pupils, for the less able or more able? Are objectives for the intellectual, emotional, spiritual, and physical development of pupils all reflected in the time-table? Is tne curriculum offered to boys and girls promoting stereotyped sex roles? Is the curriculum for able children excessively academic? Is the curriculum for the less able excessively non-academic? The evaluation will range over the relation between the sequences of learning within subjects, the time allocated to subjects and the total offer for different groups of pupils. It will be concerned with the whole rather than the parts, doing the synoptic review that a teacher within his or her own subject department finds difficult.

The review of curriculum will relate it to objectives specified by staff, or at least staff objectives interpreted by the evaluators. This will extend the evaluation to gaps in the curriculum for all or groups of pupils. Should there be social studies if being aware of social responsibilities is an objective? Why do less able children have fewer periods of mathematics than their quicker learning peers? It will take in the pros and cons of integration of subjects, the public examinations policy and the time to be taken over examination courses. Why is it that the top bands start their run up to GCE a year earlier than the middle or lower band when the reverse would seem as sensible? Why is it that integrated studies is reserved for the less able? Why are secretarial courses reserved for girls? Once the reviewers have some idea of the objectives of the staff they will be alerted to areas of the curriculum that need particular attention. They will be brought up against the assumptions that form the framework of the curriculum. Pupils go up with age not attainment. Time for particular subjects is fixed regardless of the different times taken by different pupils to attain mastery of particular skills. Examination choices have to be made in the third form and the smaller the school the more restrictive these choices are liable to be. Evaluating the curriculum as a whole will be based on previously discussed objectives. But the evaluation will inevitably lead to questions about assumptions which may or may not coincide with objectives. The act of evaluation is once again liable to be disturbing as feedback uncovers unexpected assumptions and misfit between aims and procedures.

Any contemporary review of the curriculum will need to note two social issues. The first is that schools always receive pupils from very different backgrounds. These differ by social class, by religion, and by culture or way of life. There has always been this diversity and schools have always been balanced between promoting some minimum degree of uniformity and sustaining cultural variety. This is a dilemma for teachers. It has been made more difficult with rapid immigration and cultural pluralism. The curriculum has to provide pupils with the common knowledge and skills that will enable them to find employment and enter higher education, but not at the cost of violating profound beliefs or becoming self-defeating through damaging the self-image of pupils from minority groups. There is little doubt that the curriculum in English schools has been traditionally ethnocentric. It would be difficult to find any country where this was not the case. Curriculum evaluation has to include some consideration of this ethnocentrism. It also has to balance the often conflicting views of the groups wanting a curriculum that will suit their children, and to maintain the basic, instrumental aspects of the curriculum that will enable pupils to play their part in adult life and work. Inevitably this evaluation will touch the political, moral aims held by the teachers responsible.

The second issue is sexism in the curriculum. Just as the traditional curriculum has probably been insular, so it may have included stereotypes of male and female roles. Again, whether this is seen as a problem or not will depend on the priorities of staff. But in a mixed school an annual check on the number of girls taking mathematics or physics, craft or technical subjects can provide a useful indicator. Peer evaluation in single-sex and mixed schools, particularly if the colleagues on the evaluation panel were of the opposite sex, would be another revealing way of looking at textbooks, subject choices, and staff-pupil relations.

In both the cultural and sexist issues affecting curricular design there are pressure groups at work. Teachers have to perform a balancing act between opposed parties. But evaluation of the curriculum taking into account both these issues is unavoidable. A useful solution to the dilemma is to accept the conflict and organize antagonist evaluation. Here evaluators are deliberately chosen because they support the opposed sides. The final report is in two parts and the dilemma is brought into the open. Reconciliation may be impossible given the strength of belief over both issues. But antagonist evaluation is at least educative and can be a basis for reconciliation in the curriculum.

7. Evaluation in Context

The response of many teachers to the pressure for more systematic evaluation is to point to the particular context of their school, or to the particular way in which they organize their work in the light of that context. This is the consequence of a narrow view of what is involved in evaluation. The directors of a company do not just present the output for the year and the accompanying profit or loss. They break down the profit and the product into its constituent parts. They list the resources used, the way they have been organized, the snags and successes. They show how the company is developing some lines and phasing out others. They predict what is likely to happen in the forthcoming year. They present all the statistics for two or more years, and time series for the more important figures. Above all they outline the context in which the year's results have been achieved. Any evaluation that is to guide future decisions and satisfy an audience has to include not only an account of the product, but of the context, the input and the way those inputs are organized. Schools are not exceptional in needing to be understood in context.

Most of the suspicions of teachers over evaluation are concentrated around the misconception that they are being asked to publicize a few selected measures of output torn out of context. Yet evaluation involved. You account for your husbandry of resources in, not out of, Furthermore, the common rejection of the idea of accountability in education is usually based on the same restricted view of what is involved. You account for your husbandry of resources in, not out of, context. In this chapter ways of spelling out this context are suggested. Once again the focus is on possible quantitative indicators rather than on the more likely impressions that are more usually used. The latter are still important here as elsewhere.

The product of any evaluation is information that will help in making decisions. Within a school this usually means giving priority to assessing the performance of pupils at the end of a course, a year, or a school career, and comparing the total benefits with those from similar types of schooling, or relating these benefits to the resources used. Both methods focus attention on aspects that are going well or need improving. But these aspects can only be evaluated in relation to a school's environment. In this chapter attention is on the relation between the school and this environment. The object of collecting this information is to help formulate objectives, and hence guide curriculum and organization, in the light of the experience of pupils before arriving at the school, during their time there, and after leaving it. We are asking fundamental questions. Is the school serving the best interests of the pupils? Is the school working in the light of knowledge about neighbouring social, economic, and educational institutions? Are the human and material resources of the school organized efficiently?

Many school staffs will have already decided that a worthwhile set of related aims are that the secondary school should serve the local community and be responsive to the opinions of parents, employers, social workers, teachers in feeder primary schools, and college staff. The curriculum should take account of particular characteristics of the environment. To convert such aims into objectives requires a knowledge of that environment. Once that knowledge is obtained, aims and objectives within the school might be modified. Context evaluation is a method of increasing the effectiveness of schooling by providing the information necessary to ensure continuity of education from all sources. The school comes to be seen as one agency in a total education that involves many.

The educational context

Secondary schools take pupils from a number of primary schools and prepare them for a number of colleges of further, higher education and employments. Surprisingly this crucial educational context for the work of any one school can be neglected. While teachers can organize the work of their school in isolation, pupils may be handicapped by an absence of continuity as they pass from one institution to another. It is difficult for a first year secondary teacher to establish a common base if feeder primary schools have contrasting curricula. It is even more difficult for the newly-arrived first former if he happens to have worked on a different curricular basis from that in his new school. The information that is required is firstly curricular. The curriculum of each feeder primary school should be known, particularly in the basic subjects. This is the first step. It would seem odd to an outsider not to proceed to the second step of consultation to ensure some common core among the curricula of feeder primary schools. As many primary schools will feed to more than one secondary school, such consultations would be most efficiently organized on a local education authority basis or at least in different administrative parts of it. Description, evaluation, and action are in this case inseparable.

There may be a need for a similar sequence of events to secure continuity for school leavers. Where a high proportion of these go on to a local further education college, the benefits from ensuring continuity are obvious. They are often forgotten because the external examinations are assumed to secure a common base for a minority. With the increasing variety in examination content with CSE, and the accompanying increase in the proportion of pupils taking such examinations, the need for the planning of continuity has increased. The spread of linked courses, wherein pupils still at school take courses in F.E. colleges, and the use of these colleges to rationalize A level and other sixth form work have brought more co-operation. But continuity can still be accidental. One of the most telling evaluations of the work of a school would come from lecturers in F.E. colleges, just as secondary school teachers are often in a good position to evaluate the work of feeder primary schools.

The second type of information on the educational context of a secondary school is of facilities for recreation, the youth services, and activities organized in vacation time. Formulating objectives requires a knowledge of these educational influences alongside the school. The recognition of this importance in the community school results in the sharing of facilities, joint planning of courses and a blurring of the boundaries around the school. The statistical picture of these educational facilities can be found in the booklets that most local education authorities produce for their public.

The review of links between the school, its community, its feeder primary schools, further education colleges, youth services and so on are too important not to be organized. Once again this means that senior members of staff have to take responsibility. It is usual for the responsibility for inducting new pupils and liaising with primary schools to be allocated. But other liaison duties tend to be left as a general duty. This requires at least a review that these duties are being taken seriously by senior staff. It may not be realized that there is an expectation that staff will meet new pupils, interview parents, find out the views of shopkeepers, police, caretakers, groundsmen, and so on. Part of the evaluation must be to ensure that staff have a clear picture of their responsibilities. These are often left too vague to ensure sufficient feedback.

The use of information on the context of a school

The ideal information for use in decision making by school staff would consist of the benefits that would accrue to the various parties involved in the community from alternative educational policies. The policy giving the greatest benefit for the least cost would be chosen. Obviously the information that will actually be available will not enable anything like a balance sheet of costs and benefits to be drawn up. But it should be sufficient to give the staff of a school

an idea of the nature of the service that is needed and of the preferences of those involved.

This identification of preferences is essential because the term
community, as used in 'community school', or 'the needs of the
community', or 'community action' is misleadingly over-simplistic.
The community consists of several groups who do not necessarily
share common interest and who will want different things from the
school. In this chapter we only deal with the contrasting requirements
of parents, employers, college lecturers, and teachers in feeder
schools. There will only be brief mention of other groups. Yet these
too have views. The neighbours of the school, the police, the social
workers, the shopkeepers, the youth workers, the trade unions and
the chamber of commerce, are examples of groups who will ask the
school to do different things. Context evaluation is a matter of
recognizing these demands and reconciling them as decisions are
made. The evaluation will result in a compromise, but at least it will
be a compromise based on knowledge.

The social background of the pupils

Two strange features of schools in their context, particularly in
conurbations, are the familiarity and insularity of some of the pupils,
and the unfamiliarity and detachment of some of the teachers. The
high proportion of pupils who never leave their immediate urban
patch is mirrored by a similar proportion of teachers who never enter
it socially. There are cosmopolitan pupils and locally resident teachers,
but housing policy works against the latter. Teachers are not exceptional in this. Commuting is a common way of life. But it can mean
that planning in the school can be accidentally divorced from
context. This is not necessarily harmful or beneficial. But whether
innovative or traditional, a curriculum is likely to be more effective
if it is planned in the knowledge of the social conditions that will
influence the perception of the pupils concerned. This planning is
necessary whether the objective is to prepare children for life in the
local community, or to prepare them to break away from it.

I have deliberately concentrated in this section on the available
statistics which can indicate social background. But these need
interpretation. They are rarely tailor-made to the catchment area
of a secondary school. The figures are not necessarily reliable. They
are not a substitute for local knowledge. A stroll round the local
area may be as illuminating as a set of housing statistics and the impact
will be greater. Local surveys organized as part of a geography,
history, environmental or social studies project, may not produce as
reliable evidence as the Census, but it is likely to relate more accurately
to the catchment area of the school and will be more vivid. The
figures complement local knowledge and should not replace it. But

information gathered in the school is more useful if comparable with that already available outside.

Teachers always estimate the social background of the pupils in their school and make comparisons with other schools. These estimates and comparisons are often the basis of decisions about the curriculum. In this section the sources of information to help in this estimation are listed. This is not easy. Secondary school catchment areas, particularly those of voluntary schools, do not coincide with the areas on which suitable data exists. For example, the Census, which yields important national evidence on occupations, social class, household conditions, and place of birth, is reported on a national basis, by region, local authority, and enumeration district. None of these will give data that reflects the intake into the school, particularly if the area concerned is socially heterogeneous. The best guide is therefore information collected already in the school on the pupils; information on the environment of the school should be used only as a crude indicator or for comparison. Sources of statistical information mentioned in the text can be found in Appendix A.

Probably the best single indicator of the social background of pupils is eligibility for free meals. An alternative is the proportion in the school actually receiving free meals, as recorded on the return for the Department of Education and Science. The latter is a more convenient source as it has to be produced anyway; and as it is sent through the local education authority a figure for comparison can be produced. But some eligible children may not take a free meal on the day of return. Eligibility is a good indicator as the usual procedure is for the headteacher, having received a request from the parents or form teacher, to make a recommendation to the Education Welfare Officer or his equivalent, who then visits the home to make an assessment. Another useful indicator is the proportion of pupils in the school who are in receipt of uniform grants or clothing grants, although this usually coincides with eligibility for free meals.

Many schools will also record parents' occupation. This is valuable information because of the relation between parental occupation and the motivation and achievement of pupils. Children of semi-skilled and unskilled workers are likely to need special attention if they are to benefit from schooling. A staff may need to know if some social groups are at risk of under-attaining. The Census gives this information in two ways. First, there is a five category socio-economic grouping, the fourth and fifth categories being semi-skilled and unskilled. The other information is a seventeen-part categorization, with categories ten and eleven once again semi-skilled and unskilled workers. This information enables a check to be made between the school's clientele and the occupational structure of areas of different sizes at local authority, regional, or national level.

The identification of pupils from different cultural groups may also be advisable if attainment is to be monitored to ensure that some groups of pupils are not handicapped. The simplest and most immediately useful means of identification is the language spoken in the home. Other possible definitions are either very difficult to spell out in sufficient detail, or are politically very sensitive. For example, religion may be a very important factor to take into account in planning the education of Hindus or Moslems. Similarly it may be important to know the level of attainment of Turkish Cypriots or West Indians or Chinese pupils. But the definition of such pupils is complicated. The West Indies consists of many different countries with distinct traditions. The children and grandchildren of immigrants to Britain are British. The concern may be about the Black British, but there is a reluctance to identify pupils by colour. It is necessary to be very clear about the purpose of identification before collecting statistics for school records. The sequence aims, objectives, and indicators is essential here if unexpected consequences are to be avoided.

To illustrate the nature of the information available on social background I have taken three fictitious schools in three actual areas of the country, one in a Northern industrial county borough of nearly 100,000 persons, one a London borough with 250,000 population, the other a rural district of 21,000 persons in the Midlands. In the first of these the local education authority had produced a comprehensive set of education statistics for the county. In the second there were statistics available down to ward level extracted by an intelligence unit in the borough for a public debate over development, and in the third there were no published local authority statistics, although these were available in the information of the local authority. I have included only the information available to the public in libraries or distributed to schools, or produced in the schools for routine returns or records.

School A

This school is one of five comprehensives serving a Northern industrial town. Each school has a catchment area defined by the local education authority but these do not coincide with wards. At the time of writing small area statistics from the 1971 Census were not available. The county authority produced a detailed set of annual educational statistics for public information. This was to be the first of an annual publication, so that any developing trends could be detected. Information on education in the county borough was also available from the local education authority. Local government reorganization meant that the County in 1971 did not have the same boundaries as in 1976 (Table 7:1).

School B

This school serves an area in a London borough. No rigid catchment areas are drawn. The borough has produced very detailed papers

Table 7:1

Source	Statistic	County Borough	Admin. County	England + Wales	School
Census 1971	% persons living at over 1 person per room	17.2	17.5	6.8	—
	% without hot water supply	6.9	6.4	6.4	—
	% without bath or shower	10.0	11.1	8.7	—
	% without inside flush toilet	23.2	19.3	12.0	—
	% without all three facilities above	25.0	20.9	17.9	—
	% owner occupiers	46	36	41	—
	% born outside UK	1.3	1.2	6.5	1.0
County and DES	% receiving free meals	—	13.8	17.3	15.0
Registrar General Stats. Review 1973	Infant mortality rate	17	17	17	—

to help in discussions over development. The Greater London Council also produces an *Annual Abstract of Statistics*. The statistical information has been mainly extracted from the Census 1971, including data on wards within the borough. Additional information for the discussion paper on development has been obtained from local employment exchanges, the General Household Survey, the Department of Health and Social Security quarterly returns, the Metropolitan Police, the Family Expenditure survey, the National Income and Expenditure Survey, the 1966 and 1974 Land Use Surveys, the Department of Employment Gazette, surveys organized by the borough itself, and from reports by independent researchers. Few school staffs would be able to call on such a rich source of published statistics; in the school concerned here no copies were available. Most local authorities have intelligence units whose job it is to inform decision-making through the collection and circulation of statistical information. Table 7:2 does not show data by wards which was available in the published papers.

Among the other statistics made available for this borough were the following which could be of use to teachers for comparison with school-based figures, where available, or as additional indicators of social background in the area served by the school. Source is reports from the borough unless otherwise stated.

Table 7:2

Source	Statistic	Borough	Greater London	England + Wales	School
Census 1971	% persons living at over 1 person per room	18.1	4.7	6.8	—
	% without hot water supply	21.2	7.7	6.4	—
	% without bath or shower	21.0	9.1	8.7	—
	% without inside flush toilet	25.2	8.3	12.0	—
	% without all 3 facilities above	34.5	24.3	17.9	—
	% owner occupiers	20.0	36.0	41.0	—
	% born outside UK	22.0	14.6	6.5	—
LEA* and DES	% receiving free meals	16.3	8.6	17.3	22.4
Registrar General Stats. Review 1973	Infant mortality rate	19.0	17.0	17.0	—

*Source: *Annual Abstract of Greater London Statistics*, 1973.

Socio-economic grouping—percentage of semi- and unskilled = 30.3%; Greater London = 24% (School = 46%).
(Socio-economic groups 7, 10, 15 and 11, 16 and 17)
(Source: 1971 10 per cent Census)

Ratio per 1,000 of child population in care of local authority = 19; Greater London = 10 (School = 2.5%).

Percentage of single parent familites = 17.3; Greater London = 11.2 (School = 23%).

Pupils whose medical condition was found to be unsatisfactory = 0.74%; Greater London = 0.35%.
(Source: Annual Abstract of Greater London Statistics)

Pupils found to require dental treatment at first inspection by school dental service = 53%; Greater London = 50.9%.
(Source: Annual Abstract of Greater London Statistics)

School C
This school is in a small market town serving a rural area in the South Midlands. It takes most of the children from this area, many of whom arrive by school buses. The distances to school are long. The catchment area is largely farming. No information was produced for circulation by the local education authority, but the library in the

nearest town in which the school was situated held statistics produced
in annual reports (Table 7:3).

Table 7:3

Source	Statistic	Rural district	County	England + Wales	School
Census	% persons living at				
1971	over 1 person per				
	room	8.5	10.2	6.8	—
	% without hot water				
	supply	6.5	6.3	6.4	—
	% without bath or				
	shower	7.6	7.5	8.7	—
	% without inside				
	flush toilet	12.3	11.0	12.0	—
	% without all 3				
	facilities above	14.6	14.5	17.9	—
	% owner occupiers	55.0	53.0	41.0	—
	% born outside UK	N.A.	5.1	6.5	1.5
County and	% receiving free				
DES	meals	N.A	24.2	17.3	25.0
Registrar	Infant mortality				
General	rate	—	16	17	—
Stats.					
Review 1973					

These statistics indicate the relative deprivation or relative plenty
faced by schools. They can serve as a basis for planning. The organization of schooling has to take account of such factors. They need flesh
on them if they are to be used in public. To finish this section, here is
part of Michael Marland's address on the occasion of the twenty-first
birthday of Woodberry Down School. This illustrates the power of
such statistics in bringing home the extent of problems posed by the
contexts of some schools.

There is the hard fact of need. There are many parents as well as me in
the hall tonight who live and bring up children in the area. They *know*
what a difficult kind of inner city area we live in.

How widely known, though, is the extent of the difficulties of the children
who look to schools such as ours for education? No single one of the factors
usually regarded as difficulties is an insuperable problem, but put together
the comparative figures show that our pupils' need for help is immense.

Consider one-parent families: we have three or four times the national
proportion; and sad to say, a rapidly increasing number who live in
unhappy situations after marital strife or with fathers alone with several
children; consider large families: we have 23% of families with five or more
children, compared with 18% nationally. Or financial difficulty: twice as
high a proportion of children as nationally receive free dinners.

The general medical problems of our borough are reflected in the high proportion of our pupils whom we refer for medical investigation—about one third. A sixth of each year's intake have serious medical problems affecting their education. A quarter of our pupils are referred to the Education Welfare Service. These and other inner-city distresses create very many behaviourial and learning problems.

Hard facts show that the difficulties offered to educational attainment are very great for very many of our pupils—much greater proportionately than the higher resources.

Yes, our resources *are* generous, but are the resources available to inner-city areas generous enough to cope adequately with the extreme educational difficulties?

Parental interest and support

The importance of social background factors in influencing the attainment of pupils at school is probably a reflection of the part played by parents both in affecting the motivation of pupils and in actually helping them to be ready for work at school. Strong parental motivation can overcome poor material conditions. The trend towards a more open schooling has involved parents in the schools, but no figures are available on the extent to which this is being achieved, or the extent of the involvement. An evaluation of this parental context of schooling can result in two kinds of useful information. It can indicate the pupils who are not likely to get the necessary minimum of parental support and who may need support from the welfare service, and it can indicate whether efforts to involve parents are succeeding.

One secondary school in the West Midlands, anxious to get parents involved in school activities, kept records year by year of parents who came to parents' evenings, or activities organized by the parent-teacher association. A separate note was kept of those parents who took an active, working interest so that three categories were listed, non-participants, passive participants, and active participants. The senior master undertaking this work had the common suspicion that active parents were a stage army, while the majority did very little. Keeping the figures, while helping him to obtain a Diploma in Advanced Studies in Education, also helped the school staff to track the effects of their efforts to build up participation and to pick out the successful and unsuccessful means of doing this.

In most schools the evaluation of efforts to get parental support will depend on judgements by staff. Teachers will want to look at whether parents feel that they are welcome in the school, at how they are received if they call, at the facilities for talking with them, at arrangements for open days or evenings, at the way letters home are phrased, delivered, and answers ensured. The functions of any parents' association will need to be reviewed. The form of reports will require attention. If parental support is a crucial factor in pupil attainment it has to be mobilized, and the efforts to do so evaluated. There will be some difficult decisions to be made. These reinforce the need to start at the object of getting parents involved and then decide on the form of evaluation, for many schools will be reluctant to provide parents with the information they will request. Relations with parents are changing fast and this is an area of school policy where the exercise of discussing aims, objectives, and indicators can clarify as well as lead to evaluation.

Employment possibilities

Given the concern of pupils and their parents for the qualifications and skills that will help in getting the best possible job, it is necessary for a school staff to plan their work knowing the opportunities that exist. The presence of a teacher in charge of careers information and advice, and the help given by the Careers Service means that much of the information necessary for an evaluation of the structure of available employment is at hand. Luckily there is also good information available locally in the Youth Employment Service and from Industrial Training Boards and the Training Services Agency. Information of a more detailed kind is also available from the Census.

The Department of Employment used to estimate the industrial distribution of employees from a count of National Insurance cards. Since 1971 this information comes from an annual survey of employment. Unemployment information is collected monthly at exchanges. The boundaries of local authorities do not coincide with those of employment exchanges and the statistics are subject to a number of cautions. They do, however, show the numbers of employees in 27 industrial groups, the number unemployed, the number actually seeking work, with the distribution of these unemployed between the various occupational groups. This even enables the occupations with the highest numbers unemployed to be identified.

This information enables a picture to be drawn of the local employment situation. For example, in the area around School B, the five largest industrial groups, in descending order were, Distributive Trades, Manufacturing, Utilities and Transport, National and Local Government, and Construction. The numbers in Distribution were over twice those in the next largest category, Manufacturing. But such figures should be treated with caution as an indicator of opportunities open to school leavers. In this area over 70 per cent of the residents worked outside the borough. Once the broader picture was looked at, the dominance of the distributive trades was closely challenged by professional and scientific services, the commercial sector, and public administration. The shortcomings of this information on employment do not destroy its use in formulating objectives by school staff. Particularly when the trend figures produced from successive Census figures, or from Department of Employment surveys are used, the increasing dominance of the service sector becomes obvious in such city areas. Yet it is doubtful if this is fully appreciated by pupils or their parents, or taken into account when the curriculum is being planned. Context evaluation is a means of informing decision-making in the school.

Community and communications

So far in this chapter the concern has been with knowledge within the school about the environment. But if one objective is that the school should serve the community, it is important to know how the school is perceived. What do parents think that the school is organized to achieve? Do they think it is being achieved? Do they think about the school at all? Some will see it as a means for equipping their children for adult working life. Others will see it as a place where their children are taught to behave in a civilized way. Many may just accept it as a place where they send their children, a convenient child-minding institution. Apart from evidence that most parents take a traditional view of schools as places where children should be taught basic knowledge and kept in order, we know little of the communal perception of schooling. This applies also to employers, social workers, policemen, college lecturers, shopkeepers, clergy, and so on. Their public pronouncements suggest that they all share the views of most parents. This suggests a suspicion of many of the recent developments in education. But it also suggests that evaluating the environment from within a school may result in an interpretation of communal wants and needs that might not be shared by those involved. To say that it is all a matter of communication is to reproduce one of those blindingly obvious, superficially impressive truisms that abound in the educational literature. Yet community and communications are derived from a common root. One makes the other. The crucial evaluative question from the school becomes 'how well are we getting across our objectives, procedures, and achievements to those around us?'

There are no readily available indicators of the success of a school in building up links to, and services for, the community. Evaluation has to rest on the judgements of staff. They can judge relations with local residents and shopkeepers, social workers and employers. It is useful to keep figures on services given by the school to the neighbourhood, the visitors to the school, links with local associations and so on, and to look at this activity over time. But eventually, the sequence of events has to be to spell out what both school and community are to gain from establishing links, how the success of such policies can be gauged and whose judgement is to count. It is often the quality rather than the quantity of such links which matters and statistics could be very misleading.

Further and higher education

A glance at the DES Annual Statistics destination of school leavers tables gives a good indication of the range of opportunities now available. These figures are based on a ten per cent sample of pupils from each school which could easily be boosted to 100 per cent to give the school a running record of the destination of its own leavers. The local further education colleges in particular provide an important context for the work of a secondary school. Where sizeable numbers of leavers go to any one college or any one type of course in different colleges, there should be some evaluation of the school curriculum to check that the leavers are adequately prepared before transfer. The co-operation between college and school staff is sometimes ensured via linked courses and even by college staff teaching specialized subjects in the school. Increasingly, further education colleges are taking students who would previously have stayed on to take A level or sub-A-level courses in the schools. But the need for co-operation and consultation remains. There is a curious tendency for each stage in education to blame the previous stage for inadequately preparing the students. Secondary school staff should know the problems faced by college staff and should be prepared to review their own practices to overcome them. Similarly college staff would benefit from a closer association with the staff of the schools.

A lot of the work of preparation usually lies with careers staff in the school. But it is a matter that concerns the whole curriculum. Once again evaluation becomes a way of defining responsibilities, of smoothing out the sequence of learning, and of ensuring that the methods of one stage do not make difficulties for the next. This has become a pressing need as local colleges take on students across the whole range of ability. It is not only the student arriving to take A level or a day release course who benefits from continuity. It is the student re-taking O levels or a course to equip him or her with basic skills that has to be considered. Evaluating the context of post-statutory education is no longer concerned with filling up UCCA forms or keeping an eye on the courses for craft apprentices. The variety of courses offered in further education is often not appreciated in schools. For example, the Technician Education and the Business Education Councils are rationalizing old and promoting new courses. The extended role of the Manpower Services Commission has led to a rapid creation of new programmes of courses preparing young people for work, and giving them the necessary experience of it. These youngsters are paid while on such courses.

The feeder primary schools

There are two important sets of information that are needed in the secondary school on the pupils coming in every year. One set gives a picture of the ability, aptitude, and attainments of the pupils and the other the curriculum of the primary schools from which they come. The passing of information from primary to secondary school is often surprisingly casual. Indeed there is sometimes resistance to transferring too much information in case the child is labelled on entry to secondary school. Yet the continuity of education requires that the new is based on the old. The ending of selection for secondary schooling has diminished the administrative demand for objective information on individual pupils and meant that secondary schools are liable to receive less information on their incoming first-year children. But, at the same time, comprehensive schools are receiving a more heterogeneous intake.

It is essential to check the quality of the information received, information that is missing yet necessary, and information that is transferred but not used. The first check is on the amount of information that has to be collected on pupils after the new intake has been received at the start of the school year. A second is the amount of correction that is necessary to curricular arrangements made on the basis of information received from the primary schools. A third is to find out whether staff are actually using information that has been accumulated and transferred with considerable labour by primary school teachers. The results from these checks will often be unexpected and can lead to a saving of effort by both primary and secondary school staff. There is too often repetition of testing, ignoring of carefully detailed information, and too much trust in unreliable data. Here the evaluation that is necessary is a review of the relation between the school and feeder primary schools. Sometimes primary school records and the transfer of information are standardized throughout a local education authority, but even here there will often be additional information passed on by some schools. For example, many primary schools test reading to monitor their own attainment, but others leave this to the secondary schools. Yet the secondary school teacher often finds it necessary to re-test unless he has information on reading on all incoming children and can rely on the information transferred. As each primary school will choose the reading test that suits its own curriculum there is liable to be too much variety in the information available to the secondary teacher and he may decide to test to

obtain standard information even though all children were tested
before leaving primary school.

In the discussion of the organization of examination results for
evaluation, the need for some attainment measures at intake were
noted. Without these, public examination results five or seven years
later were difficult to interpret. But a school staff may also want to
have intake data of an objective kind to help make decisions about
grouping, whether in streams or groups of mixed ability. Such data
also provides a means of building up a picture of the changing
characteristics of the intake over time. Without this, decisions about
the curriculum may be made without reference to the needs of the
pupils entering. As an example, here are figures given by a headteacher of an inner city comprehensive school. In this education
authority the aim of the transfer procedures was to secure as far as was
possible a balanced intake into every school. This was attained by
primary school staff placing each leaver into one of three bands,
containing the top 25 per cent by ability, the next 50 per cent, and
the lowest 25 per cent. As a guide, the children took a verbal reasoning
test and the primary school staff were informed of the numbers of
their leavers who should be placed in each band. As a check the
secondary school re-tested the incoming pupils on verbal reasoning
tests used in the primary schools in previous years. The characteristics of successive intakes are shown in Figure 7:1.

This graphing of intake bands seemed to show an improved intake,
on the basis of placement into the bands by primary school staff.
The school in 1975 was receiving less than its share of the most able
children and more than its share of the lowest band. By 1977 it was
receiving a more balanced intake. However, the bands used here
are very broad. Furthermore, they are based on standards in the
authority which may not be comparable with national standards.
Figure 7:2 shows graphs for the same years based on verbal reasoning
tests taken at intake.

The detail provided by the actual test scores at intake shows that
the proportion of able children who would have previously gone to
grammar school had not increased markedly. Neither was the school
receiving a balance over and under 100. The broad bands used in

Figure 7:1   Intake bands 1975, 76, and 77

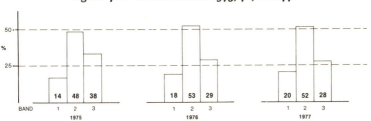

Figure 7:2   Intake bands 1975, 76, and 77

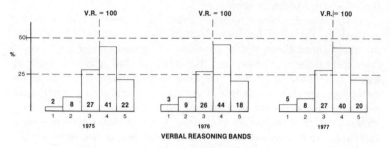

Figure 7:1 were concealing a persisting difficulty. The finer limits and national norms revealed a different pattern.

Curricular information

The decentralized nature of English education and the ending of selection at transfer means that secondary schools receiving children from more than one primary school are liable to find significant variations in the curriculum that has been covered. This occurs not only in the range of subjects covered, but in the cover of basic skills. There is reluctance to spell out even a minimum common content in a subject like arithmetic. The secondary school staff have to deal with this problem by starting at what they guess is the lowest common primary school content. But they still meet difficulties as there may have been no genuine mastery even of simple skills, particularly numerical, because of curriculum decisions rather than the ability of the pupils. The need to evaluate this curriculum match between the secondary school and its feeder primary schools is crucial, yet is rarely done systematically.

The organization of curriculum continuity is also complicated by the demands of other secondary schools who may organize a distinctive curriculum and ask the same primary schools to adopt an approach suited to this scheme of work. Thus negotiation to achieve continuity should have a high priority and must involve groups of schools. The lack of an agreed sequence seems insane to those used to centralized influence over the curriculum. The work of ensuring continuity seems to be the necessary price of ensuring the autonomy of any single teacher. Where the mobility of children between areas with different approaches may create an unnecessary penalty if there is excessive curricular variety it is difficult to argue for complete local discretion without careful planning of transition to secondary school. An evaluation of curricular continuity will involve negotiation and some investment in liaison activities. Such evaluation should extend to the primary schools and mutual adjustments can be made in the core subject areas. The involvement of local inspectors or advisors in this mutual evaluation and adjustment often helps to produce effective co-operation and should have high priority in their work.

The costs of the action following evaluation will inevitably force staff to look at the total arrangements for the induction of new pupils into the secondary school. There may have to be a choice between concentrating on securing curriculum continuity and ensuring a smooth personal transition to the secondary school. Many primary schools now arrange visits to secondary schools for top juniors. Parents visit the new school. There is sometimes an exchange of teachers, or primary school teachers bring their children with them to the secondary school so that they teach in primary and secondary school in alternate years. The first weeks in the secondary school are often carefully organized to simulate the primary school climate so that the transfer is not too much of a shock. Integrated studies and project work are often organized to give the work continuity. Yet it would be unwise to assume that this effort is more valuable than concentrating on making sure that all the newcomers have covered the work on which the secondary school curriculum is based. Evaluation can lead to tough choices. Sometimes the appeal of the mundane work of securing an adequate base for academic work is less than that of securing a happy set of first-year pupils. The evidence does not suggest that children are necessarily lost in the big school. Many look forward to it and feel resentment if they continue to be treated as juniors. They dislike the diet of projects and may be frustrated at not getting 'subjects'. Evaluation should not be swamped by the emotional appeal of the pastoral. The first weeks of the September term do need careful attention to secure the smooth assimilation of the new intake, but this includes the rapid settling down to new and interesting work as well as the rapid identification of problems and the maximization of support for the children who find the transition difficult.

There are no obvious objective indicators of the success of transfer arrangements and curriculum continuity. The important evidence is the experience of the first-form teachers. But this can be supplemented by direct and indirect evidence collected from pupils. The running assessment programme should be sensitive and intensive enough in the first weeks of term to detect weaknesses in groups of pupils that arise from a gap in their primary schooling. If one pupil from primary school Y does not know how to convert simple fractions to decimals, can the remainder from this school manage this conversion? If all find it impossible, the secondary school teacher either has to start at a more elementary level or give these pupils special help. If the former seems undesirable, he must negotiate with members of staff from the primary school concerned to see if they could include this before their children leave. This intensive search early in the secondary school is even more necessary to detect learning problems arising from the use of different methods in the primary schools. The various ways of carrying out simple arithmetic processes can lead to confusion when a child meets a new method. There may be no need for uniformity of method in the primary schools, but at some stage children have to be shown that the same processes can be tackled in different ways.

Direct evidence can be collected by systematically asking pupils about different methods of working, repetition of work already done, and wrongful assumptions about work that has been covered. One way of organizing this would be to give each child a checklist for use with any work that is being introduced in the first form. This list would have a space for the subject to be filled in under direction by the teacher. At the end of the session the teacher would ask the children to tick in the appropriate place to indicate whether the work had been previously covered or not covered. Various elaborations of such a form would be possible, but even a simple two category version would show whether the level at which the work had been pitched was justified in the light of the previous experience of the pupils. In very large secondary schools, where there may be variety between the approach in different forms, this method of checking might have advantages in second, third and fourth forms. Evaluation can serve to detect the need for immediate reorganization as well as providing evidence for longer-term action.

8. The Organization of In-school Evaluation

The evaluation recommended in this book has been considered as an integral part of the total organization for learning. Evaluation is not tacked on as an optional extra. It is an essential part of any effective curriculum. It is the way in which information on the success or failure of methods of attaining desired objectives is fed back to the teachers who are responsible for determining objectives, learning strategies, and the form of the evaluation itself. The choice is between leaving evaluation to impressions that have no necessarily consistent or even detectable frame of reference, or organizing it so that the criteria of success and failure are spelled out. It is a choice between casual and systematic judgement.

The second recommendation has been that evaluation should be accepted as being about judgement not just the production of statistics. Figures are useful but the same criteria of usefulness apply to them as to the impressions of the teachers. There has to be some planned, visible reference against which the audience for the evluation can interpret the figures or the judgements. This reference can be internal to the school. It can be the performance of other schools. It can be standardized tests, public examinations, national statistics, the judgement of fellow teachers in neighbouring schools, of inspectors or advisors, of academics, parents, employers, or the pupils. Evaluation can come from a variety of sources, some yielding quantitative and some qualitative information, but it has always to be referred to some known criteria of success and failure for the judgements to be meaningful. An aspect of school life cannot be judged good or bad without specifying the basis on which that judgement is to be, or has been, made.

The third recommendation has been to employ a variety of viewpoints in evaluation While most of these will be found among the teachers in the school, using their own judgements and using a number of techniques such as tests or the regular selection and collection of indicators, there is a place for a number of different perspectives on the same aspect of school life particularly from teachers in other schools. This triangulation of views not only makes the evaluation more convincing, it brings home the views of the public for education on whom the attainment of pupils ultimately depends. Everyone evaluates the work of schools. It is informative and politic to mobilize that interest in organizing schooling.

The fourth recommendation has been that teachers should take the initiative for evaluation. They carry the responsibility. They have to implement measures to remedy the failures and reinforce the successes. They need the information most. Furthermore, if teachers do not evaluate, make it clear to the public that they are doing so, and give the public sufficient information, the evaluation will be done for them. It is safest to assume that no news is bad news in education. Evaluation is not only a necessary step to improving effectiveness, it is the guarantor of professional autonomy.

A fifth recommendation arises from the need to obtain the maximum information from minimum effort. Data gathered for assessing the work of pupils has also to be used for evaluating the success of the school as an organization. There is a demand for new forms of assessment to contribute to the organization of new types of courses. This assessment is needed to ensure that the steps to learning are followed in the right order and that pupils are not penalized by missing some, and not understanding others. This is time-consuming work. Any data produced has also to be used to reflect on the success of the school. Significantly, worries over that success have arisen out of the introduction of new curricula and teaching methods. Staff and public want the information. This has also to come from a new form of evaluation. Neither evaluation to inform teaching and learning, nor evaluation of the school as an organization can be confined to norm-referenced tests and examinations, although these remain important. The two sources of demand for evaluation come together in requiring reference to standards attained, to indicators and criteria that are pre-specified by staff, and, where possible, to comparable levels of attainment among other pupils in other schools.

Finally, staff have to have a commitment to evaluate. A reluctant approach will ensure the failure of any evaluation programme. This is why a modest, pragmatic, incremental approach has been recommended. The organization of in-school evaluation will often involve only the pulling together of scattered, casual assessments into a routine arrangement. While education was highly selective, evaluation could remain unsystematic. There were public examinations that sufficiently measured the success of grammar schools. The secondary modern schools in their short lives soon moved to the security of fourth- and fifth-year examinations set by the Royal Society of Arts, the College of Preceptors, the City and Guilds, the Union of Educational Institutions, and many others. These examinations were largely replaced by the Certificate of Secondary Education. Comprehensive schools, particularly once they moved from having grammar and secondary modern streams within them, could use no such simple indicator of success, although public examination success remains the most valued single indicator. The production of an adequate and informative set of indicators is a pressing contemporary task. It is not easy because the determination of aims which is a necessary first step is itself dependent on working out aims for universal secondary education to at least sixteen.

The organization and the information

Most of the teachers consulted asked for a plain statement of the basic minimum organization for evaluation and of information to be collected. This is difficult given the variety of aims among school staffs. However, assuming that the form in which information will be collected and used will be determined by the priorities of teachers, here is a personal basic evaluation programme.

1 The evaluation must be built into the decision-making processes of the school. Hence a senior member of staff must be given responsibility. This responsibility must be permanent. The job will be to:

(*a*) Organize ongoing discussion of objectives as information is collected, tabulated, and considered by staff.
(*b*) Organize the collection of information inside the school, its tabulation, storage, and retrieval.
(*c*) Organize the presentation of the information to other staff, to pupils, and to the public of the school, particularly governors.
(*d*) Organize peer evaluation where appropriate.
(*e*) Organize the collection of national and local information for comparative purposes to match (*a*) to (*c*) above.

The job would require mathematical experience, particularly as some internal marks will need scaling. But the crucial part is the organization of an information base for the school so that staff can get a picture of trends in the school and comparison with external data. Inevitably this will require taking initiatives outside the school. For example, the sharing of data between neighbouring schools as described in Chapter 5 is a valuable way of obtaining comparisons where the contexts are likely to be similar. However, this requires organization to obtain genuinely comparable information. Similarly local education authorities, examination boards, and the DES may have to be approached to provide data for school use.

2 The basic information to be regularly collected should contain as a minimum:

(*a*) School rolls, year-group numbers, teacher numbers, and pupil-teacher ratios.
(*b*) Some measure of resource allocation, including teachers, selected from Chapter 6. The most powerful of these is probably pupil-period load as developed by Marland.
(*c*) Intake data, whether in the form of bands, standardized test scores, or gradings. As this data is needed to check against future

results, particularly of fifth-year examinations, it should preferably
be test scores, or bands based on test scores, with some external
reference as in Chapter 3.

(d) Some information on the context of the school selected from
Chapter 7. The basic statistic is the proportion of pupils eligible
for free meals.

(e) Selected statistics on such features of school organization as
attendance and staying-on rates.

(f) Output measures covering academic and other aspects of
school life. The basic statistics will be in the form of public examination data selected from Chapter 4. Many schools will also want to
collect and store information on the destination of school leavers.
The proportion attaining mastery in skills as suggested in Chapter
5 would widen the objectives covered in this important area.

3 The information should be stored and retrieved annually in the
form of time series where possible. This should be the basis of the
following exercises:

(a) Scrutiny by staff to detect trends, formulate hypotheses, and
plan action.

(b) Reconsideration of objectives. This will bring pressure to
change the form of the information collected, but the preservation
of existing time series should also be a priority.

(c) The preparation of an annual report for governors. One of the
recommendations of the Taylor Committee on governors was that
they should 'Keep under constant review the school's success in
achieving its objectives, and produce regularly more formal
appraisals of its performance.'[1] The stored statistics should enable
staff to anticipate and satisfy this need for information, not only
from governors, but from parents, employers, local authorities,
and inspectors.

4 Peer evaluation using local teachers in neighbouring schools, and
panel evaluation by other teachers, academics and lay people should
be used to supplement more conventional evaluation in areas where
judgement by outsiders is appropriate. This should preferably be a
co-operative exercise between neighbouring schools. Where lay people
are involved staff should still define the objective prior to evaluation.

5 Where programmes or campaigns are organized, and evaluations
are designed to monitor impact, reports should be prepared and stored
in the ways recommended above.

This book contains possibilities for use, not models for implemen-
tation. The bald statements above were produced with some trepida-
tion. But even where no statistical information is collected or stored,

---

[1] *A New Partnership* (1977), Report of the Taylor Committee on the government of schools. London, HMSO.

evaluation needs to be taken seriously and this means it has to be organized on a permanent basis. It is now possible to return to the questions asked in the Introduction by the teachers consulted. If the book has seemed prescriptive, it has been a response to their insistence that a case should be made, if only to be rejected.

Question 1
Here the teachers were concerned with the way to start evaluating their efforts, particularly in getting their pupils to learn. This question is answered in Chapter 1. The recommended start is to consider evaluation not as a separate exercise tacked on to the existing work of the teacher, but as an important, central part of the planning of school organization and curriculum. This unity of evaluation and curriculum still seems strange to many teachers because they tend to treat evaluation casually. But this is itself a symptom of a casual attitude towards planning the curriculum. Where a school staff has worked out explicit targets for its work there is no problem in placing evaluation at the centre. But in many schools the first step has to be a return to fundamental questions about what teachers are trying to achieve. In others, innovations necessitate new thinking along these lines.

It is unlikely that the rate of innovation in secondary schools has been as rapid as critics fear. Indeed, the movement in the 'progressive' direction in the primary schools has been limited. Teachers are generally a cautious profession. But in all schools it is possible for innovation to go faster than evaluation. This results in anxiety and, often, retrenchment. Ideally assessment should be built into any innovation. This not only provides information on the success of the development at the end of a term or a year. More importantly it can provide instant feed-back to teachers and to pupils. In this way adjustments can be made, pupils can be guided on the basis of assessment, and pupils will have guidance on how fast to progress through individual work, and where to work next.

The sequence of specifying aims, objectives, and indicators is less about evaluation than about the total organization of the school. The decision to evaluate is a commitment to reviewing the curriculum and the organization of resources to make them work. This need not be a 'once for all' decision worked out in fine detail. The first step need only be to get staff to articulate their implicit objectives and to get some agreement over which are common. A basic set of objectives derived from broad aims is a start. The advantages of deciding to evaluate systematically is that the sequence of events feeds back in circular fashion so that the interpretation of results can lead to a review, not only of organization, but of the original objectives, leading to their amendment or to additions to them. The starting-point has to be the recognition that some evaluation, being about judgements, can not be confined to teachers in the school. They organize it. They set the objectives and decide the criteria. But outsiders often have to be involved because governors, parents, employers, advisors, and so on will make judgements and affect attainment through their influence over pupils and teachers. Schooling is too important not to be evaluated by all those concerned with it. It is better to aim for one central form of evaluation which will be well documented. This has to be organized by the teachers. But the judgements will inevitably come from the public for education, and the pupils, as well as from the staff of the school. It is best to recognize this from the start and to build some of it into the evaluation programme.

Question 2
Here the teachers were worried about an increase in the amount of testing necessary in order to accumulate quantitative data for evaluation. Undoubtedly the commitment to evaluate will focus attention on data that can be readily interpreted and which has some easily detectable reference for interpretation. This follows from the need to make judgements about evidence, whether soft or hard, in writing or in figures. But the inevitability of judgement answers the question. The key to useful evaluation is informed professional judgement, based on reliable qualitative and quantitative information. The recommendation that teachers should organize their judgements follows from the mix of quantitative information. The sequence of moving to indicators is the same for each. But the need to be systematic in the accumulation of indicators means that staff have to arrange for regular reviews of their work. There has to be a time-table of evaluation to ensure that important aspects are not overlooked. This will involve teachers taking responsibility for organizing the collection of statistics or the collection of judgements. Evaluation may not increase the amount of testing in the school but it will increase the amount of self-scrutiny. It will mean that aspects of school life that staff consider important will be regularly reviewed. This may prove uncomfortable for some. Similarly, the involvement of outsiders in evaluation, while organized by the staff of the school, will bring external perspectives to bear on often sensitive areas of school life. This happens anyway. Evaluation replaces rumour with information.

Question 3
Here the teachers were worried about the often narrow concentration of evaluation on strictly academic aspects of the work of the school. The answer is to work honestly from the aims and objectives which are agreed to have top priority by the staff. These are liable to cover a range of academic, social, cultural, sporting, and moral activities. If they are valued they should be evaluated. If the morals of children are considered to be as important as examination results, it is important to assess the success of the staff efforts to produce a genuinely moral climate. This is part of the reason why evaluation is not just the

collection of statistics. Many of the most valued activities organized by teachers spring from their concern with the moral, social, sporting, and cultural lives of their pupils. Research evidence suggests that teachers are deeply concerned with pupils as persons, not just as examinees.[1] This is why evaluation must have as broad a sweep as the objectives of the staff. But at the heart of the evaluation will be those instrumental aspects of learning that are highly valued by staff, parents, employers, and pupils. These will have been chosen for evaluation because they are necessary for further learning or for obtaining employment. Public examinations indicate the extent of mastery of these skills, so do the records given as examples in Chapter 2. Other indicators will be the key checkpoints through which pupils have to pass in order to benefit from further schooling. There may be few such indicators, but in each case they should reflect the priorities of teachers and the milestones that they think pupils should pass.

Question 4
Here teachers were concerned with the lack of yardsticks against which to measure many of the valued aspects of schooling that they thought worth evaluating. Clearly there is limited value in standards determined internally if these are only based on the impressions of staff. But there are many indicators that are not dependent on judgement. There are possibilities of internal moderation to check on standards used. These statistics, records, and assessments take on greater meaning when stored over time. Comparisons against previous performances then become possible.

The second, and generally more useful set of yardsticks are external to the school. There are standardized tests and public examination results on one side and the collected views of experts on the other. The former are already extensively used by teachers and a lot of space has been given to possible methods of presentation. The use of peers to help in evaluation is unusual. It has been suggested that groups of schools might co-operate to provide this mutual service. Groups of schools would benefit from being able to share information. Experts and laymen among parents, employers, and the public of the school might also play a part. The organization of these different external references for evaluation brings different perspectives to bear on the same aspect under review. That review is given credence through the involvement of outsiders. Above all, the involvement of outsiders can be educative. Misunderstandings between employers, parents, and teachers are common. Evaluation is not only a way of giving the public of the school information on successes and failures. It is an effective way of presenting the objectives of the staff for their school. Provided that the evaluation is organized to reflect staff priorities it will yield information on their extent and on their attainment. It is

[1] Schools Council (1968), *op. cit.*, pp. 41–4.

also an acknowledgement that attainment in school is dependent on factors outside. If schooling is affected by external factors it seems sensible to involve external judgements. This should have the beneficial effect of showing how teachers are often struggling against the slackness of parents in doing their bit in supporting their children.

Question 5
Here teachers were worried about the time that would be involved in evaluation. There has to be work put into it. But it has been argued that it is so central to the work of the school that it is already done, or should be done, because it would yield a large payoff from a small investment. All staff have to be involved in evaluation, because it occurs inside each classroom as well as across the whole school. But the organization of evaluation might benefit from allocating the responsibility in the same way as other responsibilities in schools. Scaled posts are often given for trivial activities. Yet it is rare to find seniority being given for responsibility for organizing evaluation, even though it is central to the work of all teachers. The organization of initial discussions, the preparation of documents for discussion, the chairing of working parties to prepare those documents, steering a programme through staff meetings, arranging for external experts to help, and arranging for schools to share information all require skilled guidance. Collecting the information, storing it, and retrieving it as detailed in Appendix B requires some technical knowledge. Above all, the preparation of a routine report on the progress of the school is a very skilled job. These are not of course new roles. They are present in most schools and are the responsibility of the headteacher and senior staff. But it is rare to find the tasks organized systematically and on a permanent basis.

It is useful to involve a working party of teachers in the organization of evaluation with the senior teacher responsible for evaluation as chair person. Just as different perspectives add to the credence of evaluation, so a working party will ensure that staff interests are represented. This can be a small group elected by the staff or nominated by the headteacher. Their job is to prepare the way for an evaluation programme and to carry out that programme once agreed. There should be a member of the staff of the mathematics department on it to provide the necessary advice on scaling and the preparation of statistics. The North Central Association of Colleges and Schools which accredits secondary schools in the United States insists not only on a planned and continuous evaluation, but on the maintenance of data collection in the fields of achievement, student attitudes, teacher morale, parents' views, the follow-up of school leavers, studies of early leavers, and so on. [1] While elaborate data collection may be a

[1] North Central Association of Colleges and Schools (1974–5), *Policies and Standards for the Approval of Secondary Schools*, Chicago, Commission for Schools.

waste of resources, all schools should maintain over the years some basic minimum of statistics so that progress or regress can be assessed year by year. This data should be regularly checked for trends indicating that action is required. An important part of the organization of evaluation should consist of feeding information back to other staff after regular reviews of the time series.

Question 6
Here the teachers were worried about the release of information to the public. It is easy to recommend a 'publish and be damned' policy, but one school releasing its results in isolation may suffer as a consequence. Here the local education authority should take an active part in advising all schools. But the choice is usually between releasing reliable information collected together by the staff and being judged on rumour. School staffs no longer assume that they have sole responsibility for what goes on inside the school. There is a realization that success in schooling depends on factors, not only in the homes of the pupils, on the content of primary schooling, but on employment prospects and opportunities in further and higher education. Once this dependence is accepted there are advantages in releasing information for the guidance of the public on whom the attainment and motivation of pupils depends.

The anxiety behind these questions springs from a notion of evaluation as a package deal that will immediately affect the work of the school and expose each teacher to the glare of publicity. But evaluation has always been a part of the toolkit of all teachers. It can always be discovered in a school, even where teachers describe it as immoral or impossible. It will be used sparingly because it is time-consuming. It needs to be concentrated where a little information is likely to have a big impact. The allocation of resources is an obvious example. Another would be serious differences in the basic skills content of work in feeder primary schools. Key curricular checkpoints are others. There are dangers in this checking for it could consolidate both the content and the sequence of work. Such evaluation may not be possible in some subjects. But evaluation is a matter of choice. Resources for evaluation are short and selection is necessary, just as it is when staffing or equipping the school for the year's work. Teachers have to make harsh choices. Evaluation is a necessary part of this process.

Similarly pupils sooner or later face harsh choices. It is a more comfortable position for teachers to conceal objective information from pupils, and while they are young there is a good case for this to continue, to avoid labelling. But at sixteen these pupils will be seeking work and many get too much of a shock when this is the first time that they realize that the teachers may have concealed their true level of attainment. Too many parents complain that despite regular reports and parents' evenings, they were never told that their child was under-attaining or over-attaining. Parents have to be treated as adults capable of receiving, interpreting, and acting upon objective information about their children. Similarly secondary school pupils are too perceptive, too aware of reality not to be given objective assessments of themselves. Evaluation is an antidote to romanticism.

The positive side of the release of evaluations is also important. A school staff that keeps its public in its confidence, that supplies objective information merits support. Parents and employers should know about the examination policy of the school. They should know the shape of the curriculum, the choices available at different ages, the pastoral arrangements. There are always a number of gross misunderstandings. Parents may assume that all pupils take GCE. Employers may expect similar standards from pupils recruited progressively further down the ability range. The sharing of information is always educative. Evaluation should not consist of a few figures torn out of context. It should give the public a picture of the organization of the school, its context, the policy of the local education authority, the nature of the intake, and the support given by parents and the public.

Question 7
The problem here was about using the little time available for evaluation in the most profitable way. The first suggestion was to make use of existing returns to the DES and to the local education authority. The second suggestion was to use existing assessments of pupils, whether internal or from public examinations. It was suggested that all the indicators should be gathered together and presented rather as the directors of a business firm present an annual account to shareholders. In both cases a full picture of the year's performance has to include the context in which the staff work, the resources used, and the output attained.

The third set of suggestions was concerned with making use of professional judgement in the most reliable way. This involves specifying levels of performance that are considered to be indications of the attainment of the objectives chosen by staff as having priority. These are usually judgements by the staff of the school, but are translated from impressions by specifying in advance the levels of academic attainment, cultural activity, sporting prowess, participation, behaviour and so on that will be considered as satisfactory.

The fourth set of suggestions indicated the necessity for evaluation to involve comparisons with other schools. Most of the activities in a school have no levels that are universally recognized as satisfactory. They have to be assessed against standards in similar types of schools. Some activities are important yet essentially a matter of opinion as to whether success is being achieved. Here it has been recommended that school staffs co-operate with those in neighbouring schools, either to exchange evaluations or to become members of a group of schools providing an evaluation team that can apply similar criteria across the whole consortium. Finally, it has been suggested that other professionals and parents, employers and academics be recruited to look at some school activities and provide external references.

In the United States groups of States are covered by Associations that approve the policies and standards of secondary schools. This accreditation system usually involves teachers carrying out a self-assessment exercise in advance of a visit by the evaluation team of the accrediting agency.[1] Improvements are recommended on the basis of the visit. This is similar to a visit by inspectors in the United Kingdom. These visits also benefit from the teachers' assessment of the state of the school. Such self-assessment as recommended by the Inner London Education Authority could be combined with peer evaluation.[2] These combinations of internal and external assessment would be simple to organize and the combination of self-scrutiny and detached observations would combine insight with objectivity. The recommendation for peer evaluation rests on the flexibility of personal judgement by professionals. Inspectors, advisors, fellow teachers and experts among the public can assess those parts that other measures cannot reach. But there is even more need in employing peer judgement to go through the stages of specifying aims, objectives, and indicators in advance. Unless the evaluators know what teachers are trying to attain and the type of performance that indicates success or failure, the judgements are liable to be useless. Think of a jury judging a case at law. Their difficulty is that of teachers judging the success of their efforts. The jury has to judge the case against the law as it has been defined in advance. The law lays down the criteria for judgement. The judge in his summing-up explains what has to be established before a verdict can be made. This is the case with peer evaluation. The criteria for judgement have to be established in advance.

In all the possibilities presented as ways in which evaluation could be organized there has been a repetitive theme. Evaluation is not an appendix to the work of a school staff. It is an integral part of it. As curricula and organization change, new forms of evaluation are needed. Evaluation has to be built into the planning of new courses to ensure continuity once education is individualized. It has become the key to the successful organization of many of these new developments. It remains the way in which the effectiveness of existing procedures can be judged. The emphasis on evaluation arises from the changes that have taken place in secondary schooling. The anxiety produced by those changes has increased the demand inside and outside the schools. Evaluation has always played a central role in the organization of the school. Recent developments have made that role even more important.

[1] *ibid.*

[2] Inner London Education Authority (1977), *Keeping the School under Review.* London, ILEA.

Appendix A: Sources of data on education

Figures produced on the performance of a school have to be interpreted. This interpretation, whether by the teachers, or parents, or some other public for evaluation, is accomplished most easily when there is some set of figures for comparison. It is interesting to know that 46 per cent of a fifth-year group of pupils stay on into the sixth year. It is more meaningful if this statistic is presented alongside the local education authority figure of 32 per cent, or a national figure. It would be better still if the intake characteristics of pupils to the school were also presented. Throughout this book the value of statistics for comparison produced by groups of local school staff has been stressed. There have also been cautions about unguarded use of available national statistics. Both emphases result from the need to compare like with like. The likeness must not only be between the type of schools, their intake, catchment areas, resources and so on, but between the statistics themselves. Often figures that look identical have actually been collected in different ways, for different purposes and are not in reality comparable. Any of the sources that follow need very careful perusal before use. This necessitates a careful look at explanations of the basis of the statistics that are usually in footnotes, preface, or small print.

Official statistics

1 DES annual statistics

At present the DES publishes six volumes of annual statistics. The publications for any year usually refer to the situation two years before. Thus the 1975 figures are published in 1977 and so on. The titles of the six volumes are:

    Volume 1—Schools
    Volume 2—School leavers, CSE and GCE
    Volume 3—Further education
    Volume 4—Teachers
    Volume 5—Finance and awards
    Volume 6—Universities

The volumes likely to be of most use in school evaluation are 1 and 2 on schools and on school leavers respectively. The first volume contains the basic figures on school numbers, largely derived from the annual return Form 7. The school leavers volume is largely based on the annual 10 per cent leavers survey in which school staff give the destination of school leavers, whether employment, further or higher education, and their examination successes. Members of staff who have filled this in know that there is a large 'not known' category which makes these figures difficult to interpret. There are tables in this volume based on returns from the examination boards, but the figures are generally of leavers, not a year-group, and this makes direct comparison with figures collected by most school staffs misleading. Warning has already been given about this difficulty. It requires caution when using any such national or local figures collected for other purposes such as school evaluation.

The DES also produces small cards summarizing the statistics in each volume. The statistics also appear in other government publications. Comparable sets of statistics are produced for Scotland and for Northern Ireland.

2 Social trends

Social Trends, published by the Government Statistical Service, appears annually and presents information derived from many government sources, including the DES statistics. It is useful for providing background social data. The official sources of information containing data on education include the Census, the General Household Survey, and the publications of the Department of Employment, as well as information obtained direct from government departments, including the DES.

3 Official reports

The flow of reports from Crowther in 1956 to Bullock in 1976 provide valuable sources of information in specific areas of education. Crowther (1956) contains the results of investigations into the education of the 15- to 20-year-olds and includes unusual data on the attainments of National Service recruits. It is also an excellent source for information on the differing attainments of pupils from different social backgrounds. The Robbins Report (1963) is another source of statistics on the post-statutory age group.

The Plowden Report (1967) contains the results of a survey carried out in 1964 on parental attitudes and school and pupil attainments. The Bullock report (1976) contains summaries of reading attainment.

The DES Reports on Education, distributed free, contain statistics on selected subjects. These are themselves placed in context in the reports.

4 *Facts in focus*, Central Statistical Office
(published by Penguin)

This is a summary of government statistics published commercially. It includes a section on education extracted from DES statistics volume 1 to 6 and other official sources. It was first published in 1972 and has been revised after two years.

Semi-official sources

1 The Chartered Institute of Public Finance and Accountancy (CIPFA),
1 Buckingham Palace Road, SW1E 6HS

This Institute used to be known as the Institute of Municipal Treasurers and Accountants. They provide statistics at local authority level and are consequently an unusual source of data. Their educational statistics include:

(a) *Education Estimates Statistics*—estimates for the year of publication. Thus 1976–7 estimates of school sizes, pupil numbers, pupil-teacher ratios, and expenditure on different educational facilities were published in 1976.

(b) *Educational Statistics*—actual figures of the previous year's figures for school rolls, teacher numbers, costs per pupil, and provision of school meals and milk.

CIPFA also publishes separate statistics on school meals, personal social services, and many other aspects of local government. The *Education Estimates Statistics* is probably the most useful single publication on education for use in schools.

2 The University Central Council for Admissions

UCCA produces an annual report giving figures of admissions to universities and subjects to be read. The statistical supplement contains details of candidates for admission, their A level grades, and the first degree attainments of earlier admissions.

3 The examination boards

The CSE and GCE boards produce tables of results of candidates to their own examinations. Candidates however often take the examinations of more than one board. The statistics usually consist of tables of subjects with the proportion of candidates obtaining different levels of result in each. While the percentage 'passing' in each subject may be useful for comparison, there is not the background data that would enable the staff of any one school to make a direct comparison with the results of a board. There is also an imperfect correlation between the standards of marking between the same subjects in different boards, between different subjects of the same board, and standards of marking may differ over time.

4 The local authorities

Most local authorities produce an annual abstract of statistics. In some cases, for example the Greater London Council's *Annual Abstract*, there is a wealth of data. This council also produces booklets of graphs summarizing facts about life in London. The annual report of the Chief Education Officer or Director of Education is another source. The reports of other chief officers and committee papers of the local authority are other sources of data. Local libraries or the information office of the local authority are the most convenient contacts for teachers wanting these reports.

Other sources of useful information

There are a number of books that summarize available statistics. It is best to use the most up-to-date source. The local library should be able to advise on this.

1 K. Pickett (1974), *Sources of Official Data*, Longman, contains references to all sources of statistics from official sources, including education.
2 H. Silver (1973), *Equal Opportunity in Education*, Methuen, contains selections of readings from important historical and contemporary research, particularly that examining the relation between attainment and social class.
3 I. Reid (1977), *Social Class Differences in Britain*, Open Books, contains information on education and other aspects of life in Britain related to differences between social groups.

Appendix B: The storage and retrieval of information for evaluation

This book has not been primarily concerned with the evaluation of pupil progress. Nevertheless, records on pupils are an important source of information on the performance of the school. Reference has been made to the record system devised by the Scottish Council for Research in Education. Many local authorities recommend the use of a standard record. But teachers are often faced with the task of deciding the form of record to be kept on pupils. The sequence of planning a record system is the same as in the design of evaluation. The purposes of the records have to be thought out first. Then indicators can be selected to provide some measure of the features considered to be important by staff. The tendency is for records to be established without this planning and to persist long past the point where they are useful. Records on pupils can be used for the following purposes which should be determined first.

1 To provide information on the progress of pupils through sequences of work. This tracking ensures that pupils cover the curriculum as they move between subjects, years, options, and examinations.

2 To provide information for evaluating the progress of pupils. This progress report is used to bring advice to bear on pupils, to give them special help, and to report on them to parents and employers

3 To provide information to facilitate pastoral care. Here the information will be concerned with behaviour, social background, and co-operation with the Educational Welfare Service and other services.

4 To provide information for form-filling. Here the object is to keep an individualized data system to help the staff to fill in DES and LEA forms, and to help answer questions on pupils from inside and outside the school.

Each of the purposes listed above requires a different type of record and different data stored. This is the reason for thinking out objectives in advance. For in-school evaluation the records should include intake characteristics, scaled examination or course results, attendance and other data on the pupil's career in the school, and final attainments on leaving and destination. But these features will be a small part of most school records which will usually serve wider purposes.

There is both moral and technical confusion over the keeping of records on individual pupils in school. Some teachers object to record-keeping if it involves recording detail that can be used to label a pupil. Such objections are raised about the identification of different ethnic or social groups. They extend to the recording of personal details on behaviour or attitudes to school. They even extend to the recording of attainments, as these might lead to the child being labelled by previous performance and taught thereon with the label in mind. Other teachers acknowledge the need to keep records, but rarely consult them before taking over a class at the start of a year. There is also a difficult technical balance between recording scant facts that give too little information, and recording many aspects of a pupil's performance while knowing that little use will be made of the record. This is an area of school organization, intimately connected with evaluation, that needs attention. But evaluation, once approached systematically will provide ideas on the information that should be stored. Part of the evaluation effort should be to review records to prune out the unused and add the essential. However, some information is stored in all but schools with staff holding extreme views. If education is to be a cumulative process it seems essential for each teacher to build on the work of his predecessors. If a pupil's work is to be sequenced some form of record will be needed. If the pupil is to leave with a reliable, useable record of his attainments there has to be recording.

Pupil records are often aggregated to give an indication of the performance of the school on some aspect of work. But assessments on school performance might also need storing. In most cases this is a simple matter of filing annual statistics which can be retrieved to add a further year's figures. But a more sophisticated recording arrangement can facilitate the relating of one set of figures to another. For example, staff might want to relate test scores at input to examination results at output and this is made easy by the use of standard methods of storing the data. Most school staffs have a mathematician or someone who has taken a course in statistics and who would take charge of this exercise. It would make a useful research topic for a higher degree student in a local university or polytechnic. Most schools use a record card on which comments and marks are written. This is satisfactory for recording important features of individual performance. But the amount of information that can be stored on a card is limited. The greatest weakness is that record cards in schools are rarely designed to yield easily aggregated information. What is needed is some way of providing space on which to record summaries in words on a pupil's career in school and a way of rapidly accumulating information from the individual records to build up data for evaluation.

The punched card offers one way of storing information. These date back to around 1900 and are extensively used in offices and in research. Punch cards are also used to feed information to a computer for processing. The range in use stretches from simple edge punched cards which can be sorted with a knitting needle to the 80 column IBM card in which holes punched into one of the ten positions in each column can be read by data processing equipment such as a counter-sorter. The staff of a school do not need any technical expertise to set up a card-based system of storage. There are commercial firms eager to advise and rent or sell equipment. However, many schools now have computer terminals and might want to organize their records through a computer.

Probably the most convenient method of storage for both record keeping on individual pupils and for retrieving aggregated data for evaluation is the clipped edged card. This card is big enough to have information written on it, so that it serves the function of an ordinary but large record card. But the clipped edge can be used to store information that can be retrieved mechanically. The apparatus for preparing and extracting data is not expensive and can be used to cut down the amount of work required to fill up routine returns for the local education authority or the DES.

Many local education authorities offer a standard record card for use in schools. There would be an obvious economy in the authority also organizing a card index system that could be used in all schools. This would bring economies of scale and make it worthwhile for commercial manufacturers to produce cheap equipment for record keeping and information retrieval in schools. While teaching will always remain an essentially face-to-face activity there are already systems that use computers to back up the efforts of the teacher. Many of these systems use stored information on the learner to feed back the next steps in a learning sequence to the teacher, or to the pupil directly. This is not futuristic. It is another step in the mobilization of mechanical aids to support teaching. Similarly large-scale accounting systems maintain their quality and speed up their procedures by utilizing punched cards or computers. A school staff that decides that evaluation is a central part of their work could employ mechanical means of maintaining the quality of the information they are using in organizing their teaching. At this point they may need to seek professional advice on the possibilities of using punched cards or possibly a computer.

Suggestions for Further Reading

Sources of data on education that are often suitable for comparisons with data collected in schools can be found in Appendix A. Here is a brief list of books on evaluation that elaborate many of the themes covered.

1 *General books on evaluation as part of school management*
Barry, H. and Tye, F. (1972), *Running a School*. London, Temple Smith.
Department of Education and Science (1977), *Ten Good Schools: A Secondary School Enquiry*. London, HMSO.
Open University, 'A Case Study in Management: Sydney Stringer School and Community College'. Unit 2 of Course E321, *Management in Education*. Milton Keynes, Open University.
Poster, C. D. (1976), *School Decision-Making: Educational Management in Secondary Schools*. London, Heinemann Educational Books.
Taylor, W. (1969), *Heading for Change*. London, Routledge and Kegan Paul.

2 *Assessment techniques*
Crocker, A. C. (1974), *Statistics for the Teacher*. Slough, National Foundation for Educational Research.
Deale, R. N. (1975), *Assessment and Testing in the Secondary School*. London, Evans/Methuen Educational.
Hudson, B. (1973), *Assessment Techniques*. London, Methuen Educational.
Macintosh, H. G. (ed.) (1974), *Techniques and Problems of Assessment: A Practical Handbook for Teachers*. London, E. Arnold.
McIntosh, D. M., Walker, D. A., and Mackay, D. (1962), *Scaling of Teachers' Marks and Estimates*. Edinburgh, Oliver and Boyd.
Schools Council (1975), *Examination Bulletin 31, Continuous Assessment in the CSE*. London, Evans/Methuen Educational.
Thyne, J. M. (1974), *Principles of Examining*. London, University of London Press.

3 *Standardized Tests*
Jackson, S., *A Teacher's Guide to Tests and Testing*. London, Longman. (Revised regularly; it is important to obtain the latest edition.)
Vincent, D. and Cresswell, M. (1976), *Reading Tests in the Classroom*. Windsor, National Foundation for Educational Research Publishing Company.

Glossary

Arithmetic mean   (or *mean*, or *arithmetic average*) The sum of all the scores of a group, divided by the number of cases in the group.

Criterion-referenced test   A test constructed to show whether a detailed inventory of skills has or has not been mastered.

Mean   See *arithmetic mean* above.

Normal curve   A bell-shaped distribution of scores around a mean frequently resulting from testing large numbers of persons on some attainment or attribute. The curve is symmetrical around the mean and the proportion of cases falling under the curve cut up in terms of the standard deviation is known. Thus roughly two thirds of all cases on a test of mean 100 and standard deviation 15 will fall within plus or minus one standard deviation of the mean, i.e. between 85 and 115.

Norm-referenced test   A test constructed to measure how well a person has performed on the subject tested in comparison with his or her peers.

Reliability   A test is reliable, or consistent, if the same persons score the same on a repeat of the test, provided no learning has taken place in between.

Scaling   The process of bringing different sets of scores to the same standard of marking (see *standardization*).

Standard deviation   Measure of the dispersion of scores around the arithmetic mean.

Standardization   The process of bringing different sets of scores to the same standard of marking. More strictly, to bring different sets of scores to the same mean and standard deviation.

Standardized test   Test tried out on a large number of persons before publication to ensure that there is a standard to which persons taking the test can be compared. More strictly, a test which is designed to have a known mean and standard deviation through trials on a large number of persons before publication.

Time series   Statistics presented on a regular, for example yearly, basis to show trends.

Validity   A test is valid if it actually measures what it is supposed to be measuring.

Index